ENERGY FIX

Balancing the Six Life Energies for a Healthy, Happy Life

by **CONNIE LYNN HAYES**

Copyright © 2009 by Connie Lynn Hayes

All rights reserved. No part of this book may be reproduced or transmitted in any form or by any means, electronic or mechanical, including photocopying, recording, or by any information storage and retrieval system, without permission in writing from the publisher.

Published by Hayes Communications, Bountiful, Utah

Originally published in paperback in 2009.

Printed in the United States of America.

Cover design by Nathan Pinnock

ISBN   978-0-578-01592-7

Recent Comments About Energy Fix

"The Energy Fix is the most complete and powerful work every compiled on the subject of energy I have ever read. Her wisdom and passion will inspire you to greatness in every area of your life". — Ali Eisenach

"I have read so many books on the law of attraction, but this one is my favorite. Thank you for taking a subject that is not always easy to grasp and making it understandable and easy to implement. I enjoyed the exercises and, for once, did them all. You put so much wisdom in a concise, easy-to-read format and I have not enjoyed a book this much in some time. I have told everyone to read "Energy Fix"." — Dana Kern

"Let me just say WOW, you are so inspiring to me. This book has allowed me to open myself again, and for me to take a look at myself from the inside and get back in-sync with "Olivia"."
— Olivia Booth

"Thank you for writing Energy Fix. It is important that your knowledge is shared with the world. I have passed on so much of your knowledge to clients to inspire them. The opening information about oxygen really grabbed and impacted me. I never thought about veggies being so high in oxygen! That alone created a field of resonance in my body that allowed for much more flow. Thank you for all your decades of caring, researching, and having the courage to write."
— Linda Bienfeld

This book is dedicated to
the hundreds of students and clients
who have listened to me over the past 40 years.
I am ever grateful for your curiosity, your ability to learn new
things and your loving friendship.

I count as my greatest blessings my sweet Husband,
Norm Hayes, and my four wonderful children,
Heidi, Todd, Brad and Amy, who have all provided
most of my lessons along the way.

I am humbled and blessed by my Heavenly Father Who, I
believe, has entrusted me with this information, and
I pray that I might express within these pages
only truth as I understand it.

This book is also dedicated to those who are committed to
learning and are willing to embrace new ways of
living in a high-energy way.

CONTENTS

Acknowledgments   *vi*
About the Author   *vii*
Prologue   *x*
Author's Note and Disclosure   *xiv*

Introduction: Understanding the Life Force   *1*
   Energy Equalizer Test   *10*

Section One: Physical Equity   **11**
  1 The Fire Within   *13*
  2 Fueling the Fire   *23*
     Vegetable Recipe   *32*
  3 A Chemical Fire   *33*
  4 The Power of Fire   *42*
  5 A Raging Fire   *51*
  6 Tending the Fire   *64*
  7 Preserving the Fire   *74*
  Implementing the Physical Equity   *83*
  Recommended Reading   *84*

Section Two: Mental Equity   **85**
  8 Jumping Levels   *87*
  9 Your Mind – Master or Servant?   *97*
  10 Thinking Makes It So   *110*
  11 A Picture is Worth a Thousand Words   *120*
  12 Your Wish is My Command   *133*
  Implementing the Mental Equity   *146*
  Recommended Reading   *147*

Section Three: Emotional Equity   **149**
  13 The Language of Creation   *151*
  14 Stand For Something   *163*
  15 Living the Dream   *171*
  16 The Art of the Dream   *181*
  17 Language of the Heart   *190*
  Implementing the Emotional Equity   *198*
  Recommended Reading   *199*

Contents

Section Four: Spiritual — **201**
   18 The Unseen Power   *203*
   19 Divinity is an Inside Job   *212*
   20 Human Being – or Being Human?   *222*
   21 The Sum and Substance of Spirit   *235*
   22 What is the Purpose of All This?   *245*
   Power Questions   *257*
   Implementing the Spiritual Equity   *258*
   Recommended Reading   *260*

Section Five: Financial Equity — **261**
   23 The Abundant Life   *263*
   24 Wealth Consciousness   *275*
   25 Claiming Prosperity   *285*
   Affirmations for Financial Equity   *296*
   Implementing the Financial Equity   *297*
   Recommended Reading   *298*

Section Six: Social Equity — **299**
   26 Looking in the Wrong Place   *301*
   27 Love Is All There Is   *311*
   Implementing the Social Equity   *321*
   Recommended Reading   *322*

The Final Word   **323**
   10 Habits of High Energy People   *332*

ACKNOWLEDGEMENTS

The writing of this book has been a long-time coming and I have many people to thank for helping me make it possible. Writing the words was just one small part of the completion of this major goal.

I want to thank my family for always encouraging me, for coming to my seminars and classes, and tolerating my habit of using them as guinea pigs for all of my ideas.

This book would not have come about without the love and encouragement from my wonderful Business Partner, Natalie Wagner. Her optimism and willingness to do "whatever it takes" kept me going through the many ups and downs of the creative process.

A huge "Thank You" to Janine Freese, my dear friend and Editor, who tirelessly tried to make sense of my ramblings, and put it all so neatly on each page. I knew she had many talents; this one made this experience a happy one for me.

I also wish to recognize another friend, Keith Eccles, who brought his huge spirit and marketing know-how to this project just in time. If anyone ever reads this book, we will have Keith to thank for that.

A special thank you goes out to Nathan Pinnock for the book's lovely cover design. His talent at expressing my thoughts through his art was nothing less than amazing to me.

ABOUT THE AUTHOR

At a very young age I showed an unusual interest in "energy". As a little girl I remember going up to my Mother as I showed her my upturned palms and asking "what can I do?" Mother clearly did not understand me and my "oddities" and frequently suggested things like "go play paper dolls" (which certainly dates me, doesn't it?). I really meant to ask what I was supposed to do with all the energy I felt running through my hands.

When I was seven years old, I was playing downstairs with my imaginary friends when I was clearly told (by whom is up to you to decide) that someday I would be in charge of an "Academy of Energy", which would eventually lead to something called "The City of Light". Now before you think I am really strange, I didn't think this was out of the ordinary at the time. However, I have since been told that it was a very strange "knowingness", which is all I can call it. I have told only a handful of people in my 68 years, about receiving this information, and have just this year launched what I call the Radiance Academy.

But, my fascination with "energy" persisted. Being brought up in a religious home, I was required to read the Bible for a Seminary class. As I read it, I found myself underlining the word "light" every time it was used which, as it turns out, is over 3,000 times. I had no idea at that time why I did that.

As a dancer, I was required to workout for 4-6 grueling hours of practice, several times a week. One night after school, I came home and smelled gingerbread baking—my favorite treat. My Mother invited me to sit down and have a nice big slice of cake with lemon sauce on it, and I can remember saying, "Oh, I'd love nothing better, Mom, but, it won't create the kind of energy I need for dance practice—I'd better have an apple instead".

About The Author

As a young woman, I took up the study of Creativity as a hobby. I was intrigued by the mechanics of where ideas come from, and how it is some people are much better at developing ideas into reality than others.

People often ask me where I get all of my energy, and I have always thought it such an odd question. Energy is everywhere, I would reply, and I can't have more than you do.

But, I needed a first-class crisis to really get my attention. After my third child was born (and you'll read his story in the Prologue of this book), I became a sponge for knowledge. My life was never the same.

What, you might ask, have I been doing all these years? As I look back upon my life, I can see clearly now (not so clearly during the time) that everything I have done up to now has been necessary in order for the Academy to actually get off the ground. Most importantly, I can see that the masses are finally ready to hear about energy, and that science has come so far as to take the conversation out of "woo-woo land" and straight into mainstream academia.

For the past 40 years I have spent the bulk of my time studying and organizing this "energy stuff", and counseling people in private sessions, in classes, and workshops. Approximately 20 years ago, I was blessed with the Bio-Balance System being dumped into my head in my sleep in a relatively finished format. I take no credit for it, but I have done my best to prove its accuracy. I have taught this system in a seminar I call "The Life Force System" for many years and I know it works.

Seeing how much people were really struggling with energy, I elected at that time to re-enter the physical health arena and help people with their health and fitness. I have been counseling ever since, with hundreds of clients' Testimonials that can be viewed on my website: www.connielynnhayes.com if desired.

About The Author

The bottom line is this: I believe life is good, and that we were meant to have joy. I also know that life seems better when we feel good. But, feeling good is a lot more than just being free of pain. Having energy to do what you want, when you want, and consciously being able to create your life according to your real desires is my idea of "living". If this sounds good to you, come along with me for an Energy Fix.

The following book is my first attempt at putting this information in written format, and I hope that you find the Energy Fix both interesting and useful in bringing balance and happiness into your life. Thank you for your kind attention.

Sincerely,

Connie Lynn Hayes

PROLOGUE

My insides froze as I heard the Doctor say: "Take this baby home to die; he will not live through another attack".

As we drove home that cold January morning, I held my Baby close, still hearing the Doctor's words ringing in my ears, "He will not live, he will not live." I wondered how the sun could be shining when everything in my world was so cold. I squeezed my eyes shut to hold back the torrent of tears, as my gut wrenched. Then I started bargaining with God.

Brad was born five days after Christmas, a month premature. He had a collapsed lung and pneumonia. We had him in and out of the hospital five times in his first year and his condition gradually worsened. He had developed asthma too. His tiny legs were bruised and punctured from the daily injections. And then came that fateful day when medical science gave up on Brad; and we took our eleven-pound one-year-old home.

Brad had an asthma attack every nine days as regular as clockwork. Each attack weakened him until he became too weak to fight. He seemed to be allergic to everything, and was subsisting on Gatorade and de-carbonated Sprite. He was as tall as a one-year-old, but had not been able to sit up for over six weeks. Tick, tock—nine days to go.

Two days later a distant acquaintance called with an amazing proposal. "What if we could build Brad up so he would live through another attack?" she asked. My curiosity was peaked since all I wanted at this point was more time. "How do we do that" I replied suspiciously. "I don't know" she continued, "But, I know someone who does and he is speaking in our area tonight. Come with me to see if he can help." Dejectedly I explained I could not leave my baby since no one would watch a child that is expected to die—not even his Father. She wouldn't take no for an answer and announced that she would pick me up at 6:45, and the phone went dead. I called my Husband and begged him to tend.

Prologue

The class began and the speaker droned on for two hours as I fidgeted nervously. I would have left if I had driven my own car. When he finally stopped talking, I rushed to him and blurted out my sob story. This wonderful man instantly made me the most important person in the room and simply explained that the biggest problem Brad was facing was lack of energy with which to fight. When I asked what we should do, he left the room with no explanation. Ten minutes ticked by and I decided to leave, as I was very worried about my Son. Just then the Teacher returned with a pint jar full of a blackish-brownish, gucky-looking concoction. He told me to take it home and put it in the baby's bottle. I shook my head, explaining that Brad was much too weak to drink out of a bottle. "I feed him with an eye dropper," I said.

He left again and added some yellow liquid to the black stuff and ordered me to get as much down Brad as I could tonight and call him in the morning. I guess he saw the horrified look on my face, because he then assured me that this would <u>not</u> hurt my Baby. I left thinking I had finally gone over the edge—but, I felt strangely optimistic.

At home I found my Mother-in-law in charge, and I then made a terrible mistake. I tried to feed some of this awful smelling stuff to Brad while everyone watched. He didn't want it—I'm sure it tasted terrible; and he cried. My Mother-in-law screamed at me, "For heaven's sakes Connie, let this baby die in peace!" My feet rooted to the floor I defiantly said, "No, I will not. This is my baby, and if we go down, we'll go down fighting. I will <u>never</u> give up!"

When the house was quiet, I sat down in the rocker with my Baby, a dropper, and a jar full of hope.

I dropped some in his mouth, then rocked and sang to him. He fussed, but I just kept on squirting. Holding him close, I knew that love never got better than this—and somehow the fear subsided a bit.

Prologue

I started this routine around 11:00 p.m. At 2:00 a.m. a strange thing happened. Brad opened his mouth like a little bird and started gulping and wanting more. I grabbed a baby bottle, added apple juice to the black mixture and presented it to Brad. He sucked hungrily and within a short time had ingested the entire mysterious potion. By 6:00 a.m., without a word of exaggeration, Brad was sitting on my bed eating Wheat Chex out of a box! That night I witnessed a true miracle. Now, I don't know how many miracles you need, but, I only needed one. I never took Brad back for his daily shots. But I continued following my Mentor's advice, and my Baby continued to grow, and walk and talk just like any other one-year old child.

When my oldest Son, Todd, was five years old and ready to go to kindergarten, he required a physical examination. I decided to take all three of my children in for exams, including Brad who was 18 months old by then. When we arrived at the Doctor's office little Bradley was running around like any other toddler and the doctor asked, "Who is this?" I replied that it was Brad. He was taken aback, as I'm sure he thought Brad had died. When he asked what I'd been doing, and I told him that we were "using good nutrition to heal him". He gave me such a fabulous response that I admit I had this remark printed on a board and it hung in my office for years. He said: "Connie, you're playing with fire with this baby's life". I laughed and suggested that he check Brad over, and then we'd talk about it. To this good doctor's credit, he said he didn't understand how or why it had worked, but, he had to admit that it had indeed worked, because little Bradley checked out normal OR BETTER in every respect. He, too, had seen a miracle.

(*See footnote for information regarding the amazing product that was in that jar)

The Doctor wouldn't let me go though, until he'd given me his warning that Brad was "an asthmatic and always would be". He told me that I should never allow Brad to get wind in

Prologue

his face, which meant most sports would be out of the question for him. As I look back on that day, I am grateful for all the times I saw Brad running around the baseball diamond and skiing down the hill like a professional.

But, the best was when he moved to Hawaii and bought himself a shiny, new convertible. So much for asthma!

From that day forward I have spent a great deal of my time and energy studying *why* this worked. The following book is some of what I have learned. Enjoy!

*The product referred to in this story is Life Mate, which is an all natural product that I have used personally and in my practice for 42 years. To order Life Mate, please visit my website www.connielynnhayes.com

AUTHOR'S NOTE AND DISCLOSURE

It has been my intent throughout this book to make it easy-to-read and was never meant to be a scientific treatise. The information you are about to read has been gathered over 40 years of clinical research with hundreds of students and thousands of personal clients.

No attempt has been made to footnote all of the information given, but an extensive bibliography and has been added at the end of each section. If the reader feels it necessary to have more specific data, please refer to the bibliographies. I have mentioned the original source whenever I have used a direct quote.

I suggest that you read this book with the "spirit of my intention" in mind:

TO INFORM, INSPIRE AND WIDEN YOUR PERSPECTIVE

for the sole purpose of helping you live a healthier, happier and more abundant life.

With much love,

Connie Lynn Hayes

INTRODUCTION

Understanding the Life Force

Be not afraid of growing slowly,
be afraid only of standing still.
~Chinese Proverb~

What is the "Life Force"? Every time I ask students that question, I get a variety of answers—but, intuitively we all suspect it has something to do with energy, and it does. Think of this Life Force as a pilot light that exists in everything. This conjures up many questions, and it is my purpose to give you some answers. In reference to this Life Force:

1. Can we run out of it?
2. Can we get more of it?
3. Can we conserve it?
4. Where is it located?
5. Can we control it?

I have spent a lifetime studying energy, trying to get answers to questions like these. Most of us consider "energy" to be a positive word and, therefore, know of times when we would like more of it; and, if we could harness it to use for our chosen purpose, we think that would be desirable.

Sometimes, it would be enough to be able to conserve what we already have. We have seen other forms of energy such as electricity and steam being controlled and used to our advantage every day. And, how about highly focused energy such as the laser beam—now that's real power!

I learned a long time ago that it was not necessary to understand why or how something works in order to use it. Take the microwave or the CD player, for instance. I certainly

Introduction

could not give you a very intelligent dissertation as to why or how they do what they do, however, I am an expert at using them! So my goal in these next pages is to take complicated information that is not really necessary for you to understand, but, make you an expert at using it in your own life.

> *"As a man who has devoted his whole life to science, there is not such as matter. All matter originates and exists only by virtue of a force. Behind this force we must consider is a mind. This mind is the matrix of all matter."*
> *~Max Planck~*

Without going into a long, scientific discussion, I will summarize what we know about this energy. I use the name "life force", but it has been called by other names in different cultures. You may recognize some of them: Ki, Chi, Orgone Energy, Prana, Kundalini, Odic Force, Biocosmic Energy, Huna, Quintessence, Pyramid Power and the Dragon.

Most of us here in the West were educated about Newtonian Physics which describes the Universe as being made up largely of solid objects. This view was held by Isaac Newton and most of his colleagues in the late 17th and early 18th centuries. This was extended to the 19th century to describe a universe composed of fundamental building blocks called atoms. These atoms were thought to be made of solid matter with a nucleus of protons, neutrons and electrons revolving around the nucleus, much like the earth traveling around the sun. Everything could be described objectively and all physical reactions were seen to have a physical cause, like balls colliding on a pool table.

Those who prefer to see the world as solid and mostly unchanging find comfort in this way of explaining the Universe. But, in the early 19th Century, the discovery of electromagnetic phenomena led to the concept of a "field". A field was defined as a "condition in space which has the potential of producing a force". Thus, the idea that the universe is filled with fields that create forces was born. This helped explain our ability to affect each other at a distance through means other than speech and sight.

Most of us have just begun in the last 20 years to be able to use such concepts in our personal interactions; we are just beginning to admit that we too are composed of "fields".

Most religious writings speak of the ability to see light around people's heads (or halos). Christians show Jesus and other spiritual figures surrounded by fields of light (auras). The ancient Indian spiritual tradition speaks of a universal energy called "prana", which was seen as the basic constituent of all life, or, more accurately, the "breath of life".

The Chinese wrote of the existence of a vital energy which they called "Chi" as early as the 3rd century. They explained a system which yogis use even today to balance the two polarities of Chi: Yin and Yang. Kabbalah, an ancient Jewish mystical theosophy refers to these energies as the "astral light".

In the book, *Future Science*, John White lists 97 different cultures that refer to the auric phenomena with 97 different names. This book is not meant to be a physics primer; however, if you wish to know more about the science or religious background on the subject of the life force, be sure to look at the reading list at the end of the Physical Equity.

In *Search of the Healing Energy*, author, Mary Coddington sums up the qualities of Prana (Life Force) with the following list:

- It can heal.
- It penetrates everything.
- It accompanies solar rays.
- It has properties similar to other types of energy but is a distinct force unto itself.
- It possesses polarity and can be reflected by mirrors.
- It emanates from the human body and has been especially detectable at the fingertips and eyes.
- It can be conducted by such media as metal wires and silk threads.
- It can be stored inside inanimate materials such as water and stone.
- It can fluctuate with weather conditions.
- It can be controlled by the mind.

Introduction

- It can cause things to happen at a distance and enters into the dynamics of many paranormal phenomena.
- It can be used for good or evil.

This list, by the way, is remarkably similar to other such lists given by scholars of each of the cultural "energies", and I have therefore concluded that they are all referring to the same energy that I call the Life Force.

There are various ways for us to access this energy as well as obtain more of it or control it. I have taken volumes of difficult data, condensed it into a simplified "system" so that those who do not have the time or the interest to do in-depth research can nevertheless enjoy amazing benefits in their own lives.

In order to make this material manageable, and to make it easier to discuss, I have divided the Life Force into six equal sections. I refer to each section as an "equity". When I think of the word "equity" I immediately think of my home and the part of it that is paid for. Equity means "asset", and since these energy types are also assets and something that we all possess, we shall call them equities.

Even though I have identified six types of energy, let me make it clear that I do not, in any way, believe that six is all that exist. There are probably hundreds of divisions possible; but, our goal is to keep it simple and most of all to make this useable. The reality of it all is that there is only ONE—but we will break it into six categories in order to get our minds around this huge subject.

Here is an Overview of the Six Energies:

THE PHYSICAL ENERGY EQUITY

This is a large equity because we live on a physical planet. However, looking at the Energy Equalizer Wheel on page 10 you will notice that all equities get equal billing. You will also probably notice that other equities such as social and financial could be considered physical energy. You are right, and so together they take up half of the Bio-Balance Wheel. But, for our discussion, we will use the term Physical Energy to mean the physical body, its fuel, its health level, its fitness, the way it feels and the way it looks.

THE MENTAL ENERGY EQUITY

This category encompasses the brain, your thoughts, your beliefs, how we think, how we learn, and what we know.

THE EMOTIONAL ENERGY EQUITY

This one is magic, because using emotional energy properly can speed up your results. Think of feelings as a personal turbo charger—but, watch out, they can also be a trap.

THE FINANCIAL ENERGY EQUITY

I remember exactly the day when I realized that the energy surrounding our money and our ability to survive in this society was a very big stumbling block for many of us. That's when I added it to my Energy Equalizer Wheel as a separate category of energy. It seemed offensive to me, at first, almost sacrilegious to give finances the same amount of space as the spiritual equity. But, over the years I've seen just how crucial it is for us to learn to control this type of energy so that we can get on to the other ones.

THE SPIRITUAL ENERGY EQUITY

This is where the real power is. Spiritual Energy can control all of the other energies. That is why some people try to bypass all of the others and go straight to the spiritual stuff, which has certainly worked for some devotees like Jesus and Buddha. But, my 40 years of teaching and working with these ideas has taught me that most of us do better starting from the beginning and working up. But, this is definitely the really big one.

Introduction

THE SOCIAL ENERGY EQUITY

This equity is huge—not in size, but in impact. This is where we talk about relationships, with self and others. Hang on to your hat for this one.

TAKING THE TEST

These then are the six equities, and I have devoted an entire section to each one. Before we begin, it is necessary for you to take the Energy Equalizer Test on page 10. I suggest you make copies of this page so you can take the test every two or three months, or take it with pencil so it can be erased.

Some thoughts about this test: It's important that you answer honestly—no one but yourself need see your answers. Also, be sure that you answer the questions as of today, not where you expect to be next month or where you were last week. We want results, so we always work in the now. I take the test at the start of each new season. If you want really fast results, take it weekly to see how much progress you are making. Sunday is a good time for this. You'll be amazed to see how your answers can vary from week to week.

Notice on the test wheel there is a division line for each of the six equities and each line is divided into 10 smaller sections. When answering the questions, simply place a dot on the corresponding line to the question and on the part of the scale from one to ten that best describes your present situation. One, the line closest to the center, is lowest; and 10, the outermost line, the highest. Please don't be tempted to use all 5's—unless you really feel that is where you find yourself right now. After you have answered all six questions and placed a dot on six scales, then connect the dots. When you are finished with the test go on to the explanation which comes next. (Take the test now.)

Now take a look at your wheel. Most of us, when we take this test, notice that our wheel doesn't look very round. If yours is a very odd shape, how smooth of a ride do you think you'll be taking on this Road of Life? If balance is the goal, and it is, then we'd better get to work on how to round out our wheel and our life.

An interesting thing to note is that if you scored all #2's, even though they are all low scores, nevertheless—they are balanced. We all know people like this. They don't do much and expect very little in life, but they are happy. You also know people that seem so intelligent and talented and yet their lives seem to be one big crisis after another. Why is this? Balance—balance—balance. Those of us who become "experts" at something or another, tend to be the most imbalanced of all. That's because the better you get at one area of your life, the more you do it; and, of course, the corollary is true, too—that you then do much less of other things. Take a good look at your or any of your friend's libraries. Chances are you will find a lot more of one subject than all the others put together! We love doing and learning about something that we are good at, and we keep it up until we are a ten. But, if we are a ten in one area, then what must we be in all other areas in order to be balanced? You got it—all tens. Now, that is tough to do. Identify the equity with your lowest score—that's the one we will be working with first.

For example, I was a single mother of four children for thirteen years. At that time, I was working three jobs in order to support my family and the little free time that I did have was spent caring for my children. I had little time to spend on a social life. So it was no surprise to me when I took the test to find that my Social Equity was extremely low. My rule for my students is that once you identify your lowest energy equity, you must do something about it immediately—and I do mean immediately. Well, it happened to be 9:00 p.m. when I took this test, and not wanting my students to do something that I wouldn't do myself, I proceeded to think of what I could do about this equity right at that very moment. I came up with the idea to have a party. This might sound simple, but, since we lived in a less-than-desirable duplex and I was working three jobs, it sounded quite daunting.

Nevertheless, I plugged on. I found a date when I wasn't working and wrote up a guest list. I was so worried about the cost of this idea that I truly believed I would not go through

Introduction

with it if I waited until morning. So, I got in my car and drove to the store to get invitations and stamps. I wrote out the invitations, sealed and stamped them from my car and dropped them in the mailbox that night. Now I was committed.

I had asked each guest to bring with them someone that I did not know, so I expected around 20 people. Forty people showed up! We were definitely cramped in my tiny apartment, but, we had so much fun. That night, one of the guests that I had not met before offered me a job, which paid enough to replace the income of all three jobs combined! That evening changed my life.

Let's take a look at how this worked. By augmenting my social energy with *intention* and *attention*, (we'll discuss more of this in a later chapter), I was able not only to raise that equity by having fun and meeting new people, but, I raised my financial equity as well. This situation also left me more time with my children, as well as available evenings to enhance my social life. This is the power of the Energy Fix Equalizer Test.

IDEAS FOR GETTING STARTED

Here are some ideas that you could use to jump-start your lowest equity. If Physical is your lowest, you could go for a walk, give up caffeine instantly, order a salad instead of a hamburger, make an appointment for a massage, join a health club, etc.

If Mental is your lowest score, go to the bookstore immediately and buy a book on a subject that you know nothing about, or sign up for a class to learn a new language, or do some crossword puzzles.

If Emotional is your lowest, start a journal and write down how you feel about life, or have a conversation with your significant other about how you feel; or purchase and read the book *Love is Letting Go of Fear*, by Gerald Jampolsky.

If you find that Financial is lowest, make a budget and stick to it, open a savings account, round up useable items you no longer need and have a garage sale, or get a second job.

This reminds me of an experience. Years ago when finances were very low, I looked around the house to see what

I could sell, and to the horror of my children, I made a flier and delivered it all around the neighborhood—to sell our refrigerator. Now, this wasn't an extra refrigerator, this was the only one we had. I needed money quickly, it was the nicest thing I had and I sold it in one day. Good thing it was winter, I put the milk, butter and eggs out in the snow! The good news was that I got a raise that next week—see, it really works.

If Social is out of balance, invite friends over, get involved with a group that has similar interests, volunteer at a local charity, try out for a play, take a drama class, write a letter to a friend telling them how much you appreciate them. You get the idea.

If the Spiritual equity is lowest, make a list of all that you are grateful for, learn to meditate, pray, play with a child, go to church or synagogue, do a kind deed for a neighbor, get out in nature and hug a tree. Have some fun and do something NOW!

Remember, our goal is BALANCE. However, being balanced but low in energy is not the answer, we need to be balanced and have high energy, too. We will soon learn that balance doesn't necessarily mean "the same" in each area of our life because the power is in the frequency—and that is what this book is all about—learning to raise our energy vibration to solve problems and live a healthier, happier life.

In the next section, we are going to learn to do just that—raise our physical frequency—so read on.

Energy Equalizer Test
By Connie Hayes

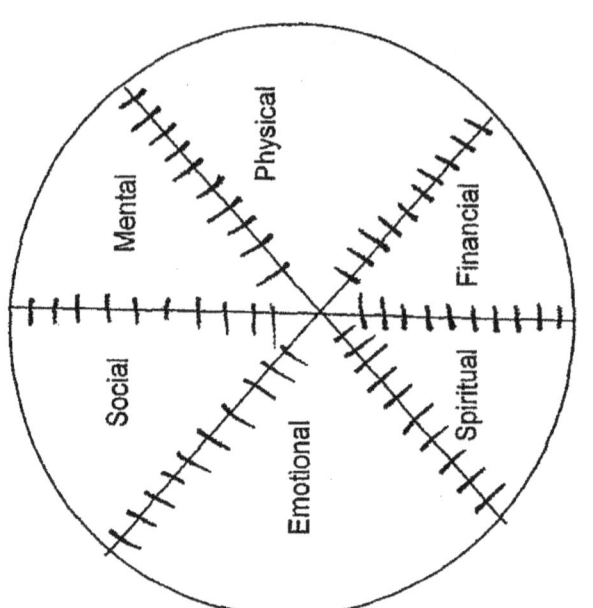

Rate yourself on each of the six equities from 1 to 10, with 10 being the best. Be honest, as this will do you no good at all if you are not. Answer the question as of today. Take the test at least four times a year. Put a mark on the line in each equity that you feel indicates your current self – 1 being the closest to the center, 10 being the outermost. Resist putting 5 on all of the equities as this is not an accurate picture. After all marks are in the equities, connect them with a line. This is now your wheel of life. Look at the lowest equities - these are the ones that need the most urgent attention.

Here are the questions:

Physical: How is your physical health right now? Your energy level? Do you like your body? Your weight? Mental: Are you purposely stretching yourself intellectually? Are you learning something new, or are you in a rut? Emotional: Do you express your feelings well? Are your emotions a negative or positive aspect of your life? Social: Do your primary relationships work? Are the people in your life a cause for joy, worry, or concern? Financial: Rate your finances for today. Do you have enough money for all of your needs, most of your wants, and enough to share? IS IT ENOUGH? Spiritual: Do you have a purpose in life? Do you have a unique reason for why you are here? Do you have goals you feel you must reach before you die? Are you working towards making this world a better place?

SECTION ONE

PHYSICAL EQUITY

CHAPTER ONE

The Fire Within

*"Fear less, hope more,
eat less, chew more,
talk less, say more,
love more,
and all good things
will be yours."*
~Swedish Proverb~

In order to really begin to understand energy, we must first understand frequency. Everything is energy—you are energy, my desk is energy, the carpet is energy—everything. However, everything is radiating energy at a different rate of speed, which is the frequency. So, we are now going to turn our Energy Equalizer Wheel into a pyramid:

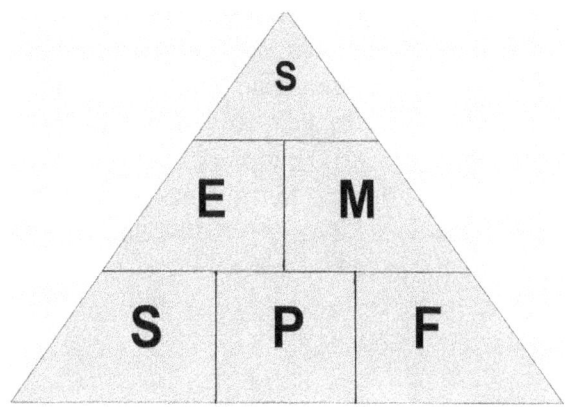

On this pyramid diagram, there are three different levels of frequency. Now, don't write to me and tell me that all these things we are going to talk about can't be broken down into only three categories of frequency. I know that. However, in order for us to get our minds around this huge subject, and most of all, to be able to use this information in our own lives, I need to keep it simple. So, for this discussion we are putting all six energy equities on three levels of frequency. Notice that physical, financial and social are on the lowest level. Low means slow. The slower the frequency, the more dense the energy. Most of our problems in this life can be found on this level. See if you agree with me. Health problems, financial problems and relationship problems—this sounds like a synopsis of most of the hurdles we try to jump over every day, doesn't it? Not only are they the most common problems we face, but, they are the least powerful of the frequencies, so that brings me to one of the most important principles I will ever teach you, which I learned from Albert Einstein: You can't solve a problem from the same frequency as the problem! This is such a critical part of this Energy Fix System that I am going to say it again:

YOU CAN'T SOLVE A PROBLEM FROM THE SAME FREQUENCY AS THE PROBLEM!

Now, it begins to make a little more sense as to why most of our huge problems are on this bottom level—because we are trying to solve them from the same level as the problem. Take money, for instance. If money solved money problems, our welfare system would change people's lives and bring them out of poverty. It doesn't do that in most cases. It only solves the problem for the moment. That's why the adage: *"Give a man a fish and he eats for a day, teach a man to fish and he eats for a lifetime"* is so true. In order to solve the problem for good, we need to raise our frequency.

On the second tier of frequency you will find both Mental and Emotional Equities. These vibrate faster, and are therefore more powerful frequencies. Facing lower level problems from this perspective gives you a much better chance at a solution.

On the top level is the most powerful Equity of all—Spiritual. This frequency has dominion over all the others, and all problems could be solved from this level if we knew how to tap into it properly. Hopefully, once you have completed this book, you will know how.

It's important to know that even though I am trying to keep this fairly simple, there are degrees of power within the levels and I will try to point those out to you as we go through each section.

BEGINNING WITH THE PHYSICAL EQUITY

It makes very good sense to me to start our study with the physical, not because it is any more important than any of the others, because, remember, they are all equal and balance is our goal; but, because physical health is a natural "springboard" to all of the other types of energy. For example: when you feel well, is your mental attitude usually better? How about your emotions? Yes, we can usually control our emotions more easily when we feel good physically. Do your relationships have a better chance of succeeding when you are physically fit and out of pain rather than feeling tired and cranky most of the time?

And, is it more feasible to do something productive about your finances when your body is cooperating with you? Yes, most definitely. I know for a fact that you take more time to help others (spiritual) when you feel great instead of always needing help yourself.

The fact is that we need a lot more physical energy than we do some of the other frequencies, because we live on a physical planet, and because physical energy is not as powerful as some of the others; therefore, it takes more of it to create balance.

I have talked to thousands of people, and most of us agree that we would like to have more physical energy. Now, I'm

Physical Equity

talking about the real thing—not nervous energy that makes us drive ourselves on, or willpower—but, the real thing; where we bound out of bed in the morning and can't wait to get to the day. And we never have to turn anything down that we want to do because we are too tired, too sick or because we are overweight.

Would you agree that most "winners" have high energy? Would you agree that high energy people are usually more physically fit than unfit? And, would you agree that most physically fit people are usually more slender than fat? In almost every case you will find that having high physical energy and being physically fit go together. The truth is that energy is yours for the taking if you know where to look.

This section of the book will teach us four important concepts about energy and what we can do with it. We can:

1. build more authentic, useable physical energy
2. conserve the energy we already have
3. stop the energy "leaks"
4. make our energy more efficient.

If you are struggling in any of the six equities, you need an infusion of energy. In our discussion of physical energy we need to know how to get more of it, how to use it efficiently and how to avoid the "siphons", which are energy leaks or thieves. Think of a burning candle. I'm going to equate its flame with energy. If I were to put a glass over the top of this flame, what would happen to it? That's right, it would go out. Why? Because of a lack of oxygen. So, we all know that we have to have oxygen to sustain the flame. WE ALSO HAVE TO HAVE OXYGEN IN OUR BODIES TO SUSTAIN ENERGY!

What if I had just a little fire in my fireplace, maybe just a few coals, and I came along with an old-fashioned bellows and gave it a good whiff or two of air? What is likely to happen? That's right, it would flame up and become a bigger fire. So, we can increase the flame with more oxygen, and WE CAN INCREASE ENERGY WITH MORE OXYGEN! Oxygen is pretty important stuff then. Let's talk about oxygen.

What do you think is the easiest way to get oxygen into our bodies? I mean the really easy way. Yes, breathing. It's a good thing we don't have to be reminded to breathe or we would all probably be dead. Breathing is one way to get oxygen.

However, if I wanted to increase my oxygen intake, is there a way I could breathe differently from the shallow breathing that I do subconsciously? Sure, I could do deep breathing. (I know this is not rocket science, but, somehow we all miss it). And, if I regularly did deep breathing exercises to increase my oxygen, could I expect to have a higher level of energy? Yes! Amazing!

I have studied various methods of breathing and have adopted two major types of breathing exercises. One is for increasing energy, the other one is to relax. I will give you directions for both of them here, since being able to control energy in order to feel great means that sometimes you want a burst of energy and sometimes you want to calm the energy field. Read through the instructions for each exercise before trying them for the first time. That way you can perform each exercise smoothly for the greatest benefit.

HIGH ENERGY BREATHING EXERCISE (as taught by Jill Johnson in *Oxycise*)

For the first month that you are practicing this method, be sure to do it sitting down, for you are sure to feel light-headed and you are sure to cough and sputter.

Bend your head over nearly to your lap, and as you straighten up, inhale through your nose to the count of five, hold for the count of five and COUGH out the air through your mouth as if someone had just hit you in the gut. Be sure to keep coughing out the old stale air before you take the next big breath. Continue with this process as many times as you can without making yourself sick. At first, you might only be able to do a couple, but, keep working at it until you can do a full set of 10 energy breaths. The goal is to do 3 sets of 10 each day. A good time to practice is when you first wake up in the morning while you are sitting on the side of your bed, and certainly any time you are feeling low in energy. At those times when you would normally want to grab a Coke or a cup of coffee, or a candy bar, try breathing instead. You can always go into the restroom to practice. I like to do deep breathing whenever I come to a stop sign or especially a red light. That way I am not upset at stopping. The person in the car next to me thinks I'm crazy, but, I know better—I'm crazy smart! Try it, you'll feel like you had a good nap.

After you get good at it, try it standing up. Bend the knees and lean over slightly with your hands resting on your knees. This also helps strengthen not only your lungs, but, your abdomen and flattens your stomach!

When you have advanced far enough to do ten at a time, visualize breathing in a beautiful white or golden light (whichever seems right to you) as you inhale, and breathing out gray or black polluted air as you exhale.

As an aside, after finishing a set of energy breaths is a goodtime to recite one of your physical affirmations or declarations which we will talk about at a later time.

BREATHING FOR RELAXATION

Lie down flat or sit comfortably in a chair. Close your eyes and drop the jaw slightly. Begin noticing your breathing.

Inhale S L O W L Y through the nose as you count 1-2-3 then exhale through the mouth just as if you were blowing through a straw making a slight "hissing" noise as you count 1-2-3-4-5 then start again. Don't force anything. Be sure to lower your shoulders.

While controlling your breathing, think "in comes relaxation" on the in breath, and "out goes the tension" on the out breath. If you do not feel your body relaxing, lift your shoulders up to your ears and then drop them before continuing your deep breathing.

Relaxation exercises are excellent tools for beginning meditation periods, and are used before visualization and affirmation sessions. Five minutes of Breathing for Relaxation will calm the most frazzled of people; but, don't despair if you haven't even got five minutes to spare. I have found that even two or three of these breaths will bring me down from a frenetic "high" and make me much more at ease with myself and my surroundings. I'm sure my family appreciates the times I take a few deep relaxation breaths before dealing with them! I, at one time, was one of the most stressed-out people you could ever know. I learned to relax with an audio tape program and I am happy to announce to you that I now have my own Meditation CD available for you, which has three meditations on it for your practice. It includes The Deep Relaxation Exercise and two other meditations. See the footnote at the end of this chapter for ordering information.

EXERCISE FOR OXYGEN

Another way I could increase my oxygen store would be through physical exercise. Isn't that the way the entire aerobic movement started? If you look closely at the word "aerobic" you'll see that it actually means "with oxygen". So, an aerobic exercise would be one with a sustained flow of oxygen. For example, if I am jumping on a trampoline at a steady pace, I am getting a sustained flow of oxygen coming into my body.

However, if I am playing tennis or golf, my oxygen intake is sporadic because my movement is not sustained. So those types of exercise are considered anaerobic.

Have you ever looked at those little charts that tell you how many minutes you need to do a certain exercise before it actually becomes aerobic? For example, the chart says that you have to run for a minimum of twelve minutes before running becomes aerobic. Why twelve and not nine? All it means is that you can be guaranteed that in twelve minutes or more of running, your body will be into heavy calorie burning—which is, of course how we make energy. So, for our discussion, think of this equation: OXYGEN PLUS A CALORIE EQUALS ENERGY.

WHAT'S A CALORIE GOT TO DO WITH IT?

That's right. Now we know quite a bit about energy. We know we can sustain energy with oxygen, and we know that we can increase oxygen. But, to create more energy, we need a calorie. Are calories hard to get? Hardly. Why? Because they are in all food. They are in hot food, cold food, new food, old food, rotten food, poisoned food—they're even in grass! Why would the good Lord put them in everything and make them almost indestructible? (One student of mine said, "I don't know, but, I'm going to have a talk with him someday about that".) They are in everything because they just happen to be absolutely essential to life. No calories, no energy.

Now, I know that a calorie is just a measurement of heat, so you don't need to call or write me to tell me that, but, for our understanding right now, just stick with me. No calories—no energy; no energy—no life. When the energy goes out of you—you are dead! So stop hating calories —they are essential. They're not hard to get, but, you must have them.

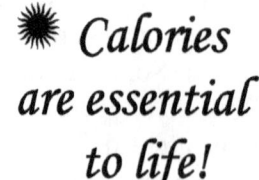
✸ *Calories are essential to life!*

The Fire Within

Now, here's the really important part. Let's say that we have a calorie—if oxygen is available right now, it will burn it for energy. Here comes another calorie—no oxygen is available right now so it will store that calorie. If your body is storing more calories than you would like it to, is it the calorie's fault? No, it just showed up, for heaven's sake. It is doing exactly what it is supposed to do. That's why counting calories is so ridiculous. It's backwards, it's working upstream, it's nearly impossible to do on a regular basis, and it's ineffective. Calories are in all food and they are essential to life. Now, I agree that we are eating high calorie foods too much of the time, in portions much too large, but, it's still not the calorie's fault. Your body is programmed to keep you alive, and therefore, it is not going to waste calories. Calories are like gold to the body. You don't dump out your purse each night and say, "well, I didn't spend all my money today, so I'll just have to throw it away." The body won't throw away calories either. It knows it can't keep you alive without calories, so if it has some left over at the end of the day, it will save them. That's the way it is programmed: burn with oxygen, save without oxygen!

So, the problem is lack of oxygen. We all know people that can eat us under the table. They can eat and eat and never put on an extra pound. Why? You might think that it's because they have a faster metabolism. Do you know what "metabolism" means? It is the rate or speed at which your body converts calories to energy. So, one person might have a faster metabolic rate than yours. But, here's the good news. You can speed up your metabolism any time you want. You could speed it up today and you don't have to know a thing about set-points. In fact, you don't need to know anything except a simple little chemistry equation that says: Hmmm! I need oxygen with my calories if I intend to burn them for energy!

Just a little note about metabolism. Each of our 65 trillion cells (or more according to some scientists) has enough energy in it to raise a 150 pound person one foot off the ground. Now, that's energy! The way that the cell actually converts that calorie and oxygen into energy is in little furnaces called "mitochondria". These little furnaces are supposed to be plentiful in each cell; however, your body is magnificent and it is not wasteful. So, if you are not using the mitochondria to burn calories, the body thinks "Hmmm, the boss is not using mitochondria lately, so don't make any more."

Wow, that means the person who is tired and overweight and needs the furnaces the most and is getting very little oxygen but lots of calories, HAS FEWER MITOCHONDRIA than the thin person has who eats like a horse, runs and is active all day. Did I say that was fair? Probably not, but, it is the way it is. So that's why the fat get fatter and the thin stay thin! Just think OXYGEN. If deep breathing and aerobic exercise were the only two ways to increase your oxygen to speed up calorie burning, most of us would be big as houses or dead. We rarely deep breathe (unless we yawn), and 95% of Americans do very little, if any, aerobic exercise on a regular basis. So, there must be another way. There is, but, hold on to your hats. You're going to love what's coming next.

*To order my Meditation CD go to
www.connielynnhayes.com

CHAPTER TWO

Fueling the Fire

*"Life isn't about finding yourself...
life is about creating yourself."*
~George Bernard Shaw~

Our goal is to raise our energy. We know what it takes to create energy; both calories and oxygen. And we know where the mitochondria furnaces are; and we know that calories are not hard to get. So, we must continue on our quest for oxygen.

You'll be happy to know that the major way to get oxygen for calorie burning is with our food! Well, that is not quite right—the number one way is WATER. Which is why I am such a fanatic about water! That's right; water is an oxygen carrier and delivers up to 85% oxygen. Did you know that the air you are breathing accounts for only 20% oxygen? Water gives you 65% more oxygen than air! Are there any calories in water? No! What a great plan! But, who's going to make any money telling you that you need calories plus water? (Who would have believed a few years ago that bottled water would become a hugely profitable industry.) What a laugh. There's only money in it when you are told to do something difficult, like counting calories.

Do you think feeling hungry is normal? You'd better believe it is normal. I'm going to create a corny scenario for you, but, I think it will help you get the point.

Let's pretend that when the Creator planned this planet and called it Earth, He said, "I'm going to put these funny little creatures on Earth called human beings, and I'm going to make them oxygen and calorie dependant. But, I'm going to surround them in oxygen so they don't even have to go looking for the stuff. Then, I'm going to put calories in all food so that they can't possibly mess up. They could even eat grass and stay alive. Also, I'm going to put more oxygen in water than anything else, and no calories. Then I'm going to dump water out of the sky, pour it down the canyons and store it in ponds and lakes so everyone can find it easily. And finally, I'm going to turn on their thirst so they can't go more than 24 hours without it. And, just as an insurance policy, I'm going to turn on their hunger so they won't forget to eat!"

Perfect plan? I'd say so. But, we have completely messed it up. We get thirsty and we drink Coke. We get hungry and we take appetite suppressants or enroll in behavior modification classes. I'm embarrassed to tell you that I had to teach those classes. We had lists we passed out that trained you do something else; like taking a bath or reading a book, instead of eating when you were hungry. Now, I say, if you are hungry—eat!

> ✹ *There is more oxygen in water than in any other food – with no calories!*

Trying to turn off your hunger all the time and going without eating is just as dumb as if I were to say "there's a law in the Universe called gravity, but, I think it's a ridiculous law so I am not going to obey it. I am going to spend the rest of my life defying gravity. I'm going to prove that I can jump off that ten-story building and not go splat on the ground." You would think I was nuts. You would probably have me hauled away before I could hurt myself. Look at all the things we have been able to accomplish by going <u>with</u> the law of gravity; such as cars and airplanes. Shall we sit around and bemoan the fact that we can't jump off buildings? Let's go **with** the law of hunger for a change and see what we can accomplish, instead of always trying to ignore it.

Fueling the Fire

The problem then is not the hunger—the problem is what we are using to satisfy that hunger—or in other words, what we are NOT eating.

FUELING YOUR FIRE WITH WATER

Good clean spring water is the best water—filtered water is just fair. Only buy bottled water if you know it is really spring water. Most bottled water isn't much better than what comes out of your own tap. The formula for figuring out how much water you need each day is this: take your weight (not how much you would like to weigh, but, your true weight) and cut it in half. (Wasn't that fun?) That's how many ounces of water you need each day just to keep you the way you are. If you want to improve your energy drink about 6-8 ounces more than that.

Are we clear then, that water is number one on our list of high oxygen foods?

FUELING YOUR FIRE WITH VEGETABLES

The second highest oxygen-laden food would be vegetables. Vegetables are approximately 70-75% oxygen. Okay, how about those little olive-green, soft peas in a can? Is there very much oxygen in that can? You know there isn't. We vacuum-packed the darned thing to purposely burp out the oxygen! We even do that sometimes in our home with our Tupperware, don't we? We are so smart, that we discovered that if we take out the oxygen, we can keep food indefinitely. We never stopped to think that we have embalmed the food and it is dead! Are the calories still in those peas? Oh, so now you know the problem—the calories are still there, but, the oxygen was removed. Anything in a can, box, bottle, jar, sealed pouch or bag certainly has lots of calories, but, little or no oxygen to burn up those calories. So, if you really expect your body to use those calories for energy, you need FRESH VEGETABLES. They can be raw, baked or lightly steamed. Fresh vegetables and lots of water is the mainstay of a HIGH

Physical Equity

ENERGY DIET! Didn't you always wonder why there are lots more varieties of vegetables than fruits or grains or meats? Maybe there was a message there that most of us missed.

The trouble with vegetables being highest in oxygen, is that we, in this culture, don't eat enough of them. Just look at our children and their diets. The government counts ketchup as a vegetable in our kid's school lunch! When I ask young clients how many servings of veggies they ate that day, they usually laugh and say "does the pickle on my hamburger count?" Salsa is about as close to a vegetable as most teen-agers get, if that! Part of the problem is that most children (my own Grandchildren included) spend a good part of their life in the car. That means that they are eating fast food almost every day. I have 22 Grandchildren, and I can think of only about four of them that truly like vegetables. And, if they do eat them, it is usually corn—a high-starch vegetable. But, green veggies?—I'd guess only two of them actually eat them on a consistent basis. This is a sad commentary on our times, and my own children know better! A symptom of the problem is that Mother's are not cooking meals like we used to every day—and it is showing up as chronic disease and obesity in our children. If we want to change results—we have to change our actions. I have included a few easy recipes in this chapter, to help get your family to eat more vegetables. Hey! I think food has to taste good, look good and smell good. Start with the freshest, most desirable-looking veggies you can find.

Of course, organic is best—we don't need all those extra toxins and sprays that most regular food has in them. We'll talk about toxins in a later chapter. Please don't overcook your vegetables—keep them fork tender with lots of color still in them. When choosing vegetables, I use the rainbow as a guide. Look for all colors—they are a different color for a reason. However, green should be your favorite color—use green vegetables freely. You need four to five servings of vegetables a day—and potatoes do not count! A serving is about a cup.

Fueling the Fire

If you don't particularly like vegetables or can't find time to cook and eat them, a juicer is the best thing for you. Juicing veggies and drinking them fresh each day is an excellent way to get your five servings. You won't get the fiber (unless you use a VitaMix), but, you will get all the vitamins, minerals and enzymes that vegetables have to offer. I personally like the Juice Man brand because it is small and easy to clean.

FUELING YOUR FIRE WITH GRAINS

The food group that is third from the top would be grains. Grains contain from 60-65% oxygen. What is one of the first things they take away from you on most diets? Bread! I told you we weren't very smart. Grains are high in oxygen, but, where in that grain would the oxygen be concentrated? In the germ, of course; therefore, in order for grains to count as high energy foods, they would have to be WHOLE GRAINS. If I took the germ out of the wheat and planted the remainder, would it grow? No, because the germ is where the "life" is and so eating foods that only have part of the grain in it, like white bread, has no oxygen and no life. I get the biggest kick out of companies that manufacture white flour and try to tell us that it is just as good as the whole grain variety. Why then don't the bugs want it? If it won't even support the life of a bug, why do you think it will be your "staff of life"? (Do you think the bugs know something that we don't?) Whole grains are an excellent food source for oxygen. Digestion of grains is another matter, and we will discuss that in a later chapter.

Because bugs like whole grains, they need to be really, really fresh. When you purchase whole grain cereals, bread or the whole grain itself, I suggest you buy it in small amounts, keep in the refrigerator and use it up quickly. A rancid grain can do more harm than good. Buy from a reputable source that turns their product over quickly—you don't want something that has been sitting on the shelf for a long time. Sprouted grains are an excellent source of both the oxygen from the grain itself, and from the sprout—which is green, our favorite

Physical Equity

color. Please don't rely on bread only for your grain source; and cold cereal is usually a poor choice. We, in this country, eat way too much bread and bread products.

Anything made with white flour is a high-calorie, low oxygen food, and that's what Americans eat the most of every day. Hamburger buns, cakes, cookies, rolls, and pastas are all useless food—and most of us can't use the calories that are densely packed in them. Cold cereals are not any better. They are not all whole grain and they are usually laden with sugar, the most calorie-loaded food possible with zero oxygen. For whole grain, hot cereals are your best bet, and small amounts of whole-grain bread. The number one reason we can't really use high amounts of grains is because even though they do contain oxygen, they also carry lots more calories than vegetables, and most of us are not active enough to burn up those extra calories. We like bread—that's the problem; so try to keep it to one or two slices of **whole grain** bread a day at the most, if you tend to store calories instead of burn them. Drink lots of water-- that will help!

FUELING YOUR FIRE WITH PROTEINS

Protein foods, such as meat, fish, poultry or eggs rank fourth on the oxygen scale. They contain about 50% oxygen if they are 100% lean. If you introduce fat into the equation, it changes the chemistry and, therefore, the oxygen content is reduced. But, what about tuna fish in a can? Well, the protein content is still there; but, since we are discussing oxygen, we know what happens to the oxygen in a canned food. What about frozen foods? That is a good question. The Bio-Chemist that I checked all these numbers with tells me that if we did a chemical analysis on frozen food, we would still see oxygen in the makeup of the food; but, it is now called "bound oxygen", which means that it is all tied up and will take the body more steps to unbind it. It most cases, he tells me, it would probably not be available for calorie-burning, so don't count on it. Fresh meats and eggs are more reliable. But, remember, you can still count the protein from frozen or canned meats—just not the

Fueling the Fire

oxygen. Eggs that are called "free-range" or "organic" are by far a better source of oxygen, because the chicken was allowed to scratch. Why are they scratching? Not to file their nails, but, to dig up something green. Organic eggs are from chickens fed live food, and not kept in "chicken hotels" and fed mash all day. Most of those poor chickens never even see the light of day. Eggs are a great protein source, but to get oxygen from them takes a little more effort. We'll be talking a lot more about dairy products in another chapter, so I'll save my comments for later.

FUELING YOUR FIRE WITH FRUITS

The number five oxygen-rich food is fruit. Fruits contain around 30-35% oxygen. Why do you suppose fruit is a full 40% lower in oxygen than vegetables? Wouldn't you expect fruit to be right up there? The reason is that most fruit is full of fructose—nature's sugar. Fructose is useful to the body for conversion into glycogen which can be used for quick energy—in case I wanted to sprint to the door. The problem is, I don't sprint to the door (or anywhere for that matter) very often and after the body has stored all the glycogen that it can hold in the muscles and liver for easy conversion to energy, it then treats fructose just like plain old white sugar—and stores most of it. The bottom line is—we like fruit, and most of us would rather eat it than vegetables because it's sweet, and we think because it is fresh and natural that we can have all we want. That is not true. We know we shouldn't eat the whole pan of brownies, why, then, do we eat the whole bowl of grapes?

The reason fruit is lower in oxygen is because fructose is bulky and takes up lots of space; and, if fructose is occupying the space, oxygen can't occupy the same space, so it is a vacancy problem. There just isn't enough room. Vegetables don't have the fructose problem so we can eat all we want of them. Fruit is great, but, don't get carried away with it unless you are doing an "all fruit day" which is an excellent thing to do now and then to let the digestive system catch up with itself. Think of fruit as nature's dessert and don't overdo it.

Obviously, the fruit that has the most water in it would be your best choice—making watermelon an ideal oxygen food. Melons and berries are good picks, bananas are usually a poor choice if looking for oxygen.--mostly because we eat them incorrectly. We tend to eat them when they are yellow-green—and they then count as a starch. Eating them speckled brown would at least count as a fruit—but, very high in fructose. Try to eat two fresh fruit a day, and in between meals as a snack is best. Fruit usually digests quickly and if it finds itself hanging around with bread or other starches, it tends to ferment and causes gas and other digestive problems.

We have now learned that it is possible to augment physical energy to a higher level by increasing our oxygen intake. The easiest way is to be drinking more clean, clear water, and adding high-oxygen foods such as fresh vegetables to our daily diet. Don't forget to do your deep breathing and/or aerobic exercise.

LET'S GET YOUR FIRE GOING!

I developed my famous 14-day eating plan when I owned a figure salon, which has proven to be extremely effective for building energy, as well as replacing fat for lean. It's the best way I know to get your little mitochondria-furnaces burning so that your body will make more of them. Even if you do not need to lose weight, I recommend this plan to make a noticeable difference in your energy level. If you are under the care of a Physician, have him or her look at it before you begin; otherwise, follow it exactly as written and be prepared to face your food addictions squarely in the face. To get your free copy of the plan, go to www.connielynnhayes.com, and click on "Free Info", then "Eating Plan". Be sure to follow all the directions exactly as written.

Fueling the Fire

Before you begin, I suggest you get a tape measure and at least measure some general places on your body. Remember, we are not only building energy by burning calories, we are replacing fat with lean. Lean takes up less space than fat (fat is fluffy) so you will lose inches on this diet. Measure your waist, your tummy at the biggest spot around your belly button, and your hips. If you have a trouble spot like your arms or legs, measure there, too. I suggest you only weigh on the first day, the seventh day and the 14th day. Don't be concerned if at the 14th day you weigh more than you did on the 7th day—lean weighs more than fat. If I am holding a pound of hamburger, the kind with the little white blobs of fat in it in one hand, and a pound of ground round steak in the other, you will see that the pound of hamburger is larger than the pound of ground round. Why? they both weigh a pound! Because, lean weighs more than fat, but, fat takes up more space. The really disturbing part of the whole "fat issue" is that by the time you see fat on the outside of your body, your insides are full of it! So the goal is to replace that fat with lean muscle which weighs more, so your tape measure is a much better tool for determining your results—and how you feel. This program is all about raising energy and quality of life. Cheers!

*The figures referred to in this chapter are approximate and are intended for understanding the concept only. Actual denominations would have lots of variables like how the food was grown, amount of pollutants in it, how fresh the food is, how it was taken care of and how it was cooked or prepared. I do not intend nor claim any numbers to be exact; I only intend that you understand the concept being explained.

Physical Equity

Vegetable Recipes

Sweet Carrots:
After steaming baby/sliced carrots lightly, just before serving, mix 1/4 cup orange juice concentrate with 2 Tb. honey and 1/4 tsp. cinnamon in a small saucepan and 2 Tb. butter. Heat and then add the carrots. Enjoy.

Spicy Beets:
After steaming shredded beets for only 2 minutes, toss with 1/2 cup sour cream, and 1-2 tsp. horseradish (adjust to taste), and 1/4 tsp. black pepper and fresh dill as desired.

Zippy Artichokes:
Steam artichokes as usual, but, as an alternative to butter for dipping, mix Thousand Island dressing with sour cream.

Vegetable Lasagna:
Layer in a buttered casserole dish, sliced zucchini squash and/or yellow squash, onions and canned, stewed tomatoes, grated cheese, making two or three layers of all of these items ending with cheese. Bake in 350 degree oven for one hour.

Cauliflower Nachos:
Toss steamed cauliflower with warm nacho sauce.

Creative Salads:
Most salads are boring with just lettuce and tomatoes. Try adding any of these to your crisp greens (I prefer leaf lettuce varieties to iceberg for better taste and nutritional value).

Black beans, almonds, toasted pecans, macadamia nuts, feta cheese, cubes of spicy cheese, dried apple chips, raisins, dried cranberries, grapefruit slices, fresh berries, mandarin oranges, sliced red onion, sliced pear, along with cucumber, radish, green onions, shredded carrots, pickled beets (or plain), parsley, or cilantro, celery and always use fresh herbs in your dressings.

*The best oil to use in dressings is fresh, virgin olive oil; use vinegars that don't have sugar in them.

CHAPTER THREE

A Chemical Fire

"Health is worth more than learning."
~Thomas Jefferson~

Now that we know where to find fuel for energy and where energy is created in the body (mitochondria), we need to have a little discussion about how this marvelous process comes about—which leads us to the endocrine glands.

The word "endocrine" actually means ductless—which refers to the glands in your body that have no ducts or passage ways that lead to anything else. This is one of those "miracles" of the human body and I spent a great deal of my research exploring these fabulous little creations. Just think: you have awesome organs and systems in your body that don't actually do much unless they are "told to" by a chemical or hormone. For example: you could have the biggest engine in your car known to man, but, if there is no spark from the spark plug, it won't turn over. This is the way your body works for the most part. Your endocrine glands are key cogs in the machine works of your body—and if they are not functioning properly, you are going to have health issues.

The endocrine glands include: the pituitary gland, the pineal gland, the thyroid gland, the adrenal glands, the ovaries or the testes, and even the pancreas. Almost all of these glands have something to do with energy, but, for this discussion I am going to focus mostly on the adrenal glands. This is one of those areas where we not only are going to build energy, but, conserve it and stop up a huge energy leak called "stress". This, then, is a three-for-one topic.

I could make a broad sweeping statement: "if I can keep your adrenal glands strong and your liver clean, I can control your health." Why do I put the adrenal glands at number one on my list? Because, these wonderful little glands are capable of doing so many things for you.

ADRENAL GLANDS – *Your built-in battery-pack*

To begin with, you have two little adrenal glands, each perched on top of your kidneys like little derby hats, and because they are part of the endocrine gland system, they produce hormones. They actually produce about 34 of their own hormones, some of which you are familiar with. You've heard of adrenaline, and how a mother is able to lift a car off her baby. You've had adrenaline rushes before which are sometimes referred to as the "fight or flight" mechanism. When a tiger is after you, hormones rush into your bloodstream to give you enough strength and energy to get the heck out of there or fight for your life. Problem is, we don't meet many tigers any more. That is why the adrenal glands are sometimes referred to as the "stress glands", because fear of not being able to make the house payment causes the same reaction in the body that the tiger does!

This is a stressful society and our bodies go through multiple stress responses every day. It is no wonder that I find more exhausted adrenal glands than any other problem. Another hormone called cortisol also rushes through your body under stress and sends all the circulation to the extremities so you can run or fight, but leaves very little help in the trunk of the body for digestion and elimination and other vital functions, which is one good reason we shouldn't eat much under stress. More about digestion later.

The adrenal glands also make a family of hormones, one of which is cortisone, which has the major function of putting out inflammation in the body. That's why, when someone has arthritis (or any other "itis" problem—which means

A Chemical Fire

inflammation) cortisone shots help. However, if the adrenal glands were working properly, they would send cortisone to the sight of the inflammation without the shot.

If that weren't enough for the adrenal glands to do, they also act as backups to the other endocrine glands. That means that if the thyroid gland is struggling, it can hook up with the adrenal glands for a little help—but, if the adrenal glands are exhausted, there is no backup and the other glands start to have problems. I call this the "domino effect", because when the adrenal glands go down, lots of problems occur; however, when the adrenal glands get up and running, other problems go away. I personally think that a lot of our thyroid problems are really adrenal exhaustion problems.

> ✸ *The adrenal glands are backup for the heart!*

Doctors treat thyroid problems, but, rarely treat adrenal problems until it is usually too late. In my experience, I find that if I can get the adrenal glands functioning, other endocrine gland issues disappear. At least, it definitely is the place to begin if you are complaining of being more tired when you wake up than when you went to bed. The number one complaint in my office and in Doctor's offices is "extreme tiredness". I suggest we take a look at your adrenal glands.

The adrenal glands are also backups to the heart—so to speak. I like to explain it this way: When the adrenal glands are exhausted, the heart has no electrical backup. Let's say that you were in the hospital operating room and the power went out. The hospital has a backup energy system for emergencies it would automatically click over to the alternative electrical supply, wouldn't it? Well your body has a similar setup. If your heart is running low on electrical energy, it can ask the adrenal glands for help. It would be like getting a charge for your car's low battery from another car's working battery.

This is a huge plus for the heart, but, when the adrenal glands are flat—there is no backup. See the problem? You are not going to hear any of this from your medical sources, but, since energy is what we are talking about, it is useful to find where your energy is low and then fix it!

Charging your batteries

So, how do we assist the adrenal glands? With nutrition, of course. There are two main ways to do this:

1. Give the glands a little "kick" to get them going –I use a product called Recharge, which is an herbal tincture; and
2. Feed and nourish the adrenals to rebuild them back to first-rate quality. The way to do this is with Dessicated Adrenal from Standard Process, Inc., and from high-quality proteins. Remember, when using natural healing methods, either with supplements and/or food, it is rarely, if ever, an overnight miracle. I have seen miracles, but, true healing is done by the body's intelligence, not ours, and it is done on the body's timetable. So be persistent and consistent.

Protein is what the adrenal glands really want to keep them running smoothly. Supplements get them up faster when they are exhausted, but, a good supply of protein daily will keep them going. Strangely enough, red meat works extremely well for this purpose. I get a kick out of women who bring their husbands to see me, and my recommendation to them is to go get a great big steak! The men just love me because their wives have been making them cut down on meat. Interestingly, the typical male body type (large shoulders, smaller hips) is referred to as the Adrenal Body Type. That body type, whether male or female, requires more protein and is able to use it. In the book about blood type diets, it is referred to as Type O (or the Hunter) body type. The danger comes when we generalize and say that all people are alike.

A Chemical Fire

They are not—and, of course, you knew that all along. Which brings us now to a discussion about protein.

The word protein actually means "to come first". Proteins are the building blocks of every cell in your body. In fact, most of your body is protein; even the fluids that make up most of your body are mostly proteins. There are some pretty important parts of your body that are composed almost entirely of protein, not just your muscles. Your major organs are 100% protein; so your heart and liver, for example, become pretty excited about your protein intake.

HOW MUCH PROTEIN DO YOU NEED?

Just for fun, take a minute right now to write down everything that you ate yesterday. List it all—even the gum and the soda pop. Now, if we use the current "nutritional pyramid" put out by the government (in the last 40 years I have seen this pyramid change at least four times—go lobbyists), you would need to have at least 4 servings of vegetables, 2 to 3 servings of fruit, 7 or 8 servings of grains, 1-2 servings of proteins and 1 serving of fat. I have been giving this test for over forty years, and I have not yet found one person who eats this way, and yet, this is what the government calls a "balanced diet". The medical industry insists that we don't usually need supplements if we get a "balanced diet"—and no one really does. In fact, if you did eat this amount of food, you would ingest around 7,000 calories. Now you know why we don't eat this much—we can't! One of the big problems with this plan, is not only the amount of food, but, the high amount of carbohydrates that it contains. The government makes no discernment between "whole grains" and typical white flour grains. If you ate 8 servings of white flour products each day (and lots of people do) you would join the 40% of obese Americans—not overweight people, but, morbidly obese Americans. That is alarming. We simply cannot burn that many calories, especially from simple carbohydrates (white flour and sugar), and our children are suffering from this oversight.

Physical Equity

The other extreme problem I have with this "pyramid" is the small amount of protein. I agree that vegetables are most important, as we've already discussed, but, if you only have two servings of protein foods, you've aged. Here is how you can tell how you're aging. Go back to your list of foods that you ate yesterday. Use the abbreviated scale below to count your protein grams for the day, total it then come back to this treatise.

Protein Source Chart

Amount	Food	Protein Grams
1 ounce	meat/fish/poultry	3
8 ounces	milk/yogurt	7
1	egg	8
1 ounce	cheese	10
1 cup	cottage cheese	20
1 slice	whole grain bread	3
1 cup	whole grain cereal	3
1/4 cup	raw nuts	10
2 TB.	nut butter	10
1 cup	legumes	20

For protein bars, powders and drinks, you need to consult the label.

The question now is how much protein does a person really need? There are varying opinions on this one, but, a good rule of thumb is: half of your body weight in grams per day to keep you the way you are. However, if you wish to replace fat with lean and/or build muscle, you need to add 15%.

Go back to your list, write down your weight, divide it in half (we did this once before for water), and you have your answer for how much protein you needed yesterday. Now, take whichever number is the highest, either half your weight or your protein intake for yesterday and subtract one from the other. If your weight was the highest number, you will have a negative total—if your protein grams were higher then you have a plus answer. All you need to know is that if your answer was a minus—yesterday you aged! All aging is, in a nutshell, is that your cells are wearing out faster than they are repairing or rebuilding. If you have a lot of minus days, your city (body) is becoming a slum district and needs rebuilding. I don't care what doctors and so-called health professionals say—we are not getting enough protein in our diets. Now, I didn't say that it had to be all meat—but, you need to know where else to get protein.

A word of caution for vegetarians and vegans

One very dangerous trend that I observed with our teens of late is that they call themselves "vegetarians", but, I found out that all that meant to them was that they didn't eat anything that "walked, crawled or swam" to use their vernacular. I told them that was just fine, but asked them how many cups of legumes they eat each day. Most of them said, "what's a legume?" Or when I asked how many cups of nuts, seeds, or tofu they ate, it turned out most of them ate none of those vegetable-type proteins. They had just dropped animal proteins out of their life; and the result—most of them suffered from chronic fatigue! You must have protein, and if you are not getting it daily, you are degenerating—fast!

Your body has to make judgment calls 24/7. If you don't eat enough protein today and the body is scheduled to make heart cells, it will probably steal protein from somewhere else in your body—like the nice little layer of protein we have under our skin. It's no wonder that our skin starts to wrinkle and sag; but, if it has to choose between skin and heart

> ✸ *We are not getting enough protein in our diets.*

cells, I'm personally glad it knows which one is most important!

Protein Insufficiency – More problems

As an aside, if you suffer from allergies and/or fluid retention, you probably have a protein deficiency. I have seen people get over their allergies completely, just by diligently seeing to it that they get the proper amount of protein each day, and your swollen ankles and tight rings will go away too, with protein, and of course, lots of water. Remember, protein is processed through the kidneys as ketones, and if you don't drink a lot of water, please don't go on a high protein diet. Water is essential.

Those with hypoglycemia will be able to balance their sugar and their energy very well if they eat half of their body weight in protein grams and spread it out through the day according to this formula: a fruit in the early a.m. followed by 20-25 grams protein in their breakfast, 10 grams in a mid-morning snack, 15-20 at lunch along with some complex carbohydrates, 10 grams protein in an afternoon snack along with another fruit, and 15 or more in their dinner. These numbers obviously need to be adjusted according to the total grams needed for each individual, but, you get the idea. I also recommend, as an aside, that if you have sugar problems, or sleeping problems, that you eat raw vegetables only during the day, and only steamed or baked veggies at dinner. We'll get to digestion later.

We know that approximately 98% of a human's cells are replaced every 120 days. Some cells only last a few seconds and others last a year or longer. But, for the most part, they are pretty much exchanged for new every four months. The problem is that most people are replacing their old cells with new cells of poorer quality! That's why we age and why our body deteriorates. But, it doesn't need to be that way— you can begin building better bodies for yourself and your family today now that you know all about protein. So, start

> ☀ *Most people are replacing their old cells with new cells of poorer quality!*

feeding your cells right; they cannot be built out of cookies and candy and soda pop! Use your head—you know that most of your foods are not quality building materials for your cells, especially the outer cellular membrane which needs protein, protein and more protein.

HOPE FOR ASTHMATICS

Bronchial problems are one of the first symptoms of adrenal exhaustion. It will amaze you how many so-called asthmatics can be free of this debilitating, and sometimes life-threatening condition, just by feeding those glands, even small children. So, if you are extremely tired, get multiple infections a year and/or have breathing problems, look to protein and your adrenal glands for help. Following these suggestions will put you back on the road to feeling and looking terrific.

*Recharge can be ordered at
www.connielynnhayes.com.

** No information in this book is meant to replace your prescribed medications or your Health Professional's advice. Always check with your Health Professional if you have questions.

CHAPTER FOUR

The Power of Fire

"As I see it, every day you do one of two things: build health or produce disease in yourself."
~Adelle Davis~

In Chapter One we discussed frequency. We know that energy with a faster frequency trumps energy with a lower frequency, which means slower. That's because the faster the frequency the more powerful the energy becomes.

We also learned that the Physical Equity on the Energy Fix Wheel is on the level of slow, dense and the least powerful of frequencies. However, it is now time for you to understand that there are levels within levels—which means that within the physical, material energies we are discussing such as health, fitness and appearance, there are levels that are definitely more powerful than others. I don't pretend to know how many levels there really are, but, I do know which ones are more powerful and how we can use them to our benefit.

In the previous chapters we have talked at great length about food, and I have mentioned some food supplements that I use. This is a great place to find many varying levels of frequency and therefore, power. In some foods, we can find next to no energy, and in others, a lot of energy. The trouble with food is that high or low energy foods both fill up our stomachs. You can tell, after you eat, whether your body liked what you gave it or not, if you are paying attention; however, most of us have anesthetized ourselves so that we no longer tune into our bodies long enough to get the message. We are supposed to feel energized after eating, not tired and lagging. How do you feel after Thanksgiving dinner? Most of us feel like we need a nap, and that is true, because we have so overloaded our stomachs that all the energy we have is now concentrated on digestion and our heads and extremities feel sleepy and incapable of doing much of anything. A lot of the "tiredness" complaints we have are just due to this behavior—we overload the stomach with too much food and our body reacts the way it is supposed to by concentrating a large portion of energy on digestion, and so you feel tired. What a wonderful system—it actually does what it is designed to do. Go figure!

So how can we tell if we are eating high energy foods? Easy—eat food as close to it's natural state as possible. In other words, the fresher the produce-- the more power there is in the food. That means that if you grew it, picked it and ate it today, that would be best, especially if it was organic and had no pesticides or chemicals put in the soil or on the food. Next best would be organic produce from a verifiable source. Just remember, every time you introduce a foreign matter into the food, the frequency goes down. That applies especially to all processed food. So anything in a box, carton, bottle or can is highly suspect. If you are truly eating for energy and not just to fill up your stomach, you need to learn to read labels.

Having said that, labels can be very misleading, and we can thank our government for that. It is important to see how many calories, fat, carbs and protein a food contains, but, don't be fooled by the percentages they give you as to the daily amount needed for the day. Those percentages are arbitrary amounts based on a 2,000 calorie a day diet, assuming that the food they are selling still has any value in it after they get through with it!

> ✹ *Eat foods as close to their natural state as possible.*

The most important part of the label is the list of ingredients—what's actually in this product? You are probably going to be dismayed when you find out that what you thought was food, was actually chemical. If you don't know what a word means, it probably isn't food, and that goes for supplements, too. I am asked all the time about the difference between a product like Life Mate and maybe a product like Centrum Multi-vitamin—which brings me to a story.

VITAMINS & SUPPLEMENTS – *Synthetic vs. Whole Food*

Scientists who work with making vitamins synthetic (man-made) take a vitamin such as Vitamin C and look at it under their high-powered microscopes and examine it's molecular structure. Then, methodically, they reconstruct that structure, exactly, with chemicals—and they pronounce it the same. That's the product you find in grocery stores and pharmacies. They named this new formula ascorbic acid and announce to the world that they now have a cheap, easily reproduced source of Vitamin C. The worst part of this scenario is since this came through the "scientific field" the government believes that ascorbic acid is vitamin C and requires all manufacturers to use that chemical name because they don't even recognize any other name. That really muddies up the nutritional waters. Now, to go on with my story—those who weren't so sure about this method of reconstructing vitamins, took sea water and put it under their microscopes. They saw the molecular structure of sea water and went about restructuring it with chemicals, molecule for molecule until it looked exactly like the natural sea water, and pronounced it perfect. The trouble was that when they put salt water fish into this man-made chemical sea water, the fish died. Why? Don't you think it is pretty presumptuous on our part to believe that what we can see is all that exists? Nutrition is a contemporary science and new things are being discovered as we speak. We just can't see all of nature's secrets yet. That's the problem with synthetic foods and supplements!

When I first started down my nutritional road over 40 years ago, we knew of only 15 B vitamins. Now, they have discovered about 23 of them (the United States still only recognizes 15); so where were the other 8 back then? They were always there; we just couldn't see them!

So, we can deduce from this situation, that if we eat things the way the Creator made them, or as close to it as we can get, we will most likely find all the nutrients that we know of **and all those we don't know of yet**. Wouldn't that seem like the logical thing to do?

Therefore, when choosing food, choose natural. How can we choose natural proteins from animals?, you might ask. Wild life is better for many reasons. First, those animals have probably eaten only foods that are wild and natural, whereas domestically produced animals are fed all kinds of chemically produced food to make them grow big and fat. Domestic animals are also given lots of steroids, and medicines to kill the bacteria in them, to make them appear as "well" to us. To make matters worse, the butcher usually adds more chemicals to the meat to make them bright and red, since we think that looks fresher than if they were brown. Even old meat can be made to look fresh with chemicals. So, if you can manage it, get organic meats which are frequently called "free range", and poultry without all the added chemicals. Wild, cold-water fish are best and can usually only be found in organic grocery stores unless you caught them yourself.

This is the reason I only use and recommend natural, whole-food supplements. You can at least count on the fact that these products come from the original whole food or foods and contain all the known nutrients as well as the, as yet, unknown ones. First and foremost, with whole-food products, you can do no harm—nothing more than the food itself could do. Watch out though for labels that read "all natural", because that term has also become very misconstrued. We think, and the manufacturers want us to think, that natural means safe. It doesn't—even aspirin is considered "natural" because it's original source was coal tar! Don't fall for the " natural" conspiracy. If you are going to go to the trouble of taking supplements, which I think you should, make sure they are the finest money can buy. You can always be sure that if I recommend a supplement to you, it is whole-food and natural, even right down to the processing of that supplement—which is another concern. You can start out with a natural food product like corn for example, but, in trying to extract the oil from that corn you use high heat (which is faster and much cheaper than a cold, expellered process), and you have then damaged the structure of the oil so much so that it has now become a dangerous source of oil—not a nutritious food at all. All oils, whether taken from the canola, safflower or any other vegetable that is exposed to high heat, has been damaged. I know that buying cold-pressed oils are more expensive, but, they really are worth it. Your best bet is extra virgin olive oil—expellered (cold pressed), of course.

I have found through research, that whole foods that have been vacuum processed are usually better than those that have been dehydrated. Both kinds have had the oxygen sucked out of them, so the oxygen is not available; however, we have to prepare them with water which usually solves the oxygen problem. But, there again, where the food came from and how it was prepared before being made into a supplement is an important part of the equation. Therefore, I only use those supplements from companies that have their own gardens, orchards and animals, like Standard Process, or companies that can verify their source of food, like Life Mate from Natural Wonders. When you read a label from any of these companies, don't bother with the list of nutrients with names that you probably can't pronounce (thanks to the government), but, go directly to the ingredient list and see if you can find names of foods that you recognize. Take Vita C, for example, the only vitamin C product that I can recommend from Life Plus. They list over 20 foods that are contained in that product, and all of them I know! What a concept!

The way you prepare food also either raises or lowers the frequency level of that food. If possible, always quick-cook foods or if you cook foods over long periods of time, like some meats, make sure that you are keeping the moisture in, such as in a slow cooker. Steaming vegetables is best if not eaten raw. Dairy products are another matter.

CALCIUM – *the most important mineral*

Dairy products have become a real enigma in this country. On one hand, they do contain good protein, which we do need. On the other hand, they also contain a lot of chemicals that we don't need or want. And in the process of pasteurization, all the enzymes have been destroyed; which renders the calcium that naturally occurred in the food, not only useless for most of us, but, down-right dangerous for some.

Calcium deficiencies are rampant in this country because of the pasteurization process. Calcium is considered a macro-mineral, which means that we need it in very large amounts. It is needed for bones, teeth and nerve health. It is also called nature's "lullaby nutrient". About 99% of your calcium intake goes to bones and teeth, and 1% goes to nerves; but, guess where we find the first deficiency? That's right, in your nerves. So, the symptoms we see are anxiety, insomnia, pain and hyper-activity as well as inability to focus. That really takes a lot of problems into consideration, doesn't it? Take for example ADD—a true scourge of our times. Children who can't sit still in school and/or are incapable of focusing long enough to learn anything are being singled out by the hundreds and put on dangerous drugs to "mellow them out". I agree that something is wrong, but, in most cases, putting children on drugs that have serious side-effects should be last resort—not first! In my experience with many of these children (and adults), I find them to be extremely calcium deficient.

Calcium absorption 101

To understand why they are deficient, let's take a look at how calcium is actually used by the body. Calcium is one of the most difficult nutrients we know of to actually be digested, absorbed and utilized by the body—and it is needed in huge amounts, especially in growing children. Dairy products, then, become our major source of calcium—but, most of them can't digest it. It's legal to say the calcium is in the milk and cheese; however, if we can't digest it—we won't be able to use it. Now, I would be happy if when we can't digest something, our body would just eliminate it; but, most of the time, it stores it instead. It probably thinks that some day it will figure out what to do with it, but, in the meantime its' frugality can really cause some problems. When it saves unusable calcium, it stores it in different parts of the body like the joints, which causes arthritis; in the soft tissue, which is known as fibromyalgia; in the kidneys, which results in kidney stones; or the gallbladder which turns out to be gallstones. None of these are very pleasant conditions to live with. Our medical industry has figured out ways of dealing with some of these problems like removing the gallbladder. Now, in most cases, that is throwing out the baby with the bath water. I know there are instances where the gallbladder is full of cancer or gangrene and removal is the only option, but, not in the hundreds and hundreds of gallbladders that are removed each year just because a person is suffering from the pain of gallstones.

> ✺ *99% of your calcium intake goes to your bones and teeth ; and 1% goes to the nerves, the first place you'll find a deficiency.*

Doctors are not really crazy about me because I tend to ask questions that they can't answer. I couldn't possibly be smarter than most of our physicians, but I have to wonder, why aren't they asking *why* people's bodies are storing calcium in weird places and causing all of these problems? I believe that is the appropriate question that is not being addressed. I had a client call me and tell me that her eye doctor had found a calcium deposit on her optic nerve. I said, "what does he plan to do about that?" She said that they hadn't come up with a **surgical procedure** yet to deal with that situation. Do you see the problem? They think the only solution is to have a way of cutting out the deposit; or worse yet, taking out the organ with the deposits in it! Wouldn't it be simpler just to figure out why the body is depositing calcium in the first place? Because, basically, there's no money in it. That is a sad thing to admit, but, that's the most logical answer.

The other part of the answer is that medical professionals, for the most part, have had little or no training or education in nutrition. Therefore, that makes them no more qualified to answer a nutritional question than your plumber. You wouldn't ask your plumber about your calcium, would you? Why, then, do we ask doctors about it? They are doctors of medicine and/or surgery. If you want medicine and/or surgery, they are the right ones to ask. If, however, you want to know about nutrition, they probably won't know. The problem I have with this situation, is that even though most doctors don't know much about nutrition, they still answer the question as if they did know. They routinely give you answers that are not only incorrect, but can be downright dangerous to your health. I will never tell you not to take your medicine; I might read to you the side effects from the PDR (guide to drugs). I don't write those books, but, I will notify you of the side effects so that you can make an informed decision about the risk to benefit ratio when taking that drug. That way, you can talk intelligently to your doctor or pharmacist when deciding which drugs to take and which ones to eliminate or exchange for a less dangerous one.

But, back to the calcium absorption problem. This is my basic rule: It is probably not a good idea to use non-pasteurized dairy products because of the potential deadly bacteria that could be lurking in them. That leads us to enzymes, our only hope for utilizing any calcium, or many other nutrients, out of our food. Taking a full-spectrum dietary enzyme product such as Digestive Formula from Life Plus, or Multizyme from Standard Process, Inc., works well for this situation. It is also necessary for most of us, especially growing children, teenagers and women to take extra calcium in supplement form.

Most calcium supplements are just as difficult to digest as is the calcium in your dairy products. That's because most supplements use calcium carbonate—which is essentially chalk. You don't want calcium carbonate—that's the one that is in the drug store variety. Calcium citrate gets a lot of press lately, and it is legal to say that it is easier to digest than carbonate; however, it still takes about 5 steps for the body to break it down and use it. I prefer in most cases, calcium lactate. This is the easiest to digest (except for calcium bicarbonate) and is relatively inexpensive. There is one knock on calcium lactate—it is bulky and so you have to take a lot of it to get the job done.

Because calcium needs to be absorbed through the colon wall, if you tend towards constipation and do not have a soft bowel movement at least twice a day, you are probably calcium deficient. This is the first question I ask kids with ADD. Many times they tell me that they only go to the bathroom once a week or so. I can guarantee they are going to have attention problems. But, before I can give them calcium to solve their deficiency, I have to get their bowels working, which we will discuss in a subsequent chapter. For now, eat fresh foods, high-quality supplements and take enzymes with every meal. Your body will love you for it!

*Nothing in this chapter should be misconstrued to mean that you should not take medicine that has been prescribed for you by a doctor. The information is intended to make you more aware of drugs and their side-effects and alternative ways of building health. Nowhere am I diagnosing disease or prescribing something for a disease. If you have further questions about your personal issues, please consult your health professional.

CHAPTER FIVE

A Raging Fire

"Smell the perfume of flowers, taste with relish each morsel, as if tomorrow you could never smell and taste again. Make the most of every sense."
~Helen Keller~

When we are talking about ways to create physical energy, we also have to realize that there are ways to lose energy. I call these "energy thieves" or "energy siphons". One of the most interesting things about nutrition is that the very thing that can bring you energy can also cause energy to be used up. Take digestion for instance. When we eat food, it takes a lot of energy just to digest and absorb that food, and, if absorbed properly, will create more energy. We've already discussed metabolism and how some people can eat and eat and never put on weight and others starve and still don't lose much weight. We learned to eat the Energy Fix way, but, now I want to explain why counting calories is not the most effective strategy—because calories are not equal. It does matter which calories you are eating. Some diets that rely on calorie counting will let you eat pie, cake, or whatever and you're supposed to stop when you have eaten all the allowable calories for the day. But, let me show you why that can be a problem.

For example, if you eat 100 calories in the form of a cookie, it takes approximately 78 calories just to digest that cookie. So, where do the extra 22 calories go? Right to your hip bank! Now, if you eat about the same number of calories in the form of a hard-boiled egg, it takes about 123 calories just to burn up the egg. So where did the extra 23 calories come from?

> ✺ *Calories are not created equal!*

You guessed it, out of your hip bank! So you see, calories are not equal and the reason is all about digestion. Now you can see why all that protein in the 14-day diet works.

Let's take another illustration. Let's say you go ahead and eat the egg, but, your stomach environment doesn't have the right acids to break it down so that you can actually use the amino acids, vitamins and minerals from that egg—then what? Believe it or not, this is what happens to a majority of us—especially if we suffer from indigestion or obesity. Then, not only are we uncomfortable, feeling gaseous and bloated, we have now created a terrible problem for our elimination system.

GOOD DIGESTION IS ESSENTIAL TO LIFE

Let me ask you a question. If I left a piece of meat sitting out on my kitchen counter for a few days, it would get pretty rank, wouldn't it? Well, that's what happens to food that has not been properly digested in the stomach, and is sent on into the intestines and colon. It becomes rotten and attracts all kinds of unwanted guests like viruses, yeast and parasites. And, as if that were not bad enough, you are still deficient in nutrients because your body could not absorb them. Is it any wonder that colon cancer is on the upswing in this country? And, to make matters worse, your body turns on the hunger again because it is starving for nutrition. Remember, your body only has one way to tell you that you need nutrition—through the hunger sensation. That's why when you eat Twinkies and Snicker Bars, you are hungry again so soon. You are still starving!

A few months ago I got a telephone call from a woman that I did not know. She said she had a question for me. This was her question. "If I could only do one nice thing for myself to

A Raging Fire

improve my health, what would that be?" Well, that was a loaded question, because I did not know anything about this woman and I knew I was being set up somewhat; however, I told her that after drinking 8-12 glasses of clean water each day, I would probably tell her to take digestive enzymes. She was surprised with the answer, but, I will tell you why I answered her that way. I had no idea what she was eating or what her health problems were, and I don't know yours either, but, I do know that if I can get you drinking lots of water and at least digesting the food you are eating, I've got a pretty good chance at improving your health. I could make this kind of generalization because I know that most of our diseases are actually digestion diseases. I personally believe, that if we could get digestion (and elimination) under control in this country, we could go a long ways in preventing arthritis, diabetes, cancer and heart disease—our four biggest killer diseases! I think we are losing the battle with these terrible diseases because we keep working on controlling the symptoms of the diseases instead of addressing the underlying causes.

There has been some attempt at preventing heart disease by recommending low-fat, low-sodium diets and increasing exercise, but, no mention of improving digestion has been made, to my knowledge. The increase of gallbladder surgeries in the U.S. is enough evidence for me to know that we are not digesting fats properly. It seems like a very drastic measure to remove a gallbladder from a person instead of cleaning it out and working on proper digestion.

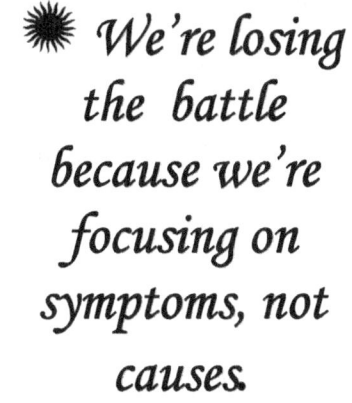
We're losing the battle because we're focusing on symptoms, not causes.

The surgery, in most cases, is taking a short-term problem and turning it into a long-term situation, in my opinion. Now, with no gallbladder, we really have to pay attention to digestion because it is permanently impaired—but, no one tells the patient that before it is removed. If you still have a gallbladder, my advice is to keep it!

Most dreaded diseases are preventable. I'm so happy to make this statement that I am going to say it again, MOST DREADED DISEASES ARE PREVENTABLE. I wonder how many of you really appreciate that statement. Only as few as 40 years ago, if I had told you that we could prevent cancer, heart disease, diabetes, arthritis and probably Alzheimer's Disease as well as obesity, I would have been put in jail. Isn't that amazing?

NUTRITION FOR PREVENTION OF DISEASE

Back in the 1960's, our own American Medical Association taught their medical students who became our doctors that, "what you eat has nothing to do with disease". I knew then that what kind of gas or oil I put into my car definitely made a difference in the way it performed, and yet, couldn't believe that what kind of fuel we put into our bodies didn't matter. We *were* told that we needed to eat a "balanced diet" to build strong bodies; but, I could never figure out why NOT eating a so-called "balanced diet" would not lead to a weak or diseased body!

Fortunately enough people in the scientific field as well as the health-related fields questioned that assumption, too. And now, the Cancer Association actually prints in their own literature that "most cancers can be prevented with the use of nature's own anti-oxidants which are found in fresh fruits and vegetables".

In the area in which I live, we have a large grocery store chain that advertises on television that they go to elementary schools as part of a community effort to educate young children as to the benefit of eating "five a day" (five servings of fruits and vegetables daily) to prevent cancer. Now, that's progress! The truth is, however, that all of the most dreaded diseases on the top ten list of killers in the USA are also preventable with proper diet—and the word isn't getting out fast enough to suit me. That's one reason I am writing this book.

For right now, I wish to make **three** major points:

First, your body is magnificent! The human body is simply awesome. There isn't a day that goes by that I do not stand in total reverence of the amazing capacity of our bodies and minds. All the conveniences that we use each day were first created in a human mind, and every material thing we possess was built by human hands. And the most amazing thing about our bodies is that they keep going, and going (just like the Energizer Bunny) with little or no thought on our part. That's why we act so surprised when we hear that "good old Joe died of a heart attack". Why, he looked just fine last week when we saw him. I wonder, what happened?

So why are we sicker than ever?

This is one of those situations where the first time we paid attention to our body—it was too late; but, the truth is that there were plenty of early symptoms that were ignored. Simply stated, because our bodies are so magnificent, and they seem to always be able to make something out of nothing, and nothing out of something, that we actually believe that it is capable of doing this magic forever. However, not only is that a lie, it is denial in the worst way.

Our physical bodies (and mental ones, too) do need care and do need certain kinds of fuel for maximum performance as well as longevity. What irks me is that most people are not interested in this information until something starts to go wrong. That's like closing the barn door after the horses have escaped! Yes, you might be able to recover the horses (or cure

Physical Equity

the disease), but, preventing the whole debacle would be a whole lot easier. That's what we are discussing here—prevention.

In my business as a Nutritional Counselor, I find that prevention is usually a hard-sell. Why? Because you can't really feel much before you get sick. That would be like curing the flu today even though you don't get it until next winter. You see, most people are only interested in fixing what's broken, and don't want to hear about the rest. You are obviously different or you wouldn't be reading this book in the first place!

I remember when I was divorced and raising four children on my own. I absolutely had to take care of the children's teeth, but, my own teeth only got attended to when the pain was so bad that I couldn't function. Then, when I finally went to the Dentist, I would instruct him to "just fix the one that hurts and don't tell me what else is wrong, I can only afford this one today." And, so it went for 17 years. Now, of course, I am paying and paying for those years when I could and should have prevented most of my dental problems. Unfortunately, this is the mentality of the young. How, then, are we going to make a difference with the next generation if we don't get past this critical error in thinking?

Years ago in China and Japan (not so much now since they have become "westernized"), doctors would only get paid if their patients stayed well—and *not* paid if their patients got sick! So, if that were the case, what is the motivation for the doctors? That's right - they couldn't afford to have 1/3 of their practice dying of cancer and up to 45% of their clients dying of heart disease, could they? We have it totally backwards now, in my opinion. Here, disease is big business. We don't have a health system, we only have disease control—and over the past 50 years, despite all the new-fangled technology, drugs and research, the occurrences of all the dreaded diseases have gone up, not down. Something's really wrong!

A Raging Fire

Unless we as a people, dare to take personal responsibility to prevent this and all other dreaded diseases for ourselves, it could be a very long time before we see major breakthroughs. I do know, personally, that since people are starting to demand second opinions and are trying natural alternative methods of health care, traditional doctors are forced to take a deeper look at some of these "other techniques", and many of the most progressive doctors are beginning to recommend them as part of the overall care of their patients. We should all seek out this kind of advice.

I was privileged to take classes from Dr. Deepak Chopra who is a pioneer in the field of merging traditional medicine with natural medicine in a hospital setting. So, there are some encouraging signs on the horizon, and we have to be alert enough to find those professionals who dare to buck the system and look at any and all methods of preventing and curing disease.

Luckily our Creator is smarter than we are; which brings me to my **second** point: Everything we need to keep ourselves healthy and help us live long and productive lives was given to us with very little effort on our part.

1. Clean air (we messed it up)
2. Pure water (ditto)
3. Nutritious food (oh, dear)
4. Opportunities to move and exercise our bodies
5. Sunshine
6. Rest
7. To love and be loved
8. Shelter from the elements
9. Meaningful work (do you hate Monday mornings?)

That's about all we really need. However, when you look at this list you can readily see how mankind has really fouled up most of these requirements.

Physical Equity

I am fortunate to live on a beautiful mountainside in Bountiful, Utah, and yet, I can still say that our air and water is not clean and pure. What does this say about the rest of the country? Not much. Every morning when I drive down off the hilltop, I see this brown "soup" hovering over the city, and it almost makes me sick just thinking about having to live in and breathe this stuff for the rest of the day. And, the water—well, we have filters on our drinking water at home, and I only drink spring water that I have to purchase, when I know God meant it to be plentiful and mostly "free". Something's wrong with this picture. What about those that can't afford to buy spring water or purchase filters? And, what about the charlatans that charge $1.50 for a bottle of water that came from the same source that we were trying to avoid?

How nutritious is your food - really?

That brings us to our food supply. Our food in America is at "crisis level", in my opinion. In many cases, as Dr. David Wimmer is known to say, "eating the cardboard box that the food comes in will give you as much nutrition as the food itself".

Dr. Wimmer and I were in the great state of Kansas giving a seminar a few years ago and we made the comment that the soils that our food is grown in is depleted and nearly void of nutrients. We had two farmers in the audience, and we called on one of them to tell us if that was really a true statement. The farmer stood and told us that he was embarrassed to admit that over 76 minerals are missing from the soil because of modern farming practices, and they are only required to put back three of them by the U.S. Government—and that those three are the ones that make the vegetables and grains grow large. He went on to say that most farmers cannot afford to rest the land like they are supposed to and we should not count on our vegetables, grains or fruit to give us adequate nutrition.

This is a travesty! The problem is that most Americans

believe that the government is looking after them so that they don't have to pay attention. Wrong! The farmers are such a large contingency (along with the dairy farmers and the cattle ranchers) and have such powerful lobbying capabilities, that the elected officials are not going to tell the people that their food can no longer be relied upon for proper nutrition.

Which brings me to my **third** point—the theory of eating the "balanced meal". I can remember being in Jr. High School and being taught how to prepare a "balanced meal". That meant making sure that each meal represented all four of the major food groups: meat (or other protein), vegetables and/or fruit, grains or other starches and dairy. We were even taught that we needed four glasses of milk a day. Our mothers worked very hard at preparing meals to insure that we received nutritious food, even though, when they were young, they often had meals that consisted of only one food group—the one that was in season or that was plentiful. My Father told me that they often had only vegetables for supper, or only mutton for lunch. The balanced meal was unheard of back in the early 1900s. But, with our "civilized" and "wealthy" society, we were now taught to eat all food groups every meal whether it was in season or not. Well, my friends, this is where a lot of our trouble started.

Why? Because it is virtually impossible for the human body to digest all of these different types of foods at the same time. It is no wonder that most of the diseases that we dread are merely digestive diseases. That's right. Our bodies are unable to break down all of these variations of foods in our stomach at the same time, so undigested particles of food are causing havoc. Let's take a look at some of these problems.

FATS ARE ESSENTIAL TO LIFE

It is common knowledge that many forms of heart disease are caused or made worse by fats accumulating in the circulatory system. This is the same as pouring fat down your sink. Eventually, you'll have a stopped-up drain. Isn't it interesting, however, that our treatment of choice for plugged arteries is to do surgical bypass and/or eliminating fats from our diets. Doesn't anyone understand that fats are a necessary part of our diet? By going on low or no-fat diets, we are not plugging up our arteries (maybe), but, we are causing good fat deficiencies because **all fats are not equal**. Wouldn't it make more sense to understand which fats we need and how we can actually use them instead of simply cutting them all out? This is especially a problem for children.

> ✱ *Low-fat and no-fat diets are dangerous.*

I've already told you that you have to have fat to absorb calcium, well, what about the children that are being forced to drink skim milk because the parents are afraid they will get fat? Now do you see the problem?

Recently, information about the dangers of trans-fats has become public knowledge, and that is a very good start. Trans-fats are deadly and should be eliminated completely. You will have to read labels to make sure you are not ingesting trans-fats. So, to prevent heart disease, we need to make sure we are getting healthy fats, the Omega 3's, 6's and 9's and not the saturated fats. Olive oil, fish oil and flaxseed oil are excellent for this; they are the good fats that actually help burn up the bad fat. That's why low-fat or no-fat diets can be so dangerous. If you take supplements for this purpose, make sure you take them with food, so they can be digested properly. Non-digestion of fats actually shows up as gallbladder problems.

Most people are aware that arthritis is partially due to the accumulation of calcium deposits. If you want to really see a hard-sell, try to tell an arthritic person that they are deficient in calcium. They will quickly point out that they have calcium deposits, which to them means that they have too much calcium. This is not true. What is true, is that they have not been able to digest and properly assimilate calcium, so the body stuffed it into joints and sometimes muscles (or other places) thinking that it will figure out what to do with it later, and because it was unusable calcium, the body is still deficient in this mineral. A bit of trivia for you: I am told that there are more undigested calcium tablets in the sewers that any other identifiable object. That's because calcium is acid soluble and that's why I suggest you take calcium lactate, and take it on an empty stomach as we discussed in an earlier chapter.

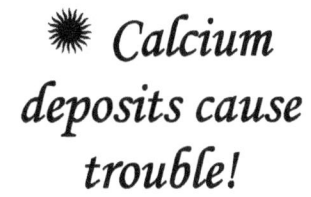

SUGAR DESTROYS GOOD HEALTH

Diabetes, of course, is the improper utilization of, or inability to break down sugars. Again, we won't get into a long discussion here about this problem, only to say that our American diet has become so loaded with sugars of every type, and the low-fat craze has made it even worse. I see obese people chomping down the no-fat goodies and never even worrying about the sugar. Without all the sugar, they wouldn't even think of eating these so-called "allowable" foods. It's no wonder Type II diabetes is on the upswing in this country. Not to mention the millions of kids who are starting and ending their days with 64 oz. of soda pop each day. If I were ever to picket against anything, it would be the myriad of vending machines housed in every one of our schools.

When I inquired as to why they allow our children to spend their lunch money on candy bars and soda pop, I was told that these machines represent a large "profit center" to the schools (somewhere over $32,000 a year per school) and one that they can't afford to discontinue. What a price we are paying for this one. Instead of giving our schools more money to operate on, we are raising a bunch of hyperactive, mean and unruly children that are even killing each other as well as the rest of us. I personally believe, that we would see a tremendous reduction in youth-related crimes and nearly an elimination of attention deficit—just by taking excess sugar from their diets. It won't happen until we take charge of the situation instead of allowing other people to raise our children. They are doing the best they can with the resources they have, but, I believe this apathy is a disgrace.

However, the bigger problem with sugar and too many simple carbohydrates is the fact that our small children are now contracting Type II diabetes—that's adult-onset diabetes in kids as young as five years old! That's because our children are being weaned on sugar starting as infants. The number of treats they are being offered on a daily basis is overwhelming. Someone needs to educate our young mothers.

Obesity is totally out of control in our country. One third of our population is more than 20% overweight and the number of obese children and teenagers is rising daily. This is a national crisis. However, as long as we treat obesity as a "beauty problem" and continue to look for the "magic bullet" that will cure it, we will not be able to control this devastating problem.

> *❋ Children as young as 5 are being diagnosed with adult-onset diabetes!*

The main reason for this is the weight-control business - a 49 billion dollar industry. And the major reason people spend this kind of money on their weight is because it is a health problem that we (and everyone else) can see on the outside of ourselves, and we don't like what we see. Being overly fat is another symptom of digestion problems. Most people cannot digest carbohydrates (especially people who find it next-to-impossible to lose weight) and with the mounting craze of diets that are pushing high carbohydrates and low protein and fats, it is only getting worse. High protein diets do work—it's just that most people can't stay on them for long periods of time because we all crave carbohydrates. Refer back to Chapter 2 of this book, and be sure to get your copy of my 14-day diet at www.connielynnhayes.com.

This chapter was meant to just scratch the surface of disease-related digestion problems. The most important thing to remember from this information is that very few of us, in my experience, have a perfect digestive and elimination system because of our incomplete diets, lack of water and high stress load. The easiest and most effective answer is to include a good, full-spectrum digestive aid in your daily meal regimen. Your health, as well as your appearance, will be so much the better if you took only this one, high-energy step towards a healthier body. I highly recommend Standard Process's Multizyme or Life Plus's Digestive Formula for this purpose. We can prevent disease in most cases and good digestion is a fabulous place to start. So, I will say it again:

Eat as close to nature as possible, drink plenty of pure, spring water, and take natural whole-food supplements including a full spectrum digestive aid with your meals.

*Nothing in this chapter or book is to be misconstrued as medical advice. If you have any of the problems mentioned, see your health professional.

CHAPTER SIX

Tending the Fire

"Look deep into nature, and then you will understand everything better."
~Albert Einstein~

If I could be sure that you would remember only one thing that I have to say, it would be this, "you are magnificent". There you have it, the most important and most truthful statement is just that. You and I are so magnificent, that most of us don't really know or understand what that means. We've discussed how marvelous our glands are and how beautifully our bodies know what to do with food and water and oxygen; but, the truth be known, it actually works magic most of the time because of all the hurdles we put in its' way to make its' job harder than it needs to be.

One of the ways we increase the load on our bodies is through stress—yes, the naughty word has been spoken. The truth is, we need stress; our hearts wouldn't even beat every day if it wasn't for pressure. A lot of us, including me, work well under pressure—that's when we get the most done, just before the deadline. We all remember cramming before a test and staying up all night to write our term paper. That kind of stress can be helpful because temporary stress is just that—temporary. The kind that does real damage is continual stress—the kind we live with every day. This kind of stress is our #1 energy siphon!

We already discussed how the adrenal glands are the "stress glands" and need to be functioning at optimum levels in order to protect us from the damage caused by stress. That's a good step forward. Remember, the body can't tell the difference between what is really happening to you and what you are imagining will happen or reliving what happened in the past. That's right, your body goes through the exact same steps when you are worrying about what possibly *might* happen (which in truth almost never happens) than it does in real time.

THE MECHANICS OF STRESS

In order to truly grasp the meaning of that last statement, let's go over the different reactions that your body goes through under "stress". These steps were first recognized by the endocrinologist, Hans Selye. I'm going to liken it to a military example for clarity:

1. When stress first appears, the body goes into the ALARM stage. This would be similar to if there was a perceived threat somewhere in the world and our President was concerned enough to put the military on alert. All troops and military personnel would be alerted and told to be on call—not to leave town because we may need them at a moment's notice. At this point, nobody has been deployed and no harm has been done.

2. If the stress is not alleviated at this level, the body goes into the REACTION stage. This would be where, in the military example, bullets are loaded into the guns, bombs are loaded into the planes and submarines, and soldiers are shipped out to the place where trouble is brewing. As of now, no bullets have been fired, and nobody has been injured. For the body, at this point it pulls out all kinds of nutrients and puts them into the bloodstream in case they are needed. They might be taken from the cells, the liver or any other storage place where the needed nutrients might be found. An important note here is that if the problem for the military is resolved at this stage, it is possible to put bullets back in storage along with bombs, etc. and send the troops home to be used at another time. However, that is not usually the case with the body. If the nutrients are called out into the bloodstream under stress, and they

are not used, most of them would not be returned to the same place from whence they came—they would most likely be lost—especially water-soluble nutrients.

Most of our bodies go through this alarm/reaction syndrome all day long and the neat thing about the body is that it is capable of coping with this stress reaction constantly—IF IT HAS PLENTY OF AMMUNITION TO RELY ON! However, as soon as it runs out of nutrition (bullets) you go into the third stage of stress.

3. The third stage is called EXHAUSTION—which always, always, always leads to disease and/or death! ALWAYS! In case you don't know, that doesn't mean sometimes.

Let look at how this process might look in a real situation: Let's pretend that you and two of your friends have been out together for the evening, and on the way home you are in an automobile accident (God forbid!) Now, just for our example, let's say that all of you go to the hospital with the exact same injuries. Unfortunately, one of you dies in the ambulance—one dies on the operating table during surgery and you are in serious condition but are expected to live. What makes the difference here? I'm not trying to trivialize accidents, nor life-threatening injuries that can result from accidents, but, stay with me here for a moment. The point is that you could have three quite different end results based only on how well the person was nourished and how much ammunition they had on hand to combat this degree of stress at the time.

In another section of this book, we will also take into consideration the person's mental and emotional health as well, But, for now, just let this fact sink in—your body's ability to fight disease depends in large part on the nutrients you ate yesterday. Most people will say that they didn't eat very well yesterday, but that they usually do. Oh, yeah? My guess is they don't MOST DAYS! That's probably the main reason I depend so much on quality supplements—for those times that I didn't do very well.

RULES FOR STRESS MANAGEMENT

1. **Eliminate the stressors you can**. Fortunately, this really includes most of what we call "stressors." We worry and fuss about things that we have no control over—like the war, death, our children's safety when they are away from us, etc. Stop it! My sweet Mother was the Queen of Worry. I don't think she felt alive if she wasn't worrying about something—and most of those things she had absolutely no control over. Do not burn your precious energy needlessly. It's a choice!

2. **Prepare for the stressors that you can't eliminate**. One thing to remember here is that stress really is relative, and we all have different levels of stress that we can cope with. Many years ago, when I was newly divorced, one of my long-time friends, who was also divorced, called me quite frequently. She was someone who tended to always see the glass "half-empty". One morning she called early, and after I said hello she began to whine about what a terrible day it was going to be. I asked her why it was going to be so awful and this is what she said: "because I have to wash my hair, go to the bank and make a potato salad—all in one day". After a long pause, I told her that I had to do all those things before I went to work!

Here's another example. Let's say that you have several small children and it is early morning, and they are playing together, making noise and a mess, like they usually do and you are going about your work happy and all is well. Now, it's 3 o'clock in the afternoon, these same children are still screaming and playing rough and tattling on each other the same as in the morning, but, because you are tired and frazzled, you are about ready to bang their heads together—that's when it became a stress and you are now in the alarm stage.

Here's another possibility: You are at work, and there is a definite, clank, clank, clank in the air conditioning that you hardly noticed in the morning; but, by afternoon, you are ready

Physical Equity

to take a sledge hammer to the darned thing—now you are in the alarm stage of stress.

If, in either of these cases, the stress is not eliminated OR if other stresses are added on to this stress as layers without rest in between, you are in alarm/reaction, alarm/reaction, which is O.K. to a certain extent, if your body has all it needs to work with to keep it from the *effects of stress.*

According to the American Institute of Stress, up to 90% of all diseases are related to stress. That's why it is so important to get rid of the ones that you can, the ones you see on the nightly news. Unless you can *directly* do something right now about any of these problems, stop worrying about them:

Here are some of the useless stressors:

1. homelessness/poverty
2. war and its fallout
3. disease
4. addiction
5. crime
6. business and political corruption

Preparing for battle

Now, about that preparation. These are the nutrients that are needed first in the alarm/reaction stage of stress: B vitamins—which you already know are water soluble and need to be replenished every day—and the bad news is that we don't like the foods that they are in which makes it even more of a problem. Life Mate, if taken in adequate amounts will fill this need for most of us. On my website, www.connielynnhayes.com, is a special stress test that you can take to see how many Life Mate you need each day, and some information about Life Mate so you can see why I am so big on this particular formula. Click on "Free Info", and take the test often, because our stress level does change with our lifestyle.

After the B complex, the body then needs lots of Vitamin C which is also water soluble, which means your body can't store it. Only use natural whole food C supplements and eat lots of fruits and vegetables (fresh, of course).

The third nutrient called out by the body under stress is calcium, which we discussed at length in Chapter Four. These, then, along with lots of protein to repair cells are the main players when a human is under stress. We will be discussing other ways to deal with stress later on in this book.

THE ROLE OF HORMONES

> ✹ *Carbohydrates supply energy to the body.*

To properly understand stress and what the body goes through to counteract all of our stress, it is necessary to understand basic nutrition and the role of the endocrine glands and the hormones that they produce. Remember, stress is an energy siphon and we are learning how to plug up the leaks. We talked earlier about the adrenal glands, which are part of this system—but, only part. Here's a little review to set the scene for this discussion: We know that carbohydrates are responsible for supplying energy to the body. Energy is the most important need of the body. Without it, all systems cease to function. For this reason, the body puts its need for energy above every other need and will take energy from whatever source is available. It is the special function of carbohydrates to provide this energy.

We also know that protein is the primary nutrient of the cells. Every part of the body is made up of cells; therefore, to have a healthy body requires having healthy cells. When the cells that make up the various organs and systems of the body are strong and healthy, those organs and systems can function properly, and the result is a healthy body. It is the responsibility of protein, composed of the proper combination of amino acids, to provide the nutrition that will build and strengthen the cells and tissues and keep them healthy.

> ✸ *Protein builds, strengthens and repairs cells.*

This is where the endocrine glands come in. Making sure that one's diet contains an adequate and balanced supply of these basic elements is important; however, it is not a guarantee of good health. Many people who have perfectly "good" diets still feel sick and tired all of the time. This problem commonly occurs when something goes wrong with the "controls" that regulate the body's ability to properly utilize the food that is eaten. When the body cannot use the elements of nutrition as it should, health will ultimately be affected. To help prevent this problem, the body has a set of controls known as hormones which are produced by the endocrine gland system. These hormones control the balance of the chemistry of the body, which actually renders the food we eat available for use in the body. These hormones also control **how** the food is used by the body. When these controls are functioning properly, they see to it that carbohydrates are burned up to provide energy and that protein is put into the cells and tissues where it can build and strengthen the body. These hormones also perform other functions that control many aspects of health. The importance of these miraculous glands cannot be overestimated.

Research has shown that when these controls are not functioning properly (because the glands are not producing the hormones in proper quantities to do their job), it commonly sets off a chain reaction that can lead to serious problems. The carbohydrates, instead of being used to provide energy, either go straight through the system and are passed off as waste, or are stored as excessive fat deposits on the body. However, the body's need for energy to stay alive must still be met. So, when the carbohydrates do not provide for this need, the body will turn to the only other source of energy available, namely protein! When protein must be burned for energy, it cannot be used to nourish, build and repair the cells and tissues of the body. When this condition occurs and is not corrected, the cells and tissues gradually weaken and deteriorate and become prey to viruses and disease. When cell destruction becomes extensive, it can cause the breakdown of vital parts of the body such as organs, bones, muscles, tissue, etc. and the results can be serious. For this reason, it is vital that the endocrine glands be in healthy condition so that they will produce the hormones that control the whole show!

Effects of hormone imbalances

One of the first and most common signs of extensive cell breakdown in the body with buildup of metabolic toxins is a condition known as "chronic fatigue". This is where people feel constantly sick and tired and yet the doctors can't find anything wrong with them. This "syndrome" is often a result of cell breakdown which has not yet developed into a condition that the doctor can recognize with testing. This problem is unfortunately becoming an epidemic—especially with our teenagers!

Research into the cause of chronic fatigue has shown that in virtually every case, the patient had undernourished glands that were not producing the hormones necessary to provide the proper food utilization and it has affected their immune response. When this happens, a person becomes more susceptible to infections, both parasitic and bacterial, multiple allergies, chronic candidiasis and viral infections such as Epstein Barr. In order to overcome these chronic ailments, feeding of these glands would be required to restore their ability to produce the essential hormones to balance the body's chemistry. It was found that when the glands were restored to a healthy condition and were producing these necessary hormones in proper amounts, the body was then able to make proper use of the nutrition it received, and this strengthened the body's immune system to the point that it could combat and overcome many of these problems.

The research referred to here was a ten year study by doctors in hospitals for the purpose of finding the cause of degenerative disease and this chronic fatigue. They took thousands of blood assays on patients to determine the relationship between hormone production and health. The actual research findings were threefold:

1. Endocrine glands were failing to produce the hormones needed to assure proper use of nutrition;
2. Due to lack of essential nutrition, cells were dying and the body was not able to rebuild healthy cells;
3. Cell destruction weakened the body, making it vulnerable to disease.

Results of these findings were that scientists found elements in *natural sources* to feed the glands and stimulate the proper hormone production thus promoting:

- proper use of nutrition to build healthy cells
- body chemistry restored to normal balance
- body able to rebuild itself and maintain a high level of physical and mental well-being

These findings revealed the need for what is now called "the chain of life". Basically, nothing in nature works by itself—all elements work in balanced harmony. Every life form requires a combination of elements to stay alive and they have a synchronistic effect with each other. There is no such thing as a food that contains only one nutrient, this is why I use only "whole food" supplements and never singular vitamins such as vitamin A. Balance is the key here—the balance of elements in the chain of life determines the status of health of the organism. If one element is lacking or is in excess, the entire chain is out of balance and this throws off the chemistry of the body.

The chain of life includes: **FATS, PROTEINS, CARBOHYDRATES, VITAMINS, MINERALS** and **ENZYMES** and a brand-new category just discovered in the past 10 years, **PHYTONUTRIENTS**.

Here's what Newsweek Magazine had to say about hormones in their cover story of January 12, 1987, "A User's Guide to Hormones":

> "That hormones govern every aspect of human experience from growth and development to reproduction, metabolism and mood has long been known. But, researchers are just beginning to fathom the full range of what they do and how they work...Everything is kept in perfect balance by hormones, not only for normal maintenance and survival, but in response to anything that comes along. Hormones regulate the body processes in such infinitely precise ways, even small irregularities in their levels or timing can lead to ailments."

So, what can I do about it?

These then, are the reasons why Life Mate was born. Life Mate is designed to nourish the endocrine glands which produce these hormones to promote the body's ability to maintain a high level of physical, mental and emotional well-being. Use the questionnaire on my website which is designed to help you determine the amount of Life Mate you need at this time in your life. Click on "Free Info"; take the test at least 4 times per year.

*To order Life Mate, please
visit my website
www.connielynnhayes.com

.**Much of the information used in this chapter was provided by Dr. David Wimmer of the Natural Wonders Company.

***Always check with your Health Professional before starting Life Mate to see if it is appropriate for you.

CHAPTER SEVEN

Preserving the Fire

*"Love the moment and the energy of that moment
will spread beyond all boundaries."*
~Corita Kent~

Just as having a savings account gives us some security against the unknown future, and a strong military is the best assurance of a country's peace, a healthy immune system is your body's protection against would-be "terrorists". In a nutshell, the immune system's purpose is to protect and preserve your health—a pretty tall order for most of us. The reason we are interested in it now is because it is one of the best ways to conserve energy—by preventing sickness and disease.

A healthy immune system is able to fight off invaders such as bacteria, viruses, parasites and fungi as well as the harmful effects of stress, household chemicals, second-hand smoke, pesticides and food additives. An unhealthy immune system not only gets overpowered by invaders, but, sometimes turns on itself—which causes auto-immune diseases such as lupus, rheumatoid arthritis, scleroderma, multiple sclerosis, diabetes type I, Crohn's Disease and thyroiditis among others.

The main players of the immune system:

1. **Thymus Gland:** This is the master gland of the immune network. It is located above the heart and secretes various hormones that are responsible for regulating immune functions. The thymus gland produces T-Cells (T-lymphocytes) which reach maturity in the thymus gland and then circulate throughout both the lymphatic system and the bloodstream. (See Lymphocytes below).

2. **Skin and Mucous Membranes:** Your skin is the first line of defense against invaders. Whenever it is compromised with a cut, burn, abrasion or puncture, there is an open door for disease-causing organisms to enter. The mucous membranes of the gastrointestinal tract, lungs, vagina, nose, mouth and so on, are the body's internal skin and are also a line of defense against intruders.

3. **Bone Marrow:** The center portion of the bone is an area rich in blood vessels and other substances. It is here that many types of immune cells are manufactured.

4. **Spleen:** This dark red organ, located on the left side of the upper abdominal region, manufactures lymphocytes, attacks bacteria, and recycles damaged blood cells.

5. **Lymph Nodes:** These tiny, gland-like structures are found throughout the body including under the arms, in the groin, and behind the ears. Swollen glands are really inflamed lymph nodes. The reason they are swollen is because these little nodes act as "inspection stations" for foreign substances, which they remove from the body's tissues. The lymph nodes prevent these substances from entering the bloodstream and finding their way to the organs.

6. **Lymphatic System:** This network consists of lymph vessels, lymph nodes and lymph, a thick fluid that is made up of fat and white blood cells. While the circulatory system is the transportation system for the blood, the lymphatic system carries immune cells to parts of the body where they are needed and carries out the garbage. You have three times more lymphatic fluid in your body than blood—and no pump. The only way to get the lymph fluid moving, and keep it moving, is through motion, especially up and down motion. That's why children bounce so much, I believe, bouncing on beds and the back seat of the car crying "are we there yet?" This actually helps their immune system.

7. **Lymphocytes:** These are a type of white blood cell which are produced in the bone marrow and are found in the blood and in the spleen, lymph nodes, thymus and other tissues. Lymphocytes perform four primary functions, all of which must work properly for a healthy immune system:

    a. They recognize the invaders
    b. They prepare a line of defense
    c. They communicate with other essential immune system cells by producing cytokines
    d. They stop the action of the immune cells once their job is done.

How your body prepares a defense

If any one of these steps goes awry, disease, including autoimmune conditions can be the result. Here are the major types of lymphocytes:

    a. B-lymphocytes
    b. T-lymphocytes
    c. Natural Killer Cells
    d. Macrophages

I'm not going to bore you with any more of the science of the immune system, only to say that this is a marvelous part of the body that functions well only if the communication between the brain and each other goes well, which opens up an entirely new perspective. Scientists know that the brain plays a key role in controlling our physical health via the immune system and this supports the idea of the "mind-body connection" which is what this book is really about. This becomes obvious when we consider the effects that emotional stress and tension have on our bodies causing headaches, neck and back pain, stomach distress and many other symptoms. When anything goes wrong with the immune network we often get diseases which are caused by either foreign toxins, or the body attacking itself (which results in an autoimmune disease). The main reasons for this breakdown are:

1. Poor nutrition
2. Genetic susceptibility
3. Environmental toxins

While conventional medicine simply treats the symptoms, we are more interested in going after the causes of the disease at the cellular level.

TRANSFER FACTORS – *The best kept secret of the 20th century*

One of the major problems in our modern culture is that our immune systems do not have the proper "education" in order to deal with the attacks that they receive. Why? Nature planned it better, but, we fouled it up - as usual. A baby is born with an empty library concerning various viruses and bacteria, with no instructions as to how to make antibodies to defend itself against them. They are supposed to have their mother's memory bank transferred to them via the colostrum in mother's first milk. This starts the child off with all the patterns for antibodies that the mother had been exposed to—so the infant that is nursed starts off with a huge head start. The problem is, not all babies are breast-fed, and the viruses and bacteria are mutating so fast that even a healthy person has a hard time keeping up with it all.

Dr. Sherwood Lawrence, NYU Immunologist, made an important discovery back in 1949. He found that there were certain molecules in colostrum that acted as "memory molecules" for the immune system to remember which "bug spray" (antibody) was needed to fight off certain foreign invaders. They called these special molecules "transfer factors" because they discovered that they could be transferred between mammals to broaden the immune system's memory bank. This was a huge discovery that was pretty much ignored by the media and the medical industry because penicillin was discovered about the same time and became the "darling" of the drug makers.

Physical Equity

David Lisonbee came across this research in the 1990's and got in touch with Dr. William Hennon who was the foremost authority on the subject of transfer factors and was doing much of his own research at the time. Together, they were able to conduct their own studies and formulate a product that now has over 3300 patents on it—which means that nobody else can make this product until the patents expire. The company is called 4-Life, is a Utah-based company and is probably one of the best health-related products I have found in the past 25 years. They call their product Transfer Factor which literally is "small proteins that "transfer" the ability to express cell-mediated immunity from immune donors to non-immune recipients." (Molecular Medicine, April 6, 2000).

If you could transfer all of your intelligence (I.Q.) to your child and increase her chance of success by 400%, wouldn't you do it? Of course you would. The Russian Academy of Medical and Technical Sciences, conducted a natural-killer cell research program that tested 4-Life's formulation of Transfer Factor against Interleukin-2 (the preferred drug at the time for cancer and other auto immune diseases). They found that Interleukin-2 killed 88% of cancer cells and transfer factors killed 97%. The overall increase in immune activity however, was 389% with Interlelukin-2 and 437% with transfer factors.

> ✱ *If you could transfer all of your intelligence to your child and increase his/her chance of success by 400%, wouldn't you do it?*

The exciting thing about this is that drugs replace or suppress the normal functions with external controls. Transfer factors strengthen or support body functions with internal controls and have **NO side effects**.

Before this begins to sound like an advertisement for Transfer Factor, I will just say that I love this product and I wouldn't be a day without it—I think it is one of the easiest ways to stay ahead of all of the environmental factors that are bombarding our immune systems every day. If you are around a lot of people every day, or you tend to get sick a lot, or you just prefer staying well all the time, get yourself some Transfer Factor and stay on it. Actually, it can sometimes be a hard-sell for reasonably healthy people, because there is no immediate notable effect—you just don't get sick! Most people think they should "feel" something and when they don't they stop taking it. I ask them if they'd been sick, and they say "no"— well then it worked. Prevention is a really hard for most people to understand, but, you who are reading this book are much smarter, I know!

Your defense line-up

Keep in mind that transfer factors are the educational system for the immune network soldiers, but, if you don't have enough soldiers, who are you going to educate? That's where great nutrition comes in—lots of protein, spring water, and loads of B complex, which you can get either from a separate whole food B complex, or from Life Mate. However, something that hasn't been understood very well until lately is the huge part that calcium plays in keeping you well. Other nutrients essential to keeping you well are calcium, Vitamin C and Vitamin D.

YOUR THYMUS GLAND – *overlooked and misunderstood*

Now for more information about the thymus gland—the center of the immune system. This gland regulates the movement of the meridian system—the energy track that runs throughout the body. The thymus is located in the area of the heart chakra, which is the crossroad for the flow of energy as it passes from head to foot. It's like the control room of a large energy plant sending energy where needed.

Illness begins with a weakening or lessening of life's energy somewhere in the body, and can have it's basis in any of the four areas of health namely: physical, emotional, spiritual or mental health. We are going to discuss the emotions in an entire section of this book, but, for right now it is important for you to know that the thymus gland is very sensitive to emotions, both positive and negative.

Since we want to keep the thymus gland strong, you need to know which emotions weaken it: hate, envy, suspicion, fear, anger, and jealousy. In reverse, those emotions that strengthen the thymus are: love, faith, trust, courage, gratitude and cheerfulness.

An interesting test showed that positive thinking and a smiling face, whether seen on a human face or simply drawn on a piece of paper, give positive strength to the thymus gland!

Here are some things you can do to strengthen your thymus gland, and that of your family or friends':

- a pat on the back
- a nod of the head
- outstretched arms in an embrace
- "thumbs up" sign
- certain colors
- wholesome music
- pets
- warm hugs
- long walks on the beach, etc.
- meditation
- breathing clean mountain air
- prayers

The list is endless when you are looking for the good. Isn't it powerful to know that you have an impact on another's health by the way you touch, talk to, look at, or respond to them. When even one person raises his total health, everyone around him is affected.

Preserving the Fire

Things that weaken the thymus gland are:

- advertisements that offend you
- pornography
- violence
- loud, offensive music
- mean expressions—vulgar language
- negative gestures
- destructive beverages like alcohol and caffeine
- tobacco
- drugs
- insincere speakers from a platform or pulpit
- unkind voices
- allergies and disease

The key then is to recognize and remove the negative influences from your life whenever possible and add the positive emotions to your natural way of "doing life", to improve your health and well-being.

There is a simple technique that you can do to strengthen your thymus gland, and thus help out your immune system whenever you are either feeling a bit under the weather or are around some negative influences. This is also a good way to start your day on the right foot. All you have to do is tap three times lightly over the thymus area and lightly rub clockwise down the breastbone to the solar plexus (above the belly button). This recharges the thymus.

One last thing about the immune system—virus and bacteria cannot live and grow if the natural pH (acid/alkaline) is balanced in the body. Most of us are too acidic because of the foods and beverages we consume, and because of the caustic environment in which we live. Too much alkaline isn't good either—remember balance is the key. You need to understand that the determination of whether a food is acid or alkaline is not gauged by its pH, but by the pH of its **residue** (ash) left from metabolism. The only thing I think you need to remember about this subject is that nature has given us a really good balance of acid and alkaline foods—if we stay close to nature. Where we get messed up is when we introduce processed foods into our diets—most of them are very high in acid. If you try really hard to get fresh vegetables and fruit (a nice variety, not only corn and peas), and eat whole grains every day along with lots of water you should be o.k.

I know how hard it is to eat perfectly all the time—I certainly don't; however, I do think that we all should make noticeable improvements each week when we go shopping. Start by not buying processed foods that are in boxes and stay with food that is as close to nature as you can get it. That's the main reason I take a lot of supplements and drink a lot of water. I also work daily on keeping my emotions positive and my environment upbeat. Just keep trying and together we'll all make a difference.

*Life Mate can be purchased online at
www.connielynnhayes.com

**The information in this chapter is not meant in any way to take the place of the advice from your health professional. If you have health problems, check with your health professional to see if this information would apply to you.

Physical Equity

IMPLEMENTING THE PHYSICAL EQUITY

1. Increase oxygen intake by doing breathing exercises, and regular exercise, drinking plenty of spring water (2 oz for every pound of body weight daily), eating fresh organic vegetables and fruits, and only whole grains.

2. Follow the 14 day cleanse to reset your metabolism and increase your energy.

3. High quality proteins build and repair cells – eat half your body weight in grams every day. They also fuel your fire, stimulating you body to burn fat.

4. Take a **whole food** multi-vitamin and mineral supplement. Don't forget the calcium lactate. You may also need digestive enzymes to breakdown your food and calcium, so that your body derives the highest amount of nutrition from you food and supplements.

5. Make sure to consume good fats – they are **essential** to good health. And lay off the sugar.

6. Eliminate the stressors that you can, and stop stressing about things you can't change or control – it's a waste of good energy.

7. Understand that everything in your environment affects your immune system, including what you put into your body, and even the thoughts you think. Strengthen your thymus gland with positive thoughts and actions, and take Transfer Factor for the strongest immune boost known to man.

Physical Equity

RECOMMENDED READING FOR PHYSICAL EQUITY

1. *The Mozart Effect*—Don Campbell

2. *Harmonics of Sound, Color and Vibration*—William David

3. *Reflexology Today*—Doreen E. Bayly

4. *Magnetic Therapy*—George G. Burke

5. *The Art of Aromatherapy*—Robert T. Tisserand

6. *Greater Energy at your Fingertips*—Michael Reed Gach

7. *Subtle Energy*—Collinge

8. *Body Reflexology*—Mildred Carter

9. *Healing with Chakra Energy*—Lilla Bek, Philippa Pullar

10. *How to Heal with Color*—Ted Andrews

11. *Color and Music in the New Age*—Corinen Heline

12. *Electrical Nutrition*—Denie, Shelly, and Shelley Hiestand

13. *Aromatherapy*—Berwick

14. *Quantum Healing*—Deepak Chopra, M.D.

15. *Energetics of Healing*—Caroline Myss (video)

SECTION TWO

MENTAL EQUITY

CHAPTER EIGHT

Jumping Levels

*"Imagination is the beginning of creation.
You imagine what you desire, you will what you
imagine and at last you create what you will"*
~George Bernard Shaw~

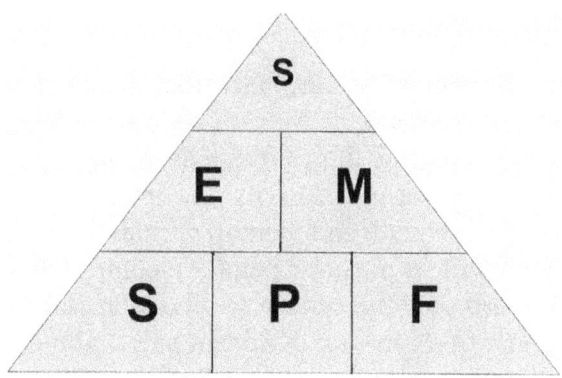

Now it is time to jump levels—by that I mean that if you look at our Pyramid of Frequency, you will see that physical energy is on the bottom row and mental energy is on the middle row. To refresh your memory, we are discussing energy in this book and I have divided it into six different "equities", only for the purpose of discussion. Breaking it down this way helps us see in our mortal minds a way to use this information in our every day lives.

Remember that all six of these energy equities have frequencies, the higher the frequency the more powerful the energy. That being so, Mental Equity, which we are now going to discuss, is a higher and faster frequency than physical energy. The reason I am jumping up a level in this book is because of the statement: **You can't solve a problem from the same level as the problem.** Therefore, I want you to see now how we can go to a faster frequency and start to solve some of our problems, especially those that are on the bottom row: health, financial and relationships.

To begin with, we need a basic discussion of the brain. The fascinating thing about science is that we are learning more about the brain and how it functions almost daily, and I am reading some pretty interesting stuff about this miraculous part of our body; but, for now, I am going to keep this explanation fairly simple.

Science can agree on the fact that our brain has two hemispheres, the left and the right. The left hemisphere, or the cerebral cortex, controls things like reason and logic; the right hemisphere is the seat of creativity and imagination. The left brain helps us learn math and memorize rules whereas the right brain helps us write a poem or paint a picture. Obviously, we need both parts of the brain to function in this world. However, most of us have a dominant side. Some people are just naturally creative and spend a lot of time using their right brain. People who do this too much are often called "spacey". On the other hand, people who are left brain dominant are logical and reasonable and may do very well in math and law, but may not be very imaginative. We are interested in creating balance.

The conscious part of our brain has two types of processes available to it; induction and deduction. The subconscious is more limited and can only use one process—deduction. This fact is extremely important in trying to understand how the mind works—which brings us to the subject of the mind. Actually, we use the word "mind" as if it were a noun—a place in the brain. It's really not a thing, but more like a process—it has no physical existence in and of itself. "Mind" is a term used to describe the action of the cells, neurons, synapses and chemical processes of the brain. So the truth is the mind is everywhere in our body! Mind is simply the name we have given to the information-processing activity of the brain. Since it is not a thing, it really should be a verb—such as "minding" rather than a noun. This means then, that all of our cells are intelligent—not just the brain—because information is being transferred from cells to tissue to organs to the nervous system every second of your life. I told you this was a miracle!

Deductive reasoning is solely a function of the conscious mind which you use when you analyze, judge, select, choose or assemble a number of different ideas and compare them. This involves thinking, a function only of the conscious part of the mind which is controlled by the left brain. For example, when you go to the refrigerator to see what there is to eat, you compare and choose certain foods, and then you decide how to use them, and even decide whether to eat standing up or sitting down. That all involves the left brain, and obviously involves thinking.

Inductive thinking, which does not involve reasoning can also be used by the conscious mind, but is the only method available to the subconscious. This fact will be tremendously important to us when we talk about programming your subconscious, because you now know that it doesn't involve thinking. The proof that this is true is in hypnosis research. The hypnotist is talking directly to the subconscious mind and bypasses interference from the "thinking" brain which has temporarily been suspended. That's why subjects in a hypnotic state can do things that they would never do if they were "consciously aware" of what they were doing. We've all seen hypnotists make people bark like dogs, or drink vinegar thinking it is water or have pins stuck in them and not feel pain as well as other phenomena.

For the remainder of this book, when I use the term "consciousness" I am referring to all the levels of the mind: conscious, subconscious, unconscious and superconscious (which we will talk more about later).

So, now we know that all cells are intelligent. Science can monitor the "activity" of thinking, but cannot find the "source" of our thoughts. Quantum physics tells us that everything can be reduced to energy and information. I have a question for you: where is the information?

Einstein's famous equation, $E=Mc^2$, actually means that energy equals matter, therefore, matter equals energy. He went on to say that thoughts=light=electrum=matter; therefore THOUGHTS EQUAL MATTER! Think about this enormous idea—our thoughts become things. This opens up huge possibilities for all of us if we understand the importance of this discovery. The Law of Attraction as well as the famous "Secret" video and book are based on this fact.

In order for you to get your mind around this amazing idea, let me show you how that happens—it involves manifested and sub-manifested thought.

Manifested thought would be everything that you can see—all things. We know that everything is energy, just different frequencies; and all things—this computer, this desk, the lamp and the glass of water sitting here—are "manifested thought"; they are considered "real".

Sub-manifested thought is what I call the "quantum soup" which is the information from which everything is manifested. This soup is the Life Force; the flowing intelligence that science cannot find but knows is there. The most important thing for you to remember about this force right now is *that it is everywhere* and it is plentiful. When you look at something (like your desk) under a high-powered microscope, you would see molecules moving around; however, the molecules that you would observe as the solid part of your desk are only a minor part of what you would see. There is way more "empty" space than there is solid matter. I once read that a comparison would be like seeing a space as large as the Grand Canyon between molecules. That means that there is plenty of quantum soup out of which to make things! So, don't worry about running out of sub-manifested thought.

So, how do we create something from of it? Good question. This is the formula for manifesting:

Thought→Belief→Attitude→Perspective→Emotion →Behavior→Result

This is an enormously important formula because it shows how we can start manifesting consciously instead of unconsciously. <u>You are creating all the time</u>. Just look around you and you will see what you have created. If what you see is not what you want, then you are creating unconsciously instead of on purpose. What we want to learn now is how to create what we want.

Think of the Quantum Soup as Jell-O water. You mix the Jell-O and then pour it into a mold. When the jello has set it takes on the shape of the mold. The thought is the mold! This is how thought works. Your thoughts start the process. It would stand to reason that random thoughts are weak, and concentrated, focused thoughts are powerful. Most of the 10,000 thoughts we have each day are the same ones we had yesterday—there are very few new creative thoughts. The ones that actually become the most powerful, and are therefore running our lives, are our BELIEFS.

A belief is a repetitious thought—one that you think all the time, or one that you have been programmed to believe from parents, teachers, religious leaders and society as a whole. These thoughts work fast and continuously because they are already in the subconscious mind. You need to seriously question your beliefs because they are creating your reality. Most of them are "weeds" in your garden and need to be pulled out, or at least seriously examined.

For instance, you've all heard the story about the woman

who always cut her ham in half before she cooked it. One day her daughter asked her why she cut it in half. The woman said that she didn't really know, except that her family had always done it that way. So, the daughter asked the Grandmother why she cut the ham in half, and she said it was because her Mother always did it that way. Not to be denied, the daughter then went to her Great-grandmother and asked the same question. The Great-grandmother said, "because I didn't have a pan big enough to hold a whole ham"! That's how beliefs get started. Some are malicious, unlike this one.

How about being told by a teacher that you can't carry a tune and shouldn't sing—do you believe that that idea would affect an entire life? Indeed! I can remember drawing a flower in kindergarten and making it blue, when the teacher said, "flowers aren't blue, Connie, choose another color". In other words, don't be creative, do what has always been done. I still say that I can't draw. Beliefs can be deadly, and they are running your life! If you dare to watch the nightly news, you will see all kinds of beliefs being passed off onto an unconscious public. Stay awake!

Here's the most important idea I will tell you in this Section:

You don't always get what you want, but, you always get what you think about most!

What, then, do you think about most? Do you think about what you want, or what you don't want? Most of the time we are thinking about what we don't want and then wonder why we get it! Take for example the bills: when you look at all your bills to be paid, do you think about having enough money, or about <u>not</u> having enough money? If you are honest, you will admit that most of the time we are worried about <u>not</u> having money. When you worry, that just adds energy to the thought and you get it faster. (We will talk more about this in the Emotional Equity Section of this book.)

Jumping Levels

That leads us to the main point: if you are not consciously thinking about what you really, really want you are creating subconsciously; which means you are creating just like you always have in the past, or what others want for you, or worst of all, what the mass mind wants. When you think of the "mass mind" what do you think of? It means what the masses—or the majority of people on this earth—are thinking.

> ✸ *Beliefs can be deadly, and they are running your life!*

Now using the best intelligence you can muster up, tell me if you think the majority of humans on this planet are thinking positively or negatively? That's a no-brainer. Just listen to people and what they say. They tell us we are all going to hell in a hand-basket, or worse. If you want to create your deepest desires, you are going to have to start taking control of your thoughts.

One of the best ways is to start listening to what you are saying. Here are some thoughts that come out of some of our mouths on a regular basis:

1. Things never work out for me.
2. My back is killing me.
3. You kids are going to be the death of me.
4. I'm fat!
5. Everything I eat turns to fat.
6. I never have enough money.
7. I'm too old; or
8. I'm too young; or
9. I was born on the wrong side of the tracks.
10. I never had any opportunities.
11. My parents didn't love me.
12. I can't remember names.
13. Nobody understands me.
14. I was not the favorite child.
15. I don't have enough education.

Mental Equity

And on and on it goes. Have you ever said anything like this? Of course you have, and so have I; then we shouldn't wonder why our back still hurts or why we don't have enough money. We need to wake up, people!

So, how do we stop saying things like this, much less thinking thoughts like these? One way that I like is playing a game called "cancel-cancel". I learned this many years ago from Wally Minto and this is how it works: whenever you hear yourself or anyone else say something negative, you say "cancel/cancel" and then that person has to say something positive. Let's say for example that your child comes home and says, "I hate math". You immediately say "cancel/cancel" and the child then has to say something positive. Now he doesn't have to say "I love math" because that would not be true, but, he could say "I love ice cream". The idea here is to understand that all thoughts and words go into our subconscious mind to be stored forever, and since your subconscious mind can't deduce whether it was a positive or a negative thought it can't tell the difference. However, when you say "cancel/cancel" you are still putting the thought into your subconscious mind, but, it now has a little tag on it that says "I don't believe this". Be sure and teach all the members of your family how to play this game, and you will be surprised to see how fast the kids pick this up and start catching you at your own negativity!

Now, there are times when you hear something negative and you can't really say "cancel/cancel". Maybe your boss or your Mother-in-Law says "my feet are killing me", and you don't feel comfortable saying "cancel/cancel". What you do in that situation is put your finger and thumb together to create a circle, and then say "Oh?" When you say "Oh" and make a circle, your mind is saying to itself, "this is something I don't believe", and puts a tag on it. It really doesn't help the other person, but, it will help you—unless they start to notice that you are "Oh-ing" them an awful lot. It's better to say it if you can, but this will work if you can't.

Jumping Levels

Now what if you are in church/synagogue/mosque or another type of meeting and you hear something negative that you don't believe? You can't shout out "cancel/cancel", and you can't say "OH" out loud—so what do you do? You still put your fingers together in a circle and think the words "cancel/cancel" to alert your subconscious mind that this is a negative thought and you are not going to accept it. Please don't underestimate the power of this simple game. If nothing else, it starts to make you aware of just how often you do say or hear negative things that you really don't believe.

Let me just say that the most destructive thinking is self-talk. This is the kind of chatter that I call the "monkey mind", that goes on all day and sometimes into the night. These are all the "what-ifs" that you can think of, plus all the judgments about ourselves and others. How often do you think "now that was a stupid thing to do?"

> ✸ *Most of the 10,000 thoughts we have each day are the same thoughts we had yesterday!*

The rest of this section, Mental Equity, relies on your total understanding of what we have just discussed. **You are creating your reality.** You are creating constantly, and the process starts with your thoughts. Unless you take charge of your thoughts and check your beliefs, you will not be able to create the life of your dreams. I want you to think about what's been said, read this chapter several times and work it into your life before we go on to any more. However, I have a little exercise for you to start doing right away:

Before you can control your thoughts and your beliefs, you have to discipline your body to take "orders" from your mind. Just reading this information will not make it yours unless you

Mental Equity

apply it. So, pick a room in your home or office where you will not be disturbed. Ideally, this room has a chair in it that you like and has a door that can be closed so you won't be disturbed. Sit down, erect but comfortable, and do not lounge. All you have to do today and every day for at least a week is sit there for 15-30 minutes. You can't read, listen to music, talk on the phone, talk to anyone else, write or DO anything else—just sit. This might be the most difficult thing you have ever done—especially for women who have mastered the art of multi-tasking! Just sit and be with your thoughts. Don't try to control your thoughts at this point, just sit and do NOTHING. That is your assignment for this week. Sit each day, without interruption for at least 15 minutes to start with and see if you can stretch it to more by the end of the week. Notice the "stories" your mind wants to tell you and how your body reacts to this strict discipline. Trust me; this will be a very valuable training that you give to yourself.

CHAPTER NINE

Your Mind— Master or Servant?

"In our unconscious mind we cannot distinguish between a wish and a deed."
~Sigmund Freud~

We know that everything is energy. The next step is to know that this energy can be referred to as "consciousness". We will go into this "consciousness" in great detail in the Spiritual Equity Section, but for right now we need to know that consciousness comes from "The Source" and is in everything. But, what distinguishes one organism from the other is the ability to adapt. The organism that survives is the one that can adapt itself to its environment. Darwin's theory of survival of the fittest didn't mean the biggest or strongest. If that were true, dinosaurs would still be roaming this planet. It means that the one with the highest consciousness can adapt to differing circumstances. Unfortunately, some humans have not learned to adapt very well to changes in their environment.

Minerals and animals have consciousness, but their ability to adapt is limited. What we can learn from the mineral kingdom is that every mineral was created with a plan, or an image. Take snowflakes for instance. There are billions of snowflakes and they all have six sides, but, there are no two flakes alike. They were all made according to a plan, just as a quartz crystal is always quartz because the pattern for that particular mineral is embedded into the atomic structure of the stone.

Plants do have consciousness, even though it is at a minimal level. They are able to produce their own food through photosynthesis, which does indicate a certain amount of intelligence. There have been many interesting experiments that show that plants have the ability to tune into all forms of life. In his book "The Secret Power of Plants", Brett Bolton tells about a polygraph expert named Cleve Backster who did an experiment using a lie detector machine. He hooked the machine to his houseplants and when he went out of town took careful note of his activities. When he compared his notes to the graph, he found that his plants greatest "emotional" response came when he decided to come home. They also registered "agitation" when he was almost hit by a car.

In another experiment, Bolton decided to see if plants could react to threats to their own well being. He decided to burn a leaf with a match, and at the very instant that he thought of lighting the match, there was a dramatic change in the polygraph tracing. The activity of the pen had gone crazy and went off the chart. Other experiments have shown that plants grow much stronger and more luxuriant by being exposed to classical music compared to hard rock.

Animals, as all animal lovers know, are capable of performing some amazing feats, so we know that they have more consciousness than plants, which is primarily expressed through instinct. We have all marveled at how geese can fly to a warmer climate thousands of miles away when they sense winter is coming, and yet in spring come back to their exact summer home. And they are led in formation by the youngest adults who have never made the journey before! According to the laws of aerodynamics bees can't fly! Of course, we see them buzzing from flower to flower, and they do it by instinct.

Humans are not bound by instinct because we possess the highest quality that consciousness manifests, and that is self-awareness. Self-awareness is called "reflective thought", which means that we are the only beings that have the ability to

The Mind – Master or Servant?

think inwardly and contemplate our thoughts and actions through reflective thinking. That makes us the only creation that has an inner world. Because of this great gift, we have a host of abilities that no other animal on this planet has. We can create systems through abstract thinking, exercise free will, creativity and foresight, so that we can plan ahead. Unfortunately, our culture does not foster reflective thinking—it tends to keep us in "outer thinking" and reducing our self-awareness through constant exposure to television, radio, computers, etc. Most people take very little time, if any, for contemplation or connecting with the inner self.

Last chapter we discussed how we create our own reality, and how the process starts with our thoughts. We are literally creating our lives moment by moment with our thinking—whether it is conscious thought or unconscious thought. We discussed how beliefs are really running our lives, because a belief is just a repetitious thought. There are three basic types of beliefs: personal, family and cultural. We create self-fulfilling prophecies through our beliefs about ourselves, our past, and what others have told us. For example: If you believe that you have to work hard for money, you will create circumstances where you indeed do have to work hard and money is "hard to come by". This makes this belief true for you. That keeps you in your comfort zone and makes your "stories" true: "see, I do always have to work hard to get any money."

> ✸ *We are literally creating our lives moment by moment with our thinking.*

We adopted a lot of our beliefs from our parents when we were children. Most of this came from people who "love us"—and they do it for our own good! The method most of us use is "labeling". Labeling someone is extremely dangerous because it is usually accompanied by an emotion, and that means it will be imprinted on the memory bank with an emphatic "YES—THIS IS TRUE". I can remember when my daughter Heidi was around 10 years old, she was a little chubby and not as graceful as she might be, and my husband started calling her "Grace". Now, he did not do this in a malicious manner and believed that he was using an endearing nickname. But, did she see it that way? I am embarrassed to say that I even had a T-shirt made with the name Grace on the back of it. This was a label that hurt and led to stories that she has told about her lack of grace.

How many stories do you tell about labels that were given to you by others? How many labels do you tend to give to others? Watch this nasty habit of labeling. Another story that comes from my storied past is when I introduced my two sons to someone new. I said "I'd like you to meet Todd—he's my honor student, and this is Brad". Now, I didn't say anything derogatory about Brad, did I? No, I didn't; but, in this case, I labeled him through omission instead of commission. Either one is destructive.

The first step in changing your beliefs and your thoughts and eventually your life, is to know that you are Cause. Now, that doesn't mean blame—we're not into blaming anyone, not even ourselves; just know that you are the start of the process, so "the buck stops here". That gives you back your power. If you are not Cause, then you have no power. If you think your situation was caused by another person or circumstance, then you have given all of your power to that experience or person. I prefer saying, "if I was powerful enough to create this mess, then I am also powerful enough to fix it!"

If you want to know what you believe, just look at your life. Look at the areas that you think aren't working for you. If money is scarce, then you believe in scarcity. If you don't have enough love in your life, then you don't believe that love is available to you. It sounds simple because it is simple—not easy, just simple.

If we go back and look at the formula,

THOUGHTS→BELIEFS→ATTITUDE→PERSPECTIVE →EMOTION→BEHAVIOR→RESULTS

you can see that after beliefs comes attitude. I break attitude down into just two categories—malevolent and benevolent. You could also say positive or negative if you prefer. When using the term malevolent, I don't mean "evil" which most people associate with the definition of the word; I mean "downward thinking" or negative. For example: my Mother, who was the sweetest little lady in the world, tended to see the world negatively. Now, she would never have admitted that, but, her natural way of responding to the world was in a rather untrusting way. She would lock up her house and worry about being robbed. She carried her purse with her everywhere, even in my house. She felt that you had to be careful, because people were mostly untrustworthy. Basically, she saw the glass half-empty. She also thought that money "didn't grow on trees" and that people were out "to get you". I, of course, drove her crazy because I tended to see most everything in the exact opposite way. Benevolent just means that you believe that most of the world and the people in it are good, and that you expect good things to happen. Some people call it "Pollyanna thinking", but, I don't think so if we are talking about a normal way of seeing things. We either are mostly positive or we're not. But, we can change that if we want to. Just becoming aware of it is a start. When our intention is to change our results, we have to change our thoughts, our beliefs and our attitudes. There's no other way if we want things to turn out differently than in the past. Check your attitude—you may be surprised to find out you are not as benevolent as you thought. I very often hear that "Oh, I'm positive, but, the person I am living with is so negative." Have you ever said that? Stop and ask yourself how you attracted that person in the first place! Maybe you did have something to do with it—hmmm!

After attitude, comes perspective. This is one of my

favorite subjects because it gets us into the topic of RIGHT AND WRONG. Imagine for a moment that I draw a half circle, or an arc, in the sand and you are standing on one side of it and I'm standing on the other. You would tell me vehemently that I had drawn a convex line, when I would argue that the line was concave. However, if we both go up on a little hill and look down at the same line, we would notice that it is in fact both. So, perspective depends on where you are standing.

You've probably heard the saying that you shouldn't judge someone else until you have walked a mile in their moccasins. That, I believe is so true. If I were to draw a huge circle big enough to put everyone in the world in that circle holding hands, then I put a certain object in the middle, wouldn't it be fun to hear everyone describe what they see FROM WHERE THEY ARE STANDING? Of course, our descriptions are going to be different, and some of them are going to be diametrically opposed! Are we wrong?—no—just different.

So the key here is to not only watch your attitude, but to check your perspective. For example: do you believe that money is evil? That can be a very powerful belief and it comes from the perspective that it is wrong to have a lot of money. Well, if that is both your belief and your perspective, good luck in creating your own prosperity! Perspective, in a nutshell then, is seeing something as right or wrong; and you will create circumstances in your life to prove that you are right! No one wants to be wrong. Are you creating a life around this type of judgment? I don't care if you do, but, I think you might care.

Emotion is the next step in the formula. When you think a thought and color it with a belief and add an emotion, it's like putting a turbo-charger on that thought—it becomes a result much, much faster. This is true for both positive and negative thoughts. So think of the implication of this statement: you get what you want <u>and</u> what you don't want much faster with emotion. So things that you really, really fear—you got it, you keep getting them, fast! So, take a look at the thoughts you think, things you are either passionately for or against—and those are the things that keep showing up in your life to make you right! We'll really get into emotions later, but, I do want you to get a heads-up on this matter right now.

When you think of something that you do want—let's call that "A", immediately what comes up is what I call "not A". What I mean by all that is that as soon as your mind settles on something that you want, all the negative reasons as to why you shouldn't want that or why you can't have it start to come into your mind. So how do we handle all these opposing thoughts? Focus on what you want and don't try to resist the negative retorts; just say "thank you very much, but, this is what I want", and turn your attention back to the desire. That is where affirmations come in.

Affirmations are like training wheels for the mind. Since we know that most of our thoughts are ones that we had yesterday and our beliefs are mostly from our culture and our families, we have to break the trend some way. Purposely writing out what we want and setting our intention to have it is a powerful way of changing our thought patterns away from what we don't want and focus on what we do want. Strangely enough, most people do not know what they want. They are really clear on what they don't want—but, the hardest step in changing thoughts and getting a new set of beliefs is being totally clear on what we really, **really** want. So, understandably, the first step in writing affirmations is to know what you want.

I have a couple of favorite ways of finding out what you want. One way is called mapping. I like mapping because it uses the right hemisphere of the brain, the creative, subconscious mind, instead of the literal left brain. What you do is take a big, plain piece of paper and draw a big circle on it. Then in the middle, write I WANT. Then, take a few deep breaths, close your eyes and let things just come up to your mind and then write them down somewhere on the paper. For example, you might say a new car. After writing this down, close your eyes, and let the next thing come up, it might be a new job. Keep writing things down. As you continue doing this exercise you will get deeper into the subconscious mind and bring up the really important things that you want. For instance: years ago I was working in the corporate world and had to wear suits every day, and I was tiring of the mind games that are played in the business world. As I did this exercise, I suddenly came up with "I want to wear sweat suits". Now where did that come from? I didn't even own a sweat suit. But, as I thought about it afterwards, my subconscious mind was telling me I really wanted a different job—and that's when I started my own business, and am I glad that I did. If you come up with something that is related to something that you have already written down—for example maybe a red car comes up—then write it down like a satellite off of the original "new car" line.

The object of this exercise is to keep going, as the last things you write down are probably the most important. Now review what you wrote, and put them in list form on another sheet of paper—then follow the instructions below.

Another more traditional way of finding out what you really want is by making lists. Here's how I do it. Take a piece of paper and list at least 50 things that you want. Now, when I say things, they can be traits that you want, or experiences that you want to have. Just keep writing until you have at least 50—more is better, but at least 50. Now go back and look at your list and grade each one as an A, B, or C. A's are ones that you really, really want and you would be very disappointed if you died and hadn't obtained or experienced those ones. B's are ones that you really want, but it wouldn't be a catastrophe if you hadn't obtained them; and a C means it would be great, but, you could live without it.

The Mind – Master or Servant?

Since knowing what you don't want is usually easier than what you do want, some people need to get to their list of "wants" the backwards way. On one side of the paper write down what you don't want, such as I don't want to be tired any more. Then on the other side, write, I want lots of energy every day. Just write down the opposite of what you don't want and see if that works for you.

No matter which way you get your list, you should have a few A's that we will now use to make affirmations. It is best if you have a balanced list of wants, which means something in all the equities because, remember, we want a balanced life.

I like to write affirmations on index cards because they're portable. I suggest making several copies of your affirmations and putting one set in your purse or your car, one by your bed and one on your desk or at a place in the house where you spend a lot of time. This way, you can refer to them many times a day which is what it takes in order to imprint this new thought on your subconscious mind.

Before starting the procedure of writing an affirmation let me give you a secret. There are two very magic words in the English language and they are "I Am". Whatever you say after you say the words I AM are most likely to come true for you. For example: I am tired, I am sick and tired, I am hopeless— you get the idea. Never, ever use those two magic words unless it is something you really want because you are bound to get it. Therefore, using the words I AM in an affirmation is very powerful. Some people don't like saying things like "I am thin and healthy" when they are overweight with lots of health problems. That's why I suggest saying in your affirmations "I Am becoming_____"; or "every day in every way I am _____". That way you are not saying something that your mind can oppose with a "not A". Knowing that, let's get on with the business of affirmations.

The three rules about an effective affirmation are that they must be:

1. Personal—meaning about you, not about someone else.
2. Positive—you would say "I am becoming slimmer each day"; not "I am losing weight."
3. Present Tense—that's why you say "I am becoming", not "I want to", which would indicate sometime in the future. The mind can't process something that is off in the future, only what is in the NOW.

Let's write an affirmation. Let's say that you would like a new car. You can't say "I am a new car", but, you can say that "I am thrilled to be driving my brand new car". That way you have made it personal, positive, and in the now. The best affirmations are ones that are very detailed. You probably are not interested in just any new car; and does it need to be brand new, or just new to you? Maybe you would say a "newer" car, but, that's still not enough detail. State the model of car, even the color and all the important details that you want it to have.

Many years ago I was a single Mom trying to make ends meet for me and my four children. I was driving an old Opal (now you know how old I am) and it was making funny noises that scared me and the gas gauge didn't work so I never knew how much gas I had in it. I really needed a newer car but, I wanted a NEW CAR. So I went down to the local Chevrolet Dealer to look at new cars and found a Monte Carlo that I really liked. It was silver, with a maroon lambo top. It had leather seats and a really neat stereo. This, then, was the car I wanted. So, I proceeded to get a picture of it and went home to make my Treasure Map (which we'll talk about in a minute) and my affirmation.

I wrote I AM THRILLED TO BE DRIVING MY BRAND NEW SILVER CHEVROLET MONTE CARLO WITH A MAROON TOP. I CAN SMELL THE NEW LEATHER SEATS AND I JUST LOVE LISTENING TO ITS' TERRIFIC STEREO. I made several copies of this and proceeded to say it over and over to myself morning, noon and night. Several weeks went by and nothing happened. So I went back to the dealership and asked about leasing. I didn't know then that you had to have even better credit to lease, and of course, they turned me down. So I went home to make my Treasure Map. This is a great thing to do to illustrate to the mind what it is that you want. I pasted the picture of "my new car" on a poster board, put a picture of me standing beside it and wrote the words LOOK AT MY NEW CAR at the top of the poster. Then I hung it in my bedroom where I would see it many times a day. Again, several weeks went by and nothing happened. So, I made a tape where I recorded my voice saying my affirmation over and over on a continuous short tape and played it to myself as I went to sleep each night. Still nothing happened.

By now, my car was really rattling and I had run out of gas once on the way to work, and I was getting really desperate. So I went to my Boss and told him that I really needed a new car and since I didn't have enough credit to get one on my own, would he consider buying it for me and taking the payment out of my paycheck? Well, what happened next I could never have expected. He said, "Oh, Connie, you spoiled my surprise". I said, "What surprise?" and he answered, "You've been doing such a great job for us that I planned on getting you a company car." I couldn't believe my ears. He went on to say that he always purchased his cars from a certain dealer and he would have him call me to get the details.

Well, you can imagine how excited I was when the dealer called and told me to come and pick up my car. So, down I went to this car lot and there was a brown, Buick Regal waiting for me. I guess the man could see the disappointment in my face so he said "you don't look too excited about this car." Well, I whined, I really had my heart set on a Silver Monte Carlo with a maroon top. He rather rudely said, "I thought this was supposed to be a company car", and I told him that it was, but, that I really didn't like brown very much. He looked at me disgustedly and said he would have to talk to my boss about this. I went away, believing that I had really blown it and that I would probably get no car at all.

Mental Equity

A couple of days went by, and I received another call that said "come and pick up your car". So down I went again, and there on the car lot was a beautiful brand new silver Monte Carlo. Before I could say anything at all the man said "I know, I know. I'm sending it out this afternoon for a maroon top, if this meets Your Majesty's approval." Needless to say, it did.

> ✸ *Make sure you know what it is you really want.*

Now for the good part. Whenever you write an affirmation, be sure to add at the end, THIS OR SOMETHING BETTER. Because we are mortal beings, we don't always know what the best is for us, so I always put this caveat at the end to make sure I am getting the best. "Something better" was not only was the car paid for by the company, but so was the gas, the tires, and the maintenance. You see, I was willing to pay all of that myself, but, I didn't have to; I got it all for free! That's the power of affirmations.

Let's break this story down just to make sure you understand all of the parts. First, I knew exactly what I wanted. I was so clear that I immediately recognized what it wasn't. Now, I know that Buicks are supposed to be better cars than Chevrolets, and if I believed that, I might have accepted the Buick as my "something better". But, to me it wasn't better, and it wasn't what I really wanted. Make sure you know what it is you want—and stick to it unless something comes that is definitely better.

The main part of the story was that I never gave up—which is critical. I just kept trying something else to help imprint my affirmation on my subconscious mind. I read the affirmations, I looked at my Treasure Map, and I even listened to my tape to reinforce my desire. Then, I took the chance of being rejected by going to my Boss. You see, I never gave up—and you must not either. Now get busy and write your list, or do your Mind

The Mind – Master or Servant?

Map and find out what you really want. Then make your affirmations on cards. You can handle about six different ones at a time. I like to put the cards on a loose-leaf ring so I can carry them with me and flip through them as reminders. Try it—it really works.

The key to controlling your thoughts and changing your beliefs is understanding the concept that the Universe always says "YES"—it is impossible for it to say "NO", and that is why you always get what you think about most. If you say your positive affirmation and then negate it with a thought like "oh, sure, that's not really going to happen", your subconscious mind says "yes" to the last thought, "that's not really going to happen". So, you not only have to say the positive statement frequently throughout the day, you have to focus on it and cancel out any thoughts that might turn it the opposite direction. We will talk more about this in a later lesson.

Always remember: What you think about comes about, and when you state what you want, you create it.

Now for your exercise this week: Go to the same room as before and sit in the same chair. Last week we were working on controlling the body, now we are ready to advance as we try to control our thought. Be perfectly still, as before, but try to stop your thoughts. You'll be able to do this for only a moment at a time, but, keep trying. This exercise exposes you to how many thoughts you have roaming around in your head; but, more importantly, it shows you the "space" between thoughts which is where the power is. Don't beat yourself up, just watch a thought come, and ask it to leave. Do this for at least 15 minutes each day for the rest of the week. Be proud of yourself for finally taking charge of your mind and body. You are awesome!

CHAPTER TEN

Thinking Makes It So

*"The mind is its own place,
and in itself can make a heaven
of hell, a hell of heaven."*
~John Milton~

We are talking about how to increase frequency and make our energy more powerful in order to solve problems. We know that mental energy is more powerful than physical energy because it is a faster frequency. We have learned that our thoughts are the mold that starts the sequence to bring us our reality. What you think is what you get. We also discussed the fact that beliefs are repetitious thoughts—those that we say or hear over and over again that literally make a rut in our brain and become the story that is running our lives and brings us our results. If we want different results—quite simply we need to think different thoughts and create new beliefs.

We live in an ever-changing world, one that moves so fast that it is difficult for us to keep up with it unless we are making a concerted effort to do so. If you purchased a computer today, by the time you got it home and hooked it up, it would be out-of-date. It used to take a generation for information to change, then, it was a decade; then it became a few months; now, what we know to be true can become obsolete within hours. This presents a daunting task for us mortals.

Which brings us to the subject of knowledge. You are either moving forward in life, or you're moving backward; which means you are either growing or dying. There is no standing still.

Socioeconomic studies show that in the average low-income household you might find a National Enquirer and maybe a Bible. In a medium-income home there might be a book by the toilet and maybe a gossip magazine in the family room. However, in a high-income home you will find a real "library" which is usually the prized room of the house. Which of these do you think is the true statement: The high income brought about the library; or, the library brought about the high income? Trust me, poverty isn't just a financial issue, it is a state of mind!

Raising your frequency also means expanding your consciousness. You will never grow by reading tabloids or listening to the nightly news. Statistics also reveal that 85% of North American households in 2007 didn't buy one non-fiction book, not one—and 95% of those that did buy one didn't read it! However, during that same period of time we spent $85 billion dollars on movies and an average of 6 hours and 44 minutes a day watching television. I'm reminded of the Mark Twain quote, "The man who does not read has no advantage over the man who cannot read."

I cannot stress enough, that in order to create the life that you really want, you have to change your thoughts and you need to do it consciously—if not, you are buying into what the mass mind wants for you. It has been proven that when you are watching TV your brain goes down into alpha level, which is the ideal frequency for your sub-conscious mind to accept, without question, what it is hearing. Do you want to believe everything that is said on television? If not, then you had better remain awake and listen carefully

> ✹ *Your sub-conscious mind can't tell the difference between a "real" experience and an imagined one.*

to what is being said to determine if it is what you believe or want to believe. It is especially dangerous for you to actually fall asleep in front of the boob tube, because your subconscious mind is then accepting all the ads and late-night ridiculousness that comes over the air waves. Be careful!

I mentioned "alpha brain waves" which probably needs a little explanation. Since we are discussing frequency, you need to understand that our brain also works at different rates of speed. These waves are called Beta, Alpha, Theta and Delta. Basically all that means is that Beta is your "awake" frequency, when you are supposedly alert and aware of what you are doing. Alpha is that nice calm frequency you experience just before you fall asleep; everything slows down a bit, you can still hear if the baby cries, you know what is going on around you, you just don't care so much. This is an excellent state of mind in which to recite your affirmations. At this frequency, your brain doesn't give you all the arguments as to why this isn't true or all the reasons why it can never be true for you. Theta is light sleep, your conscious mind is turned off but, it doesn't take much to awaken it. Delta is deep sleep which is where your mind and body really get to rest and where you actually go into the dream state. I want you to make sure you are in Beta frequency whenever you are reading, listening to a speaker or watching television, so that you can make a deliberate decision as to whether what is being said agrees or disagrees with your values and your beliefs. Most people go in and out of alpha and beta as well as theta when they are in Church or watching TV, and this is one of the reasons our world is in such a negative state. Make a commitment to yourself that you are going to surround yourself with high-energy people and focus on high-caliber information.

Transforming your life into the life of your dreams takes work, knowledge, and a deep commitment to change. Most people are not open to new ideas. In fact, psychology tells us that whenever a new idea is presented, it is first met with resistance, then with vicious opposition, and finally accepted.

Thinking Makes It So

I'm asking you to stay open to the new ideas presented in this course, test them against your own beliefs and values, and give them a try. I am a voracious reader and researcher, and every time I come across a new idea and am not sure what I think about it, instead of just dismissing it, I "hang it on a hook" in my mind. Then I wait to see if something else comes along that might clarify it, or help me to truly understand the concept and give me the chance to determine if it will fit into what I already know and believe, or whether it is a new and life-changing principle I want to adopt. This works for me, I think it will work for you. Remember that resistance is a reflex—and if you are always looking for certainty in your life you are asking for a life of boredom—because variety and change are necessary for continued growth.

In addition to our own beliefs, we also need to become aware of all the "cultural beliefs" that come to us from the groups we belong to—our families, clans, countries, ethnic backgrounds, religion, clubs, organizations, etc. A good example of how this affects us is what Presidential candidate Barrack Obama is going through as I write this, with his Reverend, Jeremiah Wright. Apparently, Obama has been attending this church for over 20 years, he was married and had his children baptized by Reverend Wright. It came to the public's attention that Reverend Wright has given extreme, anti-American lectures and is a black racist—encouraging his flock to go against the American government and the white population. The question then is, at what point did Mr. Obama start to "hear" these remarks from his Pastor? He says he didn't "hear" them, but, he also said he attended this church regularly. The point here is, you must really, really listen to what is being said and what is accepted belief by all the groups you associate with, because you will be judged by the company you keep. But, for this discussion, I am not worried about who judges you, but, what beliefs you are either "hearing" or think you are "ignoring". If you don't know the difference, you may have some serious belief "weeds" that are lodged in your sub-conscious mind that are bringing you the results you see in your life. If they are aligned with what you want, fine; but, if the results are not what you want, you had better check in with your group beliefs to make sure.

For example, you might think you want to have a lot of money, but, if subconsciously you believe that "money is the root of all evil" you are doomed to poverty. Also, if you long for a happy, romantic relationship, but, you subconsciously believe (picked up by your gossipy girlfriends) that all men are creeps, say goodbye to a romantic relationship.

Remember the story I told you of my friend (chapter 6) who was stressed and complaining about having to make a potato salad, go to the bank, and wash her hair all in one day? Well, here's the rest of the story. I had to finally tell her that I was struggling to staying positive, and I was doing everything I knew how to keep myself going forward. I told her if she couldn't be positive on the phone, I didn't want her to call any more. Now, that was a really hard thing to do, because I knew she didn't see herself as negative. I then offered to bring to her attention every time she said something negative, which I did—and she was shocked to see how often she spoke of what she **didn't** want. You need to do the same thing. You can play cancel/cancel with the people you live with and your best friends; but, refuse to surround yourself with negative, low-energy people and organizations that bring your energy down. It is imperative for you to stay positive and focused on what you really, really want.

Visualization is a very powerful way to start bringing to you your heart's desire. Remember, the subconscious mind cannot tell the difference between a real experience and an imagined one. That's why I like for you to envision the end result—how it will look when what you want is really here. And, if you add an emotion, remember, you get it faster; so if you can think, envision and feel it, your subconscious mind thinks it has already happened and calls forth an encore performance in the material world.

We probably need a little explanation as to how this really

Thinking Makes It So

happens. I am happy to tell you that science has now caught up with metaphysics and can explain some of these phenomena for us.

This is where it gets really fun. The physics that you learned in high school was probably Newtonian Physics which explains laws like gravity (what goes up must come down), and how every action has an equal and opposite reaction. This kind of physics explains the material world as we know it. Remember our Pyramid of Frequencies?

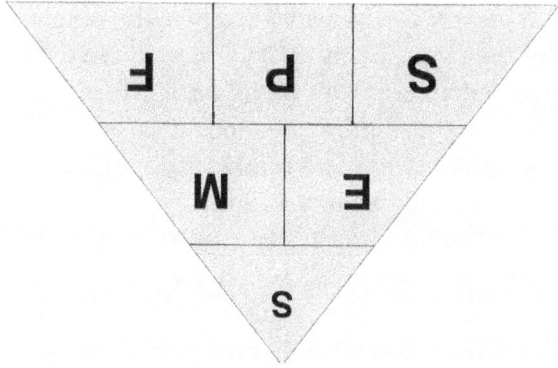

Now, looking at it upside down with the top pointing down I want you to draw wavy lines right under the three "top" ones, physical, financial and social, which will represent the ocean waves. What is above the wave line is the material world—those things that we can see and what we call "real". Below the line you will find mental, emotional and spiritual—all frequencies that we can't necessarily see with our physical eyes. These bottom ones are like the iceberg below the sea—we know they are there but we can't see them. I really don't understand how a microwave oven works, but, I am pretty good at pushing the buttons. Do you think that microwave frequencies were always there? Of course, but we just didn't have the knowledge and information with which to "see" them? These unseen frequencies are governed by Quantum Physics, which changed everything. I am told that Physicists even jumped off buildings to their death when quantum physics came along, because it challenged the beliefs upon which their entire careers and life had been based. There is good reason to be flexible and open and willing to learn.

Quantum Physics has an entirely different set of rules which deals with the particles and waves that everything is comprised of; and as we now know, these waves and particles contain only energy and information—and have all possibilities and all potential already contained within them—we're calling this the Quantum Soup. Now add to that the Heisenberg Principle, which is almost mind-boggling. It tells us that these waves and particles are influenced by the "Observer"—which means that the person focusing on the waves creates the outcome. WOW! That means that you, being the Observer, have the ability to influence the outcome if you focus on the final result that you desire. Now, that is a miracle—and, it is scientific fact! So, get busy visualizing what you really want. Most of us are very good at "imagining" what we don't want—I call them the "what ifs". What if I can't pay my mortgage? Then they'll repossess the house, then I'll be on the street, then I'll starve and then, and then, and then. Sound familiar?

So, in a nutshell, Newtonian Physics involves direct cause and effect, or linear thinking, in our material three-dimensional world. Quantum Physics deals with the non-linear which operates on the subtle energies which are on dimensions that we can't see with our physical eyes. Our job is to balance these two worlds. We will continue our discussion of this Quantum Soup when we get to the Spiritual Equity.

I do want, however, to give you a basic understanding of how your thoughts and beliefs become tangible results by using The Law of Attraction. Simply stated, this principle says that like vibrations attract like vibrations and dissimilar vibrations repel.

In science, the Wheeler-Feynman Absorber Theory tried to explain how the charged particles, due to your intention and attention, actually turned into a material desire. They said that when a particle gets emitted from a source (you) it interacts with one of two detectors, which are known as future possibilities. So, as the particle leaves you it sends out a wave of probability called an "offer wave" which goes out into time and space to the detector—that wave is your intention. When it reaches the detector, the detector sends a confirmation or what is called an "echo wave" that basically says "message received." These two waves have various ways to react—they can cancel each other out, they can build on each other and become larger, or anything in between.

I know that this might sound like gobblygook, but, stay with me here. What this means is that your thoughts, feelings and intentions are going out into the Quantum soup as offer waves and go back and forth between now and the future (which is another discussion for later), and these waves can interact and intersect with what is called an interference pattern. Now remember that we already know that everything we see as "real" is just stabilized light, and science tells us that everything that we see in our outer world is just a projection of our inner world. So, if your thought is "I am healthy and energetic" and this thought goes out into the ether and comes up against an interference pattern that says "no I'm not, I'm always tired", it cancels out the offer wave. If, however, it comes across a "resonance wave" that agrees with the original offer wave, it starts building on that frequency to make it more powerful, and the more offer waves there are that agree with this thought, the stronger the frequency becomes and the sooner it appears in your "real world". The most important fact to remember is that the possibility of what you desire is ALREADY CREATED IN THE QUANTUM SOUP, and all you have to do is offer a high-level vibrational wave that pulls you to it—you don't have to create it, just resonate with it! Your job is just to align with it. It's like Aladdin's lamp—Your wish is my command! If you send out an offer wave of lack and scarcity—your wish is my command—you get lack and scarcity, when you wanted abundance. Remember: you don't always get what you want, but, you will always get what you think about most.

If this information doesn't excite you, I don't know what would. It sends chills down my spine to know that we humans have this much power. We literally are creators with a little "c"—not The Creator with the big "C". We are creating our lives moment by moment, and we are either doing it on purpose or we are doing it half asleep. What you see in your world at this moment is a direct reflection of what you have been thinking. Do you have the determination and discipline to, first of all, know what you want, then visualize the end result and continue to send out offer waves that match your desire? Do you have the courage to stick to your dreams, and not be brought down by people who do not share your intentions?

> ✹ *You don't always get what you want; but you always get what you think about most.*

To summarize the information in this chapter:

1. Your thoughts are the mold that mobilize the Law of Attraction.
2. Your beliefs are running your life and bringing you results that you may or may not really want.
3. You have to be clear on what you really want—your intention.
4. Attention to your desire is focusing high energy towards the offer wave.
5. Visualize the end result.
6. Continue to send out positive frequency towards your desire.
7. Ignore or cancel out the negative.
8. Be aware of the people and groups you associate with and what they believe.
9. Surround yourself with high-energy people, books, music, programs.
10. Never give up.

Thinking Makes It So

In closing, I want to remind you to do your affirmations, and always add at the bottom, "this or something better". I also add this: AND I WILL NEVER GIVE UP!

When I say "I'll never give up", I can literally feel my feet rooting to the floor and I think the Universe responds with "Gee, this Gal really means this; we had better get it to her fast". That is intention, attention and high-energy offer waves. Now, get busy making your dreams come true.

Here's your exercise for this week: How did you do on last week's exercise, trying to control your thoughts? It's not as easy as it seems to be, is it? This week we are going to learn to relax. This is something really foreign to most Americans as well. It is very important for you to train your body to relax so that you can program it or deprogram it to match your desires. Relaxing does not mean sleeping! It is critical that you learn to be both relaxed and alert at the same time. It was easier for me to learn to do this with help from a relaxation tape which led me through it step by step, because my muscles, at the time, were made of steel! You can do this on your own, by methodically going from the top of your head down to your toes, section by section, tensing and then releasing in order to feel the relaxation take over your body. However, I have recorded a new Meditation C.D. that has the relaxation exercise on the first track, so you can put on head phones and let me guide you through this important exercise. Either way, this week, for at least 15 minutes a day, sit in your chair and relax your body and watch how your mind slows down as your body cooperates with you. If you can stay there longer than 15 minutes without falling asleep, go for it. And if you can find the time to do this exercise twice a day instead of just once, so much the better. You are learning to take control of your mind and body. Give yourself a big old pat on the back!

*The CD mentioned in this chapter is called
Energy Fix Meditations
and is available on my website
www.connielynnhayes.com

CHAPTER ELEVEN

A Picture is Worth a Thousand Words

*"Silent thought, is, after all,
the mightiest agent in human affairs."*
~Channing~

    We are learning in this section to take control of our mental activity, which includes our thoughts, beliefs, attitudes, perspective, emotions, and our behaviors which gives us our results. If you don't like the results you are getting in your life, you need to look at all of these parts of the manifesting formula to try and determine where you err. One part that I think needs more explanation is in your "self talk" or the stories you tell to yourself and about yourself.

    First of all, let's clear up one point. Ideas are different than thoughts. Ideas are fresh, creative and sometimes new, even if it is a simple idea like "let's go out to eat tonight". That is an idea and we encourage ideas. Thoughts are different, and most of them are not only the same ones we had yesterday, but, most of them that rumble around in our heads are a case of "mistaken identity". The difference is to know this principle: I am not my thoughts; I simply have thoughts, just as I am not you, or this car or this house. Did you get that? If not, go back and read that sentence again. As simple as that idea is, you can see how we get mixed up "thinking" that we are our clothes, our job and the car we drive. That's where we get involved with not only our "stories", but where other people's stories get imprinted onto us!

A Picture is Worth a Thousand Words

Let's face it, our past is what is controlling the present and our future—if we let it; what that means is that if we don't take control of our thoughts, those beliefs that we have carried with us thus far will continue to be true for us. Now, that's alright if you are living the life of your dreams; however, if you are not quite on target with your strongest desires, you need to investigate your past and the stories you have adopted about that past. For example, there are lots of groups that exist as "support groups" for people who have been mistreated, such as rape or incest, etc., and there are groups supporting those who either have a dreaded disease, or are so-called "survivors" of that disease. I'm not against support, but, I am against groups who perpetuate the thinking that you are still in some way connected with the problem. I know people who wear badges that say they are a cancer survivor and people who, when asked who they are, lead with "I am an abused child survivor". If that becomes your identity, and you constantly tell the woeful story about your horrid past and all you have been through, you can certainly understand how difficult it is to move on to bigger and better things. There is always some good that comes out of the horrible experiences that we have in this life. I admire people like the founder of Mothers Against Drunk Driving, who, after losing her son to a drunk driver, decided to do something positive to try to prevent other parents from losing children in the same way. That's turning a lemon into lemonade. That's not what I am talking about here. I am referring to the person who constantly tells the story of the "problem" over and over again to anyone who will listen! Remember, the mind can't tell the difference between an actual event, and an imagined one, so why put your consciousness through the problem continuously? The reason we do it is because we are always getting something out of it. Our job is to see what we are getting out of the constant retelling of our grievances and decide if that's what we really want or not.

One of the problems with this constant retelling of stories is, that after so many repetitions, they become so powerful and convincing that we actually internalize these tales in our physical muscles and tissues and it changes the way we walk and talk and, it sends out a powerful energy that affects how other people treat us. When we see ourselves as a victim, our personality changes to match that role; just the same as it does for an actor who is playing the part of a victim in a movie. Actors very often watch footage of people who are "victims" of the same sort as their role, and imitate the way they walk with their heads downward and talk with a certain "negative" inflection in their voice. Make no mistake, the person you believe yourself to be will be the person you embody, and because of your body language, you will signal to others to treat you as that person.

> ✸ *When we see ourselves as a victim our personality changes to match that role.*

What, then, could we possibly be deriving from carrying around negative stories about ourselves, even though they could be causing us suffering? The main reason is because whatever our story, we are the star of that drama—and we all want to be the star! Your ego has convinced you that if you let go of that story, you won't know who you are and you, heaven forbid, might disappear—at least be ignored. In a perverse sense, these stories give us a false sense of security, because at least we know who we are, don't we? Some people say, "Well, Connie, I'm only speaking the truth about my past". That may be true, but, the operative word here is "past", and you are bringing the same so-called truth into your present and future and continuing to make it true for you. Is that what you want? I don't think so. Whatever stories you tell, your subconscious will make true for you because the Universe can only say YES. So, if you want to continue being a victim, then you are doing the right thing; however, if you really want to be something more interesting, then telling the old, tired stories of your past is not the right thing to do.

A Picture is Worth a Thousand Words

Many years ago, when I was newly divorced I had several girlfriends who had been through the same experience and we would call each other and revel in who had been "done to" the worst. We would tell and re-tell our story long into the night and fall asleep with our poor-me tales on our lips. One night, after a particularly difficult set of circumstances, I found myself on the floor praying mightily and begging God to help me. I distinctly heard a voice in my head that said, "If you don't like what you see, choose again". Now, that made me mad at first. "You think I am choosing this?" I argued. Again, quietly and patiently the voice affirmed that I indeed did have the right to choose again. I quickly ended the prayer and crawled into bed, feeling indignant that I was being *blamed* for *choosing* my circumstances. After thinking about this mind-boggling experience all through the night, I finally started to laugh and immediately gave thanks for such an intelligent insight. Just imagine, little victim me, who had definitely had it handed to her, having a right to choose. Now that was a revelation. That also was the day my life turned around. The reason this is such a powerful thought is that if I have the power to create problems, then I also have the power to fix problems—and that gave me back my freedom, and I began to watch my language and the stories I was telling.

If you continue to see yourself as a victim at the hands of someone else or some situation, one of the pay-offs is that you can blame others for your predicament. That keeps you from taking responsibility. But, if you're not willing to take responsibility for the problem, you can't change it either. I prefer to say, "The buck stops here", and go ahead and design a life I really want; and that can only be done if I take charge.

Another way we tell our stories is by the many characters we play in this drama called life. Most of us can name numerous "roles" that we play daily such as: Mother, Daughter, Wife, Mother-in-Law, Granddaughter, Great Granddaughter, neighbor, American, Caucasian, Author, Lecturer, Consultant, Friend, etc, etc. One of the most powerful exercises I've ever done was in an all-day training seminar that I took many years ago. The Instructor had us all go outside and gave us two hours to do this exercise, which was to write down all the roles we play. Actually, there are hundreds of them and I would encourage you to do this exercise for yourself. After we completed this part of the exercise, our assignment was to again go outside and, one by one, cross out each role that we were willing to give up until we only had one left. Now, that was really, really hard. We were given four hours to do this chore, and I needed every last minute of it. I got down to Mother, Teacher and Student when I got stuck. I finally crossed out Teacher, and as I looked at the final two, I really didn't know which one I could cross out. Finally, I crossed out Mother, which brought a pang to my heart; but, I felt relieved, because I knew that if I were ever to stop learning, I would surely die. So that was the only persona I was willing to keep.

Now the truth is that you really don't have to give up the roles, you just have to give up identifying yourself *as* the role. Elizabeth Taylor was equally as convincing in the role of Cleopatra as she was in Virginia Wolfe, but, she didn't have to go on identifying with the role after the drama was over. To understand this principle, I can go on mothering, which is a verb, without seeing myself as "only a Mother". A lot of women announce themselves as "only a housewife" which to them is somehow a lowly position on the totem pole. The fact is we are multi-faceted, complicated individuals that are capable of accomplishing many tasks and roles, but without telling constant stories about that role as if that were the same as our "identity". Can you see the difference? Every character in your story is actually false evidence of your true nature, and when you keep on seeing others, no matter what role they are playing in your life drama, as singular roles, you are keeping yourself and the other person from experiencing who they really are as well. This is especially true with our children. If we see them as "our kids" and fail to see who they really are, we can expect to be treated as "the kid's Mother" and not as our real selves either.

The way to see this differently is to see our roles not as who we ARE, but as what we DO. We can go on doing nursing, but, not limit ourselves to being a nurse. Why do we want to do this? Because it frees us from the limited script that is associated with any particular role in life and that gives us the total freedom to design our life as we wish it to be. I've told you over and over again that the subconscious mind cannot reason, it can only take orders from the conscious mind; so the object of this game is to imagine ourselves to be as we want to be. That brings us to visualization.

If you are going to spin yarns about your life and the journey you have been on, make them of epic proportion. See yourself as a grand, noble hero who saved the poor damsel in distress. None of your stories are really true; they are just scripts, so let's create new scripts that are more in line with your desires. These new stories aren't who you are either, but, they will be a more empowering map that will take you to where you want to go—up the tallest mountain!

So, let's get busy reinventing ourselves. Remember, to make this work for you, you need to keep in mind a basic principle: <u>Everything you see in your outer world is only a projection of your inner world.</u> That means that since you are the creator of every incident in your life, no one is doing anything **to** you and nothing ever happens **to** you, so nothing in your outer world needs to be changed. That is the most powerful concept I can teach you today. Everyone is trying to change their outer world by fixing their outer world. That is a low energy way of doing it—and very slow—and most of the time doesn't work. Remember, we are engaging mental energy because it is a higher, faster and more powerful frequency than most problems; so start fixing your inner world if you want your circumstances to change. Once you understand that you can do this anytime you want, you will no longer be a victim or an innocent bystander in life—but, instead, a powerful life designer.

The way we begin is by "conscious dreaming"—or visualizing. Visualization is another word for imagining, and is the process of making mental images which become a mold, like our thoughts, to serve as a pattern for our future. When I was doing interior design work, I had to first spend a lot of time imagining in my mind what I wanted the room or home to look like. When we decided to build our home, before we decided on a plan we thought about not only what we wanted the house to look like, but how we wanted to feel living in this house, and the kind of things we wanted to be able to do in this home. I put in long hours imagining the rooms, the yard and the décor. Each night before I went to sleep, I imagined myself walking in the front door and going methodically through each room and noticing what I wanted to see there. I "saw" the floors, the color of the walls, the furniture placement, the light fixtures and so forth. Before I ever put anything on paper, I already had a good idea of what it should look like. It was really easy after that, because as I went shopping for various fixtures and other elements, I would know immediately if I was looking at something I wanted or not.

Most of us take a lot more time planning a house than we do designing our life—which is a shame. Take a look again at the formula for manifesting:

THOUGHT→BELIEF→ATTITUDE→PERSPECTIVE→ EMOTION→BEHAVIOR→RESULT

We haven't talked about behavior much yet, but, notice that it is right next to the result. Behavior means ACTION. You do have to do something, you know. Have you ever heard the saying "think before you act"? That is the correct order, but how many times do we all do something and think after the fact and wish we had done something different? What you have to understand is that we can go from thought clear through to behavior lickety split—so it seems as though we acted before we thought. That can't be true, there is always a thought, and it is always filtered through our beliefs and perspectives and emotions before we actually do something—it is just really,

A Picture is Worth a Thousand Words

really fast. That's why if you don't inspect your beliefs and adjust your attitude, your thought will probably turn out just the way all the other thoughts you have had in the past. The trick here is to take charge! You can do that with visualization, but, you will have to actually DO SOMETHING. In our weekly exercises, we have been working on disciplining the body and trying to control our thoughts, and now we need to learn how to visualize.

When people say they don't know how to visualize, I tell them what I am going to tell you now—you are always visualizing. The problem is that you are usually visualizing either what you don't want to happen, or all the "what-ifs" that could happen; but, make no mistake you are visualizing. All of us like to daydream, and this is a license to do it! We're not talking about wishful thinking—which is weak; we are talking about scientifically imagining your ideal life, making it your intention, and applying energy to it through attention. That's it—imagine, intend and attend.

Here are some hints to get you started: start with the idea of what you want—this must come first. Remember, most people don't even know what they want—they skip this step and if you skip it, too, your visualization will be off. When you get down to the practice of visualizing, you need to already know what you want. Get very clear about what you want so your imagination can take off—that's when it gets fun. All buildings were first seen in the mind of the architect before a pencil was put to paper. You are going to be the architect of your life from now on, and you have to construct it in your mind before you will see it anywhere else!

Once you have the idea of what you want to create you have sown the seed. Now you are going to picture in your mind the completion of your desire. See it in detail, one thing leading to another. Make the image clear, designing it exactly as you want to see the finished product. The more details the better. Put colors, and even smells into your dream if it applies. One caution here: don't bring other people into your visualization to "make" them be part of your desire. You can't control other's lives with your desires. For example: if you desire to be married, you can visualize all the details of the wedding, see yourself in the exact gown or dress, hear the words you want to hear—but, don't put a groom into the picture, just know one is there. You can, however, imagine the groom to be all that you want him to be—imagine him loving you dearly, treating you the way you wish to be treated, having all the great characteristics that you long for—but, no particular individual in the image. And, don't forget, we always say "this or something better", because even our best imaginings are not always as good as it could be.

Once you get it "right" so that you can actually feel how it will be to have this dream come true, all you have to do is stick with it. That means, DON'T KEEP CHANGING THE DREAM. Persistent attention and adding energy to the dream every day is all the action you need to take at this time. Each time you repeat the visualization it becomes clearer and the excitement builds. How many of you have children who have asked for something in particular for Christmas? How do they act for the weeks and days before Christmas morning? They KNOW that they are going to get that bike and all they have to do is wait, and continue to imagine how they are going to ride it and how swell it is going to look when they show their friends. Do they ever doubt that they will get it? Not unless you put the doubt in their minds first. This is the way you are to act with your dreams, too. Anticipate the realization of your dream, add emotion and excitement, and just wait for it to materialize. It is helpful to write out a summation of this dream, if you wish, and carry it with you so you can repeat it to yourself many times a day; but, affirmations don't take the entire place of visualization, which is what you do while sitting in your chair, relaxed and in an alpha state of mind.

One thing that most people don't like to talk about is the fact that once you home in on what you really, really want—all the "not-A's" start to appear in your life. Not-A's are all the reasons as to why you can't have what you want, so controlling your self-talk is vitally important at this point. Every time I think, "who do you think you are, wanting something like that?" I just say "cancel/cancel, thank you for sharing, but, this is what I want", and I go right back to what I want. At first, you might have to do that hundreds of time during a day, but, it is worth it.

The other truth about this whole business of manifesting is that as soon as you get very clear about what you want, the opposite seems to instantly manifest in your outer world. That is a fact, and none of us like it! But, I don't suppose anyone, including the very popular movie The Secret wanted to tell you the reason why this is true—but, I will.

We live in a world of duality—black and white, up and down, hot and cold. Did you ever wonder why we have a planet of opposites? It's because the Creator knew that the only way you could experience anything at all, and KNOW that you were experiencing it, was to see it against a field of exactly the opposite. Here's a good example of what I mean. We say there is light and darkness, don't we. There really is no such thing as "darkness", there is only the absence of light. You can't experience the light, however, unless you had degrees of light and the POTENTIAL of no light at all—which we call darkness. Hot and cold is another example: there are only degrees of heat—and without the degrees of heat we would not be able to experience what we call "cold". Therefore, when you visualize abundance, you are bringing up a field of what we call lack or scarcity, so that when the abundance materializes—you can experience abundance. You wouldn't know what abundance was if you didn't already know what lack was. Get it? The problem with this situation is that people usually stop at that point and say "this stuff doesn't work", and they let go of their dream and sure enough, it doesn't work. Remember, the Universe always says YES, it cannot say NO. It will always make you right.

Mental Equity

The best way I can explain this to you is to have you imagine a busy place like Grand Central Station in New York City. Even if you have never been there, you can probably imagine what it would look like to a person who didn't know what was happening there. You'd see a lot of train tracks with trains coming and going 24/7 and people scurrying everywhere. People get off trains and it looks like total chaos when they all start going different ways—some to other trains, some to doors that take them outside to taxis and buses, some who stop to eat, some who don't know where they are going. It looks like total chaos. But, soon everyone is either making new train connections or has arrived at their final destination in quite an orderly manner, even though on the surface it looks quite unorganized.

Once you make up your mind what you want, do you have any idea how many actions have to be put into place to pull off your dream? Sometimes it involves bringing people into your life, sometimes it means taking people out of your life. Sometimes it takes a change in job or home or city where you live. Lots of things have to be orchestrated to bring it about— and if you give up on your dream before you see it in reality, you stopped the process and probably fouled up a lot of things. Synchronicity takes place on a level that none of us really understands. But, nothing is too hard or complicated for the Universe. "Your wish is my command" is how it sees it. The best way for you to accept this fact is to remember that everything has already been created. Think about that computer program you use every day called Microsoft Word (which I am using to write this chapter). I am always amazed that it knows when I make a mistake — not only spelling, but,

> ✸ *Anticipate the realization of your dream, add emotion and excitement, and just wait for it to materialize.*

A Picture is Worth a Thousand Words

grammar and size of type, indentation, numbering, bold type, etc. The reason it can do all of that is that the creators of this wonderful software thought of everything you could possibly do wrong as you write, and because the mistake is already in the programming, it can tell me what to do to fix it. Think of the Quantum Soup that we already discussed as the computer disc that has all possibilities already on it; so, that when you make a choice, the Universe already knows what it has to do to bring it to you. Of course, it has to make corrections depending on where you are positioned in the "field of all possibilities" (which we will discuss fully in the Spiritual Equity), but, for now, just know that it knows how to do this. For now, let's just concentrate on your part of the equation.

I will summarize what we have learned in this chapter for you:
1. Stop telling your stories—especially the "victim" ones.
2. Get very clear on what you want.
3. Visualize, in detail, how it looks when your dream comes true.
4. Use your imagination—have fun.
5. Be prepared for the "not A's", and turn them away.
6. Know that when the opposite of what you want appears, the Universe is setting up the "field" so you can experience your desire.
7. Your behavior comes right before the result; therefore, you must do the work—which includes intention and attention to your desire.
8. Spend time daily imagining your desires in a relaxed and focused state.
9. Add "this or something better" to all of your affirmations.
10. Anticipate the results with great excitement.

Now, for the exercise of the week: Go to the same room and sit in the same chair you have been using for your relaxation. This time, take a picture of either a person or a thing, like a car or a flower. Sit and look carefully at this picture and take in all of the detail of it—color, texture, facial expression, wrinkles, flaws, etc. Get very familiar with all the picture has to offer.

Then close your eyes and see how much of this same picture you can visualize in your mind. Keep trying until you think you have it exactly and with all the details of the original picture. Practice this exercise every day for at least 15 minutes. This is how you train your mind to be a great visualizer.

If, by now, you know of something that you really want, or some situation or experience that you want, you can, after you have relaxed (with or without the C.D.), visualize in detail, your desire. Take time to see how it would look when you have materialized it in finished form—feel the excitement and the anticipation of actually getting what you want—thank the Universe for this opportunity and add, "this or something better in the highest good of all concerned".

I know this is a lot of information to take in, and it might be fairly new to some of you, but, believe me, it is worth the time and effort you are taking to learn this. I suggest that you read all chapters in the Mental Equity at least once per day, so that you can not just know about this information, but, that you will own it.

CHAPTER TWELVE

Your Wish Is My Command

*"Ask, and it shall be given to you;
seek and ye shall find;
knock and it shall be opened unto you."
~Matthew 7:7~*

This Chapter will act as a summary for the Mental Equity. We will go over some of the concepts we have already learned and I will say them in a little different way to make sure that you thoroughly understand this equity, since all the other equities depend on this knowledge. I'll also throw in a few twists to keep you awake!

We have been discussing Mental Energy and ways to bring the process of manifestation into our conscious minds. But, let's not forget that this entire course is about "frequency", and remember that there are different levels of frequency within each Equity. What that means is that in the Mental Equity, there are higher and lower frequencies of energy, and it is our job to raise our mental energy to the highest possible frequency to solve problems.

Since you now know that thoughts are the first part of the manifestation formula, it only stands to reason that we need to not only watch our thoughts, but, to consciously bring them up to a powerful energy. How do we do that? First, start by watching your words—words are not only thoughts, but, thoughts IN ACTION—which brings you directly to results. Words are extremely powerful, either for positive results or negative results. Unfortunately, most of the words we say each day are not doing us much good. The object of this game is to make each word that we speak count—meaning that they take us closer to our goals. Idle talk is weak; constant idle talk, especially if it is similar to what we say each day, creates a brain pathway that takes us closer to WHAT WE DON'T WANT. Gossip is another form of low energy talk. We will talk more about judgment in a future chapter, but, for right now, just know that idle and gossipy conversations are very low energy and will lead you away from the kind of magic we are talking about here.

Other kinds of language that get us into a low energy rut are foul words, attack words, and threats. Remember the research scientist who found out that plants react just to the THOUGHT of burning it with a match—imagine how much damage a verbal attack or mean-spirited threat can do. Unfortunately we use this kind of conversation every day, even with our children! We throw idle threats around like "I'm going to kill you if you don't finish your dinner". Now, I know you don't actually mean that you are going to kill the child, but, the verbiage is a threat and carries with it negative energy that goes out into the room and into the memory banks of both you and the child.

One of the most interesting studies about the power of words was done by a Japanese scientist names Masaru Emoto. His original book called "The Hidden Messages in Water" became a bestseller, and I highly recommend that you read it. He also made a video about this phenomenon which is highly educational for you and your family. In a nutshell, Emoto found that words have a terrific, physical effect on water. What he did was type certain words like "love" or "hate" and tape them to bottles or glass containers of water and freeze them. Hours later, he would take a crystal from each container, and through a very sophisticated method of photography, capture a picture of each crystal through a high-powered microscope. He was utterly amazed at what he saw. The frozen water droplets from the bottle with the positive word on it were in beautiful shapes and colors, while the water crystals from negative words were malformed, even hideous, and discolored. He went on to test this remarkable finding with many different words and phrases and the results were the predictable—words had a profound effect on water.

He also tested music, art and photographs on the water and the findings were equally amazing. This not only brought out the huge possibilities for using water for healing purposes; but, since our bodies are more than 2/3 water, it also showed what good or damage words, music, art and literature can be doing to our human bodies! When you look at one of his books which are loaded with photographs of these tests, be sure and show them to your children—and then, make it a family project to clean up the language in your home. This would be an excellent place to begin raising the energy in your personal environment, and then taking the next step by watching your words away from home.

> ✸ *Words, music and literature can do damage to our bodies.*

I told you in the last Chapter that the Universe always says YES, and is incapable of saying NO. This is another way for you to raise your mental energy—by seeing how many times during each day that you can say YES. That will train your mind to look at the possibilities instead of looking at the impossibilities. Every time you say YES, you are emulating one of the highest frequencies available to us mortals. We're actually jumping to a Spiritual frequency by doing this simple thing; but, I wanted to mention it here since it includes speaking. I think you will be appalled when you see how many times in a 24-hour period you, either with words, or by body language, say NO to what is going on around you.

Mental Equity

I'm not saying that you have to agree with everything and everyone, or go along with destructive people or a destructive situation; I'm only saying that when you think or verbalize what you are seeing in a negative format, the Universe says "Your wish is my command", which is saying YES. Learn to reformat negative situations, experiences, and conversations into a positive statement that you can agree with.

Here's an example of this principle that I learned from Louis Tice. He trains sales people all over the country and he has about 15 foster children in his own home. When he sees a child doing something that is negative or destructive in some way, all he says is "Stop! I think too much of you and too much of myself to allow this behavior to go on". Notice that this statement is a positive one—one that you can say YES to, even though it is dealing with a negative situation. I have used this tact many times, and believe me, it really does work!

This higher frequency "choosing" also applies to our attitude. When you go into a situation with a negative attitude, you are already saying NO to whatever is happening, other possibilities don't stand a chance. I encourage all of us to keep an open mind—that's where all the fun is located. If you already have your mind made up before something happens, there's no room for surprise. Being flexible and always ready to learn something new is a wonderful way to approach life; which brings us to the subject of knowledge.

I am imparting loads of information to you in this course. When you take the information in and mix it with what you already know and believe, it becomes knowledge. Once the knowledge is "used" and becomes experiential, it is then wisdom. That's why we "seniors" are said to have more wisdom than the younger souls. Experience takes the information into the "known"—not just knowing <u>about</u>. You can know a lot <u>about</u> a subject; however, when you have actually experienced it—you know it for sure. That's where I hope you will take this information—by keeping an open mind, understanding the concepts intellectually, and then trying them out for yourself, you will see how they work. The most important step comes next. Any concept that is new to you, try teaching to someone else within 24 hours after learning it—then the concept becomes knowledge. Doing or being the concept takes it to the level of wisdom.

Remember that if you are not growing—you are dying. The Universe is always expanding, and if you are, too (I'm not referring to your waistline), you are in harmony with Consciousness. In the now famous book and movie called "What the Bleep Do We Know?", authors William Arntz, Betsy Chasse and Mark Vicente have shortened the manifestation formula down to DESIRE—CHOICE—INTENT—CHANGE. One of the contributors to that movie, Fred Alan Wolf said: "It really is a question of desire; desire and only desire. It has nothing to do with ability, talent, brains or anything else."—and I agree. In order to make any of this information useable in your own life, you have to desire to do so. And, the bad news is, it can't be just a mediocre, luke-warm sort of "want" either. The desire to make something out of your life has to come from a deep-down desire to do better. Sometimes we have to hit rock bottom or have a terrible crises before we decide that "there must be a better way". That's O.K., but, you really don't have to wait for disaster to hit; you can decide in a moment that you deserve to have your heart's desire.

Just for fun try saying out loud "I want_____ (finish the sentence with what you have on your list. Then say "I desire _____ (such and such), and feel and hear the difference in your voice. Wants are not only weak like wishes, but, if you keep saying I WANT—The Universe says "your wish is my command"—and you will keep wanting. The word "desire" actually means "of God"—so you can see that it holds a much more powerful frequency than want or wish.

Once, you know what that desire is (and remember it has to

Mental Equity

be clear—not wishy-washy) and you can feel that desire deep down in your soul, you have taken the next step—<u>choice</u>.

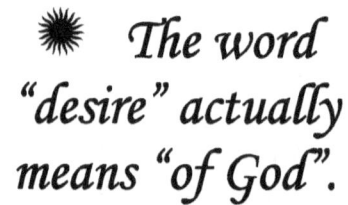
The word "desire" actually means "of God".

Making a choice as to what you want is the part where most people mess up. But, do you really understand why a human being's brain is different than other animals? It's because you have a frontal lobe, which gives you the ability to make choices. I'm often reminded that a tree, which cannot make choices, always becomes "all that it can be under the prevailing circumstances". Humans are the only species that have a choice <u>not</u> to be all that they can be—which, is of course, what most people are choosing. Why? Mostly because of laziness and because they are leaving the "choosing" up to the part of the brain that is labeled with a "repeat button", which just keeps choosing what they have always chosen—and they wonder why their lives don't change. Hmmmmm!

If, after having the desire and making your choice, you don't see results, it's because INTENT was not strong enough. This is where focus comes in—persistence, perseverance, constancy. This is where the rubber meets the road, so to speak. The reason most people have a hard time with this step is because there are so many distractions in this culture. Science tells us that we are only aware of about 2,000 bits of information out of 400 billion bits of information thrown at us EVERY SECOND. Even 2,000 sounds like a lot—but, remember, most of them are either the same ones we had yesterday (which become habits and beliefs), and/or we schitoma them out because we don't have anything in our memory bank with which to compare them. The thoughts that make an impact are either ones that agree with what we already believe, or are new thoughts that we wish to consider (if we are open to new ideas). Most of us have already made up our minds on most subjects—let's take politics for example. When you already consider yourself a Republican or Democrat or Independent or Conservative or Liberal, or whatever label you wish, you will find articles in the newspaper and magazines, hear commentators on T.V. and radio who reinforce what you already believe. Those that say things you don't agree with, you either ignore or downplay or attack. You very seldom hear really good discussions about the difference in *perspective,* without the personality being verbally attacked or abused. Personal attacks are always low energy and if you want to partake of the higher frequencies to solve problems and live a smoother life, you need to not only watch your foul words and attacks, but also refuse to listen to others who participate in this kind of language. You have every right to say, "Stop! I think too much of you and too much of myself to allow this kind of talk to go on". Once you set the guidelines for your environment, others will respect you for it. Your energy will rise exponentially!

So, intention is, in summary, the amount of energy you wish to put into your desire and choice. We have talked about ways to do this—writing out your desires by mapping, or creating a list and making affirmations is one way. I love to take one of my affirmations that I am working with and set it to music and then singing it when I am alone (definitely alone) in the shower or the car. That helps focus energy on the words and makes it more fun. Writing out your ideal day or even your ideal life is another way to focus on your intention. I recently wrote out what my Ideal Life would look like when I am living it and I read it to myself each morning and evening and I get really excited just thinking about this wonderful life I am creating. We spend more time planning a vacation than we do a life!

Once you have isolated your desires, made a choice and set your intent, you must wait for the changes to happen. Like I told you in a previous chapter, you can expect chaos to start and you might even see the opposite of what you want popup—that's part of the process and a good chance for you to restate your desire, increase your focus and stay the course. Some results happen almost instantly—but, most take a little

Mental Equity

time. However, keep an eye out for synchronistic signals and/or opportunities. Remember, the Universe has to coordinate a lot of people, places and things in order to bring about your desire—and you might have to do something. I haven't ever observed a million dollars dropping out of the sky. But, I have seen million dollar opportunities come along. Keep an open mind and be ready to act. Here's an example.

When I was doing interior design work, one of the assignments I had was to coordinate the interiors of a huge condominium project. Once the project was started, a terrible thing happened—the lender went into bankruptcy; not the builder but, the lender. Needless to say, all building stopped abruptly since there was no money forthcoming. The problem was that some units had already been sold, and people were really upset when they saw no action. That wasn't the only problem—as time went on, prices on materials went up and by the time they were able to start construction again, glass, lumber, cement, etc. all cost more than the original bids. That's when it became my problem. One of the few places the Contractor had money to spare was in the interiors and he was going to cut my budget severely if we didn't come up with another way by a week from Thursday. I did a little research and found out that the heating and air conditioning system was one item that had gone up considerably, and that was going to eat up much of my budget. So, I went into meditation and did what I call The Problem Solving Meditation. (By the way, this meditation is on my special CD.). This meditation involves getting relaxed and then pulling down a white screen and seeing the problem written or pictured on this screen. You then allow yourself to wallow in the problem for a few minutes, and then erase the screen.

Then you see the word SOLUTION written in big, black, bold letters across your screen; and then you wait. Well, I did this, and the first day nothing happened. Neither did anything happen on the second, third, or fourth days. On the fifth day, after I saw the word SOLUTION, I saw the picture of a cactus on the screen. Well, this didn't mean anything to me so I asked for "more information please." Nothing, just a cactus came up—and so it did for three more days. I was really getting frustrated by now, because I only had a few more days left before my big budget cut, but, I persevered with my meditation. On about the 9th day, I decided to go to lunch alone. Not only did I go alone, but, for some odd reason I went to a small place that I had never been to before, and then I did something really strange—I sat at the counter in between two gentlemen who were already sitting there. This was highly unusual for me—I never sit at counters and I would always find a lone seat somewhere; surely not sit between two men. To make matters worse, one of the men had papers strewn about and he acted quite put-out when I sat down because he had to move his papers. After ordering, I glanced down at the gentlemen's paper to my right, and low and behold, the very cactus that I had been seeing in my meditation was on his logo! No kidding! Of course, I immediately struck up a conversation with him and he turned out to be the answer to our heating and air conditioning problems. He was from Arizona, was used to doing large construction, and had a unique way of setting up the system so that it not only cost less to install, but, cost the tenants less to run it, too. What a win-win that was. You can imagine how excited I was when I took this man to meet my Contractor and sure enough, it saved my budget! I should have had a raise!

This story illustrates how you can use these higher energies to solve problems. I first had to get very clear about what I wanted—to save my budget. I didn't sit by and do nothing—I researched and found that the heating and air conditioning which hadn't been installed yet might be a place to save money. I put in the time to meditate with lots of intention, and persevered. When I got a partial answer which I did not understand, I asked for more information, and even though I didn't get it immediately, I kept on. And best of all, I was open and went with the flow when I was urged to do things that I normally would never do. Those are the steps in manifesting.

Mental Equity

Remember when we learned about the Quantum Soup—which is the field of all possibility. It's from this soup (actually energy and information) that the unmanifested becomes the manifested. Let me tell you another story about how this actually works.

In another instance, when I was an interior designer, I went to Furniture Market in San Francisco. Whenever I went to market, I would go to buy furniture for my clients. On this particular occasion I also went to purchase a few things for myself. My children and I had just moved into a new condominium and I was doing the interiors myself. I needed a new sofa and some sort of drapery treatment for my living room. I spent quite a bit of time dreaming about what I wanted and finally sat down and drew a picture of the new sofa and drapes. The design I drew had a little bit of an oriental feel to it and I colored it navy blue with large, white lotus flowers on it. Then I went to market to find the fabric.

Furniture Market is huge—eleven floors of non-stop shops and stores carrying everything you can imagine. I went into this tiny shop and liked some of the fabrics he had but, didn't find exactly what I was looking for, so I meandered back into his backroom which I'm sure he didn't appreciate. There I found a swatch sample book of fabrics and there was the exact, navy blue material I had drawn. However, there was one problem—the manufacture didn't have any more of it and that's why it was in the back room. I pleaded with the salesman that I only needed about 7 yards to make the sofa and a couple more to make a cornice. He finally agreed to call, but, he couldn't promise anything.

A few days later, I was going up the escalator at the old Weinstocks Store in Murray, Utah, where they had a furniture department just where the escalator ends. Right in front of me, in this department, was my sofa! No, not just any sofa—my sofa, exactly the size and shape that I had drawn with the exact same navy blue fabric on it. I thought someone was playing a joke on me, so I went up to it only to find a famous manufacturer's name on it! The salesman informed me that it had just come in that day—and now I knew why there was no more fabric available—this manufacturer had purchased all of it. Well, to make a long story short, I bought the sofa and the market clerk called to tell me he had found only 3 yards of the desired fabric, which I bought, and had a beautiful matching cornice made.

The question you are probably asking is how could I have drawn the exact same design that someone else had obviously drawn many months before I did? The answer is that everything possible is already in the field of all possibilities, and any of us, yes, you, too, can tap into it at any time. It just so happens that I tapped into it later than someone else did—but, because I had known exactly what I wanted, did the work, put the intention on it, the Universe delivered it to me—and it actually cost me less than if I had had it custom made. That's why you always say "this or something better, for the highest good of all concerned."

I hope you are getting excited about creating your life instead of just waiting for it to happen "to you". Here are a couple of exercises I would like you to do this week to help you get going.

First, I want you to take out a tablet of some kind—or a special journal that you can keep and refer to often. Hopefully, it's the same one you did your mind mapping in or your desire list. This time, choose one of your desires and write it at the top of the paper. Then start writing—and don't stop for fifteen minutes. Write down everything that you are "thinking" about this desire—positive and negative. Just keep the pencil on the paper and put it all down. After fifteen minutes take a look at what you have written and see if you can see any blocks that are there which are keeping you from having your desire. You can say affirmations all day long, but, if just after you've stated the desire—your mind negates it by saying "just how do you think you're going to get that?" you are pushing and pulling at the same time and you aren't getting anywhere! Identifying these negative thoughts will help you let go of the ones that go against your desire and keep the ones that are in favor of it. This is a powerful process and I kindly encourage you to take time to do it.

The second exercise is for you to get a box of some kind—preferably one that looks special in some way or one you can decorate to look special. This will be your Dream Box—a sort of mailbox for you to send your desires to the Universe. This exercise is fun if you will just get into it. Write down all of your desires that you are currently working with on slips of paper and put them in your box. Say the desire aloud as you "mail" it and know in your heart that it will be received. Remember, you only have to mail it once—but, you do have to keep the energy focused on getting it. Remember the child at Christmas, and recreate that feeling of excitement and expectation.

Now, all you have to do is stay open to synchronicities that occur—and they will. Watch for them and then act upon them because action is the step next to results. Here's one last story for this week.

One of my interior design assignments was to help create a shopping mall—which was entirely new for me. I had to learn all kinds of things about construction and coordinating the design with the Contractor and Architects. One particular problem showed up on which none of us could agree. I wanted it to look pretty, the architect wanted it to function and the contractor wanted it to be simple and inexpensive. We were at a stale-mate. I did my problem-solving meditation and, of course, got no solution for many days. One afternoon I was killing some time in a book store (which is normal for me) and as I walked down the aisle, a book fell off the shelf and hit me in the foot. It hurt, and as I picked it up to replace it, it fell open to a page that had a drawing on it, and, you guessed it, it was exactly what I needed to know to solve the construction problem. I bought the book, took it to the architect and he was also thrilled at the simple solution it provided. This is the power of manifestation. Now, get busy manifesting your dreams.

Don't forget to continue doing your meditation every day for at least 10 minutes and try to get better every session at visualizing what you want to create. Remember, to see the finished product—how it is going to look when it comes.

This concludes the Mental Equity section of this Course. Next chapter we will start the Emotional Equity which will give you even more power to create.

In the meantime, check out the Bibliography on page 147 and get some of the books to have in your own library. Some of your "action steps" can be reading, listening to uplifting music and instructional audio CD's, and spending time in nature.

IMPLEMENTING THE MENTAL EQUITY

1. Thought→Belief→Attitude→Perspective→Emotion→Behavior→Result. We are creating our reality each minute with every thought we think. Watch the destructive and incorrect thoughts you have about yourself. You always get what you think about most.

2. Find out what you **really** want by doing all of the exercises on pages 103-106.

3. Examine your beliefs, and those of the organizations and groups you belong to – make sure you agree with and truly accepts those beliefs as your own. Weed out the ones that don't resonate with you.

4. Examine the roles you play, notice where, or if, you are being a victim. Remember, that everything in your outer world is a reflection of your inner world. If you don't like what you see, choose again. Start visualizing the outer world you want, and then take action.

5. Remember Masaru Emoto's work with water and words. Consider the fact that you are mostly water, and, therefore, the impact words do have on you and others. Find ways to say "YES", turning negative situations into positive ones. Watch the movie "What The Bleep Do We Know".

RECOMMENDED READING FOR MENTAL EQUITY

1. *You'll See it When You Believe it*—Wayne W. Dyer (audio)

2. *What to Say When You Talk to Yourself*—Shad Helmstetter

3. *As a Man Thinketh*— James Allen

4. *The Master Key System*—Charles Haanel

5. *Key to Living the Law of Attraction*—Jack Canfield

6. *The Greatest Secret of All*—Marc Allen

7. *The Code*—Tony Burroughs

8. *Mind Magic*—Marta Hiatt

9. *How to Get Everything You Ever Wanted*—Adrian Calabrese

10. *The Intention Experiment*—Lynne McTaggart

11. *What the Bleep Do We Know*—William Arntz, Betty Chasse, Mark Vicente

12. *The Biology of Belief*—Bruce Lipton

13. *Real Magic*—Wayne W. Dyer

14. *The Power of Intention*—Wayne W. Dyer

SECTION THREE

EMOTIONAL EQUITY

CHAPTER THIRTEEN

Learning the Language of Creation

"It is the combination of thought and love which forms the irresistible force of the law of attraction."
~Charles Haanel~

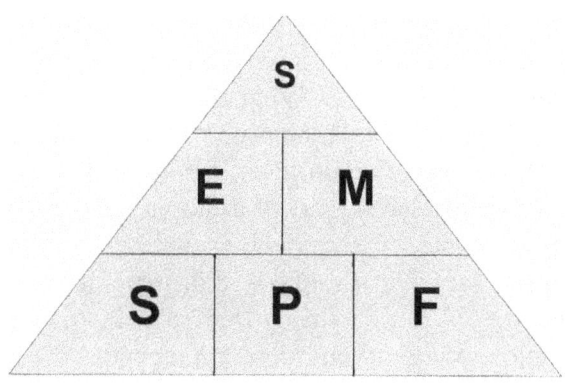

At this point in our studies I certainly hope that you are becoming very aware of your thoughts, words and beliefs and how they are creating your life. Bringing all of this up to the conscious mind is the goal—because we cannot take charge if we are not first aware. Now we are going to continue along our road to becoming "conscious creators" by learning to speed up the results. "How do we do that?" you ask—with emotions!

Let's go back to our formula:

Emotional Equity

THOUGHTS→BELIEFS→ATTITUDE→PERSPECTIVE →EMOTIONS→BEHAVIOR→RESULTS

We touched a little bit on emotions earlier, but, now we really need to get familiar with this subject since, as you can see, emotions are right next to behavior. We all have had many experiences where it seemed like the emotion came first, and before we even had time to think, we acted—most of the time to our chagrin. As I have said many times, we can go from thought clear through to behavior in less than a second—and that is because emotions are so powerful.

The most important thing to remember at this time about emotions is this:
YOU WILL ALWAYS MOVE IN THE DIRECTION OF THE STRONGEST EMOTION!

If that is true, and it is, then we probably need to know what the strongest emotions are. What do you think the strongest emotion is? Most people answer "love" when I ask that question. If love was the strongest emotion, this world would be a very different place—sort of a utopia. However, it is not the strongest; in fact, it's quite low on the list. It probably won't surprise anyone to know that fear is the strongest emotion on this planet. Why is that? Well, the truth is that love is the most powerful emotion, but, because the masses are focused on fear (and other fear-based emotions), it overpowers love just by the sheer numbers.

Here is the actual list in order of strength:

1. Fear
2. Worry
3. Guilt
4. Anger
5. Resentment
6. Hate
7. Enthusiasm
8. Humor

Learning the Language of Creation

9. Love
10. Joy
11. Pride
12. Contentment
13. Trust
14. Compassion
15. Faith

When you look at that list, it is easy to get discouraged to find that it takes until #7 to even get to a positive emotion; and love comes in at a distant 9th! However, when you think about the billions of people on earth, and you watch the evening news each night, it becomes easier to see that love and joy are not the emotions of choice for the masses. This then becomes a serious problem for us—if we do not become aware of our thoughts and emotions, we fall right in step with the rest of humanity! That should be a scary thought for most of us.

The truth of the matter is that there really are only two emotions: LOVE and FEAR—all of the other ones are derivatives of these two. So whenever you feel a strong emotion, ask this question: "Is this coming from love or fear?" The important thing to remember is that they both can't exist at the same time.

If you are worrying about something, it is fear of what might happen in the future. If you feel guilty—you fear something from the past. Jealousy isn't on the list, but, it is a strong emotion and it is fear of not being good enough. The bottom line of fear is that it is just a <u>call for love.</u>

For example: if your small child comes crying to you in the middle of the night because she is afraid of the "boogey man", you don't say, "you stupid kid, there's no such thing as a boogey man, so get back in bed and go to sleep!" You more likely would say: "let's go turn all the lights on and look under the bed and in the closets to make sure everything is safe, and would you like to sleep with me tonight?" You see, it is natural for most of us to give love when there is fear.

However, how do we respond when someone is angry or hateful to us? Often, when this happens, we tense up and return anger with anger, etc. And then we wonder where wars come from. HMMM!

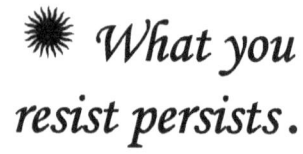
What you resist persists.

A good thing to remember is that what you resist persists. How do you feel when someone comes up and pushes you? The natural response to being pushed is to push back. I think it humorous when watching a basketball game to keep your eye on the person with the ball as he backs up, backs up towards the basket—all the while being defended by a big player on the opposite team. Since the player with the ball is expecting resistance, it is funny when the defender suddenly stops resisting and the offensive player falls down and gets called for a foul. That's the way most of our days go—we expect resistance; but, if someone refuses to push back, and instead extends love, we immediately think something is wrong with this picture! Try it sometime—it can be loads of fun when someone is ranting and raving at you, shaking their fist and going red in the face—just stop, watch the show quietly and say something kind or loving. Sometimes, I have to admit, it just makes them madder to see you so calm, but, that's their problem.

The reason emotions are so powerful is that they will manifest your thoughts FASTER. They are like little turbo-chargers on your thoughts and beliefs. So, whenever you add an emotion to an affirmation <u>that speeds up the results</u>. Of course, that also means the opposite—what you don't want comes faster, too, if there is an emotion involved. This is one of the reasons I am so insistent on your desires being something that you are really passionate about. Passion is a strong emotion and works wonders when hooked onto a desire. This would be a good time for you to go back and look at your affirmations and add emotional words to them. For example you could say: *I am so excited to say that I am now the proud owner of a new Buick Enclave.* Oh! that's my affirmation. But you get the idea.

There is a difference between an emotion and a feeling. Emotions actually trigger a physical response in the body that is communicated through feelings. It is very interesting that science has now proved that emotions are physical molecules—called "molecules of emotion"—that are actually special amino acids called peptides. These are real molecules that can be measured in a laboratory. Dr. Candace Pert has devoted a good part of 30 years to this study and can now explain to us how this actually works. I'm only going to give you the short version of her findings. If you are interested in knowing more, I highly recommend that you read her books "Molecules of Emotion", and "Everything You Need To Know To Feel Go(o)d". She actually believes that emotions <u>are</u> the subconscious mind. Let me explain.

Dr. Pert tells us that every one of our trillions of cells has thousands of little structures on it called "receptors". Just like our eyes and ears, these receptors are supposed to pick up signals that are coming to them from the environment. She says that these receptors are so important that a full 40% of our DNA is devoted to making sure that they're perfectly reproduced from generation to generation.

Once a signal has been received, the information is sent into the cell's interior where tiny little engines initiate key activities. For example, information coming in this way might tell cells when to divide and how to grow, or might inform them to repair or attack enemies, or create energy. These signals come from other cells and are carried by special juices that are contributed from glands or organs, and this sets up a very sophisticated communication that goes on in the "bodymind". These juices are more commonly called hormones, neurotransmitters and peptides, and they are all known as "ligands"—which means "to bind". This word is used because these juices latch on really tight to the receptors.

These information-carrying ligands transfer about 98% of all data in the body and the brain. The remaining 2% of communication takes place at the synapse between brain cells firing and releasing neurotransmitters across a gap to hit receptors on the other side. One of these ligands is the peptides that I mentioned before. Scientists have mapped over 200 peptides in the brain and the body, and the interesting thing about them is that each one is responsible for a complex emotional "chord" such as bliss, anger, hunger, relaxation, when their signal is received by the cell. I was amazed to learn that most of these ligands have a chemical equivalent outside of the body like valium, marijuana, caffeine, cocaine and alcohol to name a few. You can see why these drugs become addictive, since they replicate the emotions of euphoria, relaxation or pleasure.

The question then becomes, how do these ligands find and hook up with the receptors and then transfer this vital information to the body and/or brain?

The original explanation for this phenomenon was by using a lock and key model. The reason this made sense was because each receptor is shaped to fit one, and only one, ligand. They thought the peptide floated around until it found the right match. This turned out to be partially correct; however, scientists now confirm that it happens by something called "vibratory attraction" because these receptors apparently wiggle and shimmy and are in a constant state of flux—which creates a specific vibration (there's that word again). When a ligand vibrates at that same frequency, they begin to resonate together, sort of like a dance. You have heard of cellular resonance before, such as when you pluck one string on two different guitars in the same room—one will resonate with the other playing the same note.

Here's the neat part — the attracting vibration IS THE EMOTION, and the actual connection of the peptide to the receptor is WHAT YOU FEEL. Why is this important? We now know that our emotions influence our physical bodies and our BODIES CAN BE CHANGED BY THE EMOTIONS WE EXPERIENCE. Through a complex set of these receptors and ligands, these molecules of emotion are affecting how you think! Make sure you understand that these molecules are not causing emotions—they *are* the emotions, causing the feeling that you experience.

The other really important thing to remember is that this process is going on whether you are consciously aware of it or not. In a nutshell then, for our discussion, I want you to know this: The mind and body are connected—they are really all one. The ancient Chinese and Eastern Indians have been telling us this for centuries, but, of course, we had to prove it with science before we believed it. Now we know that the emotions are an extremely important part of this whole process, and they are actually creating our reality!

Why is this important? I am extremely bothered by the number of anti-depressants that are dispensed in this country. People are feeling down because of depressing situations in their lives—but, they don't have the disease called "depression"; however, they are being treated as if they do. These drugs connect with the receptors and cause the feeling of pleasure, or at least less depression. However, they are taking up receptor space with an addictive drug when we can manufacture our own just by finding passion or joy in our lives. Some people would rather pop a pill than take a deep look at their lives. Introspection is the only way to find out what is causing the depression and how to counteract it—because remember, these emotions are affecting your mind and your physiology. Our job is to find out how we can find joy and happiness without drugs. Of course, I am not referring to people who really do have a chemical imbalance called "depression".

Emotional Equity

Emotions are stored in the body and can cause a lot of pain and disease. I had a perfect example of this in my own life. I was attending an all-day seminar a few years ago where we were learning how to connect with these "stored emotions" and heal ourselves. I had been having terrible headaches for many years and I had tried almost everything I could think of to cure them. We went into a meditation and we were instructed to take our attention to a part of the body where we felt pain or discomfort. I immediately went to my head—but, when I did, my attention switched to my elbow. I didn't want to work on my elbow, I wanted to work on my head. So I turned my attention back to my head—and again my attention went directly to my elbow. This happened a few more times until I finally gave up and concentrated on my elbow (which was not hurting). As we continued the exercise I immediately was taken back to an experience from many years before. I could see myself driving along with my arm around my little 18-month old daughter, Amy. (This was back before they had infant or booster seats for children). Amy was standing next to me and I had my right arm wrapped around her tightly, when up in front of me I saw my Husband's car—and a blonde sitting right next to him. I followed him, and when he spotted me in the rear-view mirror, he pulled over into a store's parking lot, she got out and ran into the store and I, of course, confronted my Husband. Needless to say, this was a very emotional experience, which ultimately led to our divorce. The interesting thing about me seeing and re-living this experience was that when I concentrated on that right elbow, felt the emotion that was stored there and asked it to release, one of the types of headache I had lived with for years left, never to return. (I had been diagnosed with six different kinds of headaches—this experience was responsible for only one type).

> *The mind and body are connected – they are really all one.*

Learning the Language of Creation

I highly recommend using this method for releasing pain or chronic discomfort. It is called "Focusing" and is usually done with another person helping you. There is a book out that describes this method, but, I created a little different process that you can do by yourself. It is a combination of processes that I have learned from various people and I don't take credit for the origination of the idea. This is how I do it:

First, get into a meditative, relaxed state where you have quieted your thoughts and won't be disturbed. When you are ready, focus your attention on the part of the body that is hurting. Really concentrate on the pain and try to describe it—how big is it, what shape is it, is it hard or soft, does it have a color. Get as many descriptive words as you can that you feel perfectly describes this pain. Does it have a pulse, a texture? You get the idea. After you have fully described it, ask your Self these questions and wait for the answers:

1. Could I release this feeling?
2. Would I release this feeling?
3. When?

It is very interesting to observe your answers. Of course you "could" release this feeling, but would you—that's not always so easy, and now you're being asked to say **when** you intend to release it? Sometimes, you find you are holding on to these feelings and are not about to give them up. Why would you not want to release an emotion that is causing you pain? Well, there are lots of reasons, but, most of the time it has something to do with the fact that IT IS GETTING YOU SOMETHING THAT YOU WANT! Now, I know that sounds sadistic, and most of it is at the subconscious level—but, nevertheless, we do hold on to things that we think either creates our "identity", or gets special attention, or something equally ridiculous. I'm certainly not saying all pain falls into this category—but, if you have chronic pain it is certainly worth looking at. Massage and Myofacial Release Therapy can do miracles in helping you release some of these stored emotions that you are not even aware of. I have had great success using both of these therapies on the rest of my headaches. Now I'm working on my back!

Louise Hay has done a masterful job of connecting emotions to certain physical ailments. Her book "Heal Your Body" has some marvelous ideas as to which emotions could be causing your discomfort. I heartily recommend this book. She also offers affirmations for you to use to help dispel the negative emotion and change it to a positive emotion. You now know that this works, because your body responds to the molecules of emotion and produces the feeling the emotion is calling for. So, if you are feeling depressed, the message is going to go out to all your systems that says "The boss wants to feel depressed, so shut down NOW" and you wonder why you feel so lousy.

Here are a few of my favorite excerpts from Hay's book:

1. Arthritis—Feeling unloved—criticism, resentment:
    "I am love. I now choose to love and approve of myself. I see others with love."

2. Asthma—Smothered love—inability to breathe for one's self, feeling stifled:
    "It is safe for me to take charge of my own life. I choose to be free."

3. Lower back problems—Fear of money—lack of financial support:
    "I trust the process of life. All I need is always taken care of. I am safe."

4. Constipation—Refusing to release old ideas—stuck in the past, sometimes stinginess:
    "As I release the past, the new and fresh and vital enter. I allow life to flow through me."

Learning the Language of Creation

5. Heartburn—Fear. Fear. Fear—clutching fear:
"I breathe freely and fully. I am safe. I trust the process of life".

Well, I think you see what I mean. Get the book if you want more of this.

Emotions, if used properly, can get you anything you want. We are going to go into how to do this more extensively in upcoming chapters. For right now, this is what I suggest you do.

 a. Go back to your affirmations and add emotional words;
 b. Every time you feel a negative emotion coming on, ask "is this coming from love or fear?"
 c. Check your feelings and see if you can change them to a happier one;
 d. Check out your pain and see if the focusing exercise helps to release the emotion and the pain;
 e. Contact a good therapist to help you if you have chronic pain.

I hope that you are now in the habit of doing your meditation and/or relaxation exercise every day for at least 10-15 minutes. If you are getting good at visualizing what you really, really want, this week be sure to "feel" the emotion that you will have when this desire materializes. A good thing to remember is, once you are into the deep relaxation you can say your affirmation over and over to yourself as a sort of mantra—and adding a positive emotion to the meditation will get you the results much faster.

---

*Nothing in this chapter is meant to replace medicine or traditional pain therapy; however, doing the suggested exercise and contacting professional therapists can certainly complement other methods you might be using.

CHAPTER FOURTEEN

Stand for Something

"Gratitude is not only the greatest of all virtues, but the parent of all others."
~Cicero~

In the last chapter we learned about the molecules of emotion and the fascinating research done by Dr. Candace Pert. Another scientist, Bruce Lipton, has also worked extensively with these ligands and receptors and he found that there are three kinds of stimuli that our cells respond to—positive, negative, and innocuous. The truly fascinating part of this study was the discovery that when our cellular receptors recognize a positive, growth-promoting stimulus, they actually move <u>towards</u> the stimulus and open up. However, when it senses a negative stimulus, it <u>moves away</u> and closes itself down, to protect itself. This shows the magnificent intelligence of our physiology.

Why would this be of concern to us? Well, imagine that you are on a cruise ship somewhere in the Caribbean, relaxing in the sun and having a good time. Do you suppose that your receptors are open and full of life? Contrast that with going to a job you absolutely hate, or worrying about the bills—would the emotions that you are feeling cause your receptors to retract and close down? I'd say yes to both of these examples. The result is that if we continue over long periods of time with the negative stimuli, our cells contract, wither and die and this affects our immune system and our body becomes more susceptible to disease. This is one way that we know that mental and emotional stress affects our bodies.

We know now that emotions can enter the body and attach to a cell anywhere, but, the place that we experience the emotion as "feelings" is in the heart area. A lot of research has been done with the heart and some of its secrets are just now being discovered. Joseph Chilton Pearce, the renowned authority on child development and education has done a lot of this research on heart intelligence. To make it simple, he says basically that our heart is a very complex, communicating device that relays messages of feeling to our brains and to cells all over our bodies, and it does this with hormones. Depending on the emotion, which is what sends the signal, it relays either natural states of joy, enthusiasm and wonder, or depression, grief and sadness. The significance of this study is THAT WE CAN CONTROL HOW OUR BODY RESPONDS BY THE EMOTIONALLY STIMULATING MESSAGE THAT WE SEND. When we learn to master both our thoughts and our feelings we can bring happiness and contentment into our lives every day!

One of the most important things to remember about this whole process is that the body will always respond to the most dominant emotion—so you can't fake it; and, it will, of course, respond to the one that is repeated day after day.

We also know, from the HeartMath research (founded by Doctor Childre), that when you voluntarily shift to a positive emotion, your heart rhythm pattern changes and your body is instantly relieved from stress. One of the techniques that they teach at HeartMath is that when you feel a negative emotion (such as fear), immediately place your attention on your heart area and think, for a short time, about love or appreciation or caring. This is a healing method that should be taught to everyone you love, because we now know that the body <u>instantly</u> changes its response mechanism the minute you change your mind and your feeling.

This reminds me of an experience I had recently. I had just been told that my son, unbeknown to me, was using cocaine—and his wife was leaving him and taking my two granddaughters with her. I think you can probably understand the flood of emotions that instantly rushed through my body. I felt pure terror, worry, sadness, responsibility, "out-of-controlness", and every other negative emotion that you can imagine. Physically, I felt like I couldn't breathe. I felt paralyzed and couldn't even speak or cry. I remember lying down on my bed that night in an exhausted state of shock and looking up at the twirling fan above my head. I thought, "I am grateful for that fan, because it is helping me breathe. And, I am grateful for this bed, because I don't think I could stand up any longer. And, I am grateful for my sweet Husband lying next to me because I feel so alone. And, I'm glad that nobody is dead, and…and…and. Before long, my body calmed down and I started to breathe normally for the first time that day. That experience taught me what I now know is the way to change any negative emotion—with gratitude.

I have since taught this method to all of my students and it works—not only with horrible experiences like this one, but even when I am ticked off because I got in the slowest line at the grocery store. I immediately start with my Gratitude Generator. I look around and say, "well, I am grateful to have such a nice store for my shopping convenience, and I am grateful that I have money in my purse to pay for this food, and I am grateful for the farmers and the truckers who brought this lovely food to the store"—and, and, and— you get the idea. This is one of the most important tools I have come across—so simple, but the desired effect is immediate. I usually end up laughing when I get through with my litany of appreciation. Try it, it works!

> ✸ *The body will always respond to the dominant emotion.*

So, the bottom line of all this is that since we are learning how to increase our energy and create the life of our dreams, we need to know that our minds can produce millions of thoughts; but, it is the <u>quality of our feelings</u> that produces our reality. Denying our feelings doesn't work. Just like we need to bring our thoughts up to our conscious mind so we can work with them or negate them, so do we need to bring our feelings up and face them squarely so we can decide whether to keep them or change them. Remember, our body responds to our emotions whether we are aware of the emotions or not - so burying our feelings doesn't fool the body. I think the answer to this riddle is to learn to live by, and with, the emotions that we choose—on purpose.

That brings us to the subject of values. I am continually surprised to find that most people have never taken the time to sit down and think about who they really are and what they stand for. Oh, somewhere in the back of their minds they think they are honest and decent…but, they've never even heard of "core values". Well, you're hearing about them now. It's sort of like having a mission statement for a business—only more important in my estimation— but, a personal mission statement created for you, by you, A UNIQUE, LIMITED EDITION OF ONE. So let's get started. Here is a list of values. Go over them and put a check beside all those that are important to you—at least ten of them:

Beauty	Honesty
Innocence	Simplicity
Strength	Faith
Meaningful work	Intelligence
Responsibility	Relationships
Compassion	Prosperity
Hope	Service to others
Discernment	Love
Cleanliness	Self-discipline
Forgiveness	Gratitude
Being trustworthy	Integrity
Competence	Creativity
Spontaneity	Learning
Independence	Inner peace
Self-expression	Companionship
Balance	Adventure

Emotional Equity

Excellence   Order
Humor   Freedom
Living within my means   Comfort

Other values that you might think of:

_____
_____
_____

Now, look over the values that you have checked. Close your eyes for a moment and ask your Inner Guidance for your top 3-5 values that your Soul wants you to express in your life at this time.

1. _____
2. _____
3. _____
4. _____
5. _____

Remember, this doesn't mean that the rest on the list aren't important, or that you can't live by them; it just means that we are whittling the list down to "core values" for your mission statement.

Now we are going to create your personal mission statement. This statement becomes a ruler for you to measure all that you do in the future against. It makes deciding what projects or people to get involved with much easier because you just have to ask, "If I do this will it be in harmony with my core values?" If not, don't do it.

Begin your statement with the words "I am" and then describe the person you are and the things you do using at least three and maybe all five of your core values. Here's an example:

Stand For Something

I am a <u>loving</u>, curious person who lives life in <u>peaceful prosperity</u>. I am passionate about <u>learning</u> and growing <u>spiritually</u> and I come from a constant state of <u>gratitude</u> for all that I have and all that I am.

As you can see, I used six of my core values in this statement. When I took the next step that I am going to tell you about, it just didn't sound right until I went back and added the word "gratitude" to the statement. You might find that you will add or subtract values after you write yours, too.

Now that you have your statement written, read it out loud. After saying it out loud several times to yourself see if you get a feeling of expansion or contraction when you say it. What I mean is, do you feel your heart expanding and a feeling of pride or a feeling of "YES!" when you say it? Or do you feel like it doesn't really say what you mean, or that it doesn't sound like you? If it doesn't feel quite right, go back and close your eyes and ask for inner guidance on the core values that you missed or ones that you included that don't quite fit. Take time to do this exercise properly, because when it is done to your satisfaction, you will have something that will prove to be a valuable guide for the rest of your life.

When you have your statement in its final form, make several copies of this statement and put it in places where you will see it several times a day. I like to carry mine on the first page of my Day Planner and next to my bed where I can read it first thing in the morning and last thing at night. If you work at a desk, that is also a good place to put it. For this next week, I suggest that you repeat your core value statement many, many times each day, saying it out loud if possible, and with deep conviction and emotion. It should invoke a powerful feeling of "YES!" within you each time that you say it. Remember, this statement is a ruler—something to measure each of your days by. At night I not only like to review my day and see if I was productive or not, but, I like to ask "did I live this day with honesty and love? Did I learn anything new? Did I grow spiritually in any way? Have I remembered to show gratitude?

Emotional Equity

And, am I at peace? If I find that I did not live up to these values, I make a commitment to myself to make any corrections necessary to make sure that it doesn't happen the next day. I'm not going to tell you that I do this perfectly every day—but, I am trying and if I didn't have a statement to guide me, I wouldn't know how close I've come to doing it perfectly or how far away I am. This is a measuring stick to be used to help you be the person you intend to be.

The beauty of this system is that nobody is telling you which values should be important to you, and I don't recommend that you pick values that you feel you "should" pick. Choose values that mean a lot to you—and only you. The more personal you make this exercise, the better it will work for you. A good time to recite your value statement is when you are experiencing negative emotions of some type such as fear, anger, hate, resentment, jealousy, guilt or worry. Remember, we can change our body's response instantly when we change the emotion!

If I could have one wish for you it would be that you could live a passionate life. Now it might surprise some of you that I didn't say world peace, or unconditional love or whatever else. The reason I say "passion" is that I firmly believe that if we were all doing what we feel passionate about, it would be a more peaceful and loving world. Let me explain.

Living a passionate life means that it is exciting, exhilarating, fulfilling, purposeful, and the person living it is having fun and feels unstoppable and forever motivated. Doesn't that sound like a life worth living? We all want to feel that our lives are purposeful and I sincerely believe that our Creator really intended it to be that way. Remember,

> ✸ *The more you dwell on what you love, the healthier your mind and body will become.*

"Man is that he might have joy". Where did we go so far astray? The real problem, as I see it, is that we either have no idea what we are passionate about or are too afraid to find out!

Before we go any farther with this passionate discussion, let me say this. Being passionate and angry at the same time doesn't work. I know a lot of people that are passionate about "anti-war", but, they are among the angriest people I've seen. This sort of passion will not serve you or the world. You can be *for* stopping global warming, *for* animal rights, etc., but, make sure that the passion you are feeling is bringing you joy and peacefulness, not anger or hatred. Always know what you are for—not what you are against. Passion can be used for good or bad.

A good rule is to focus on what you love. The experts tell us that as you concentrate more on what you truly love and desire, the "volume gets turned down on those parts of the limbic system (in the brain) where the destructive emotions of fear, anger, depression, and anxiety are controlled. This allows you to think more clearly." This also makes it possible for other parts of the brain to turn up the volume so they can generate positive emotions. When this happens, the brain releases dopamine, endorphins, and a variety of stress-reducing hormones and neurotransmitters. Therefore, the more you dwell on what you love the healthier your mind and body will become, and the less you will experience the effects of stress. That is a pretty amazing statement: you get a double-whammy. You can both decrease negative emotions and increase positive emotions just by focusing on what you love and what is most important to you—such as your core values.

Your passions are not the same as your destiny or your purpose in life. We will talk more about purpose when we get to the Spiritual Equity. But, for now, let's focus on passion. I like this statement by Joseph Campbell:

Emotional Equity

When you follow your bliss…
doors will open where you would not have thought
there would be doors; and where
there wouldn't be a door for anyone else.

We learned back in the Mental Equity that you first have to have intention; then, you give yourself the permission to focus on it. When you are passionate about something, it's not very hard to put your attention on it.

In a following chapter we will explore the idea of living an "ideal life"— the life of our dreams. We will be taking all that we have learned so far, what we desire, what we believe, what we value and what we are passionate about and put them together into an actual "life design". Until then, be sure to verbalize your core value statement many times each day and check at night to see if you are living according to those values.

In your meditation exercise each day, I suggest saying your core value statement over to yourself until you can feel that "expansion" in your heart which means you are in a positive state and your heart is open. This is an excellent state to be in before you visualize or state your desired mantra.

I love you and value you because I know who you <u>really</u> are!

CHAPTER FIFTEEN

Living the Dream

*"Today a new sun rises for me;
everything lives, everything is animated,
everything seems to speak to me
of my passion,
everything invites me to cherish it."*
~Anne de Lenclos~

In Chapter 13 I made the statement that there are really only two emotions—love and fear. That statement is only partially correct. There really is only ONE emotion that is **real**—and that is LOVE. However, remember that we live in a world of dualities, opposites, so that we can see the difference between black and white. Imagine for a moment a screen where everything is plain, pure white—no other color is visible. Now, if I put one little dot of black on that screen you immediately understand what "white" really is, because you have its opposite to compare it against. That is why we have fear in this world, not because it is real, but, because we need the contrast in order to understand love.

We looked at the strength of emotions in a previous chapter; but, remember that the strength of that emotion was only based on the amount of it present in this world, which is why love came in at number 9. Now we're going to look at emotions from a different point of view—frequency of vibration. The purpose of this course is to learn to raise our energy, and the only way we can do that *consciously* is to learn which emotions are on the low end of the frequency scale and which ones are on the higher end. Just remember that even though we will be talking about different emotions, the bottom line derivative of all of them is either love or fear—so when in doubt, always ask "is this coming from love or fear?", and you will know for sure.

The best description of this principle that I have been able to find is in the book series by Esther and Jerry Hicks, one of which is called "Ask and it is Given". They offer a list of emotions they call the "Emotional Guidance Scale" which is in order of frequency, making it easy for us to see where we are at any given time. However, there are a few basic tenets that we should cover first.

You are most likely familiar with the sensational movie and book called "The Secret", and with all of the books that have been written around the idea of the law of attraction. I personally believe that they have done a lot of good, bringing to the attention of the public the idea that what you think is creating your reality. However, I also believe that the Secret, and most of the other treatises concerning this principle, have missed a couple of extremely important points that would make it useable for the average person. Most people are disappointed when they can't make that red convertible appear in their driveway—and some writers have condemned the making of this movie because it gives people false hopes and makes them think this law should be used to make us all greedy and materialistic. I think both points of view are not wrong in and of themselves, merely incomplete. Let me explain.

We have been discussing emotions and the fact that they appear in our formula right before behavior; this is one of the important missing factors of "The Secret". Writing down what you desire is a first step, but, as you have seen from earlier chapters it is only the first step. Controlling our thoughts and being able to stay focused on what we want is critical—because we can recite over and over that we want to be healthy; but, as soon as we go up the stairs and our knee hurts again, aren't we thinking about "not health"? We continually go back and forth all day long on what we want and it's opposite—what we don't want. So, staying focused with *attention* is vital. But, how do we do it? And since we have over 10,000 thoughts a day, how can we possibly monitor our thoughts all day long to make sure they stay positive? Luckily there is a way, and it is through our feelings, which are much easier to keep an eye on than our thoughts.

Here's the important rule to remember: If you feel good—you are going in the direction of your desires; if you feel bad—you are going away from your desires and towards what you don't want!

The goal then is to check in with yourself many times a day and see how you "feel". If you are in a rotten mood, it shouldn't be too hard to figure out that you are not in vibrational "match" to what you say you want. What do you do if that happens? Choose to a better thought immediately. To start to make sense of this powerful principle, I'm going to give you the essence of the Emotional Guidance Scale as given by the Hicks' so you can get a feel for where your emotions are at any given time. Their scale goes from Joy/Love/Appreciation being the highest frequency all the way down to #22 which is described as Fear/Grief and Depression. In between you'll find the rest of the negative emotions we have referred to like guilt, greed, anger, boredom, etc. I highly recommend that you get their book and refer to the entire scale; but, for now, know that according to the Hicks', there are only 7 out of 22 emotions that we would consider positive! However, since we are talking about frequency here, even going up one step from fear to guilt would raise your frequency a bit higher.

The way to use this concept is to remember that the goal is only for you to **feel good**. So, let's see how this works. Let's say that you are in one of those ruts we all find ourselves in from time to time, and nothing is working for you. Nothing feels good, nothing sounds good, and you are basically feeling discouraged about your life. Now, nobody is going to tell you, especially not me, that you should be able to pull yourself up by your bootstraps and immediately feel "joyful" about your life. That is probably going to be too big of a jump to make all at once—and it isn't really necessary. What is important is that you stop and notice that this is NOT what you want, and take the time to get clear about what you do want; and then raise

Emotional Equity

your emotional vibration a little bit at a time.

What if you went from depression up to jealousy? That would be a higher frequency than depression and despair. But, the way to tell how well that works for you is to monitor how much relief you got from at least getting out of despair. If you feel better being jealous of what your neighbor has, good! But, we don't want to stay there too long, because it is still a low enough vibration to be taking you towards what you DON'T WANT. Next stop might be anger. I have been known to counsel my clients to raise their vibration from depression to anger. I tell them to get right good and mad at their situation, rant and rave, shake their fists, write nasty letters (which they destroy, not mail) and then, SEE IF THEY DO, IN FACT, FEEL BETTER THAN THEY DID BEFORE! Most of the time they do; and then they laugh, which really moves them up the scale in a hurry. They aren't always able to keep themselves up that high for good, but, they can then start to creep up the scale and admit that they are frustrated or disappointed. So, do you see how this works? Just see if you can go up the scale, higher than where you are now—to a point where you FEEL BETTER. Relief is a good thing, and if you feel relief of any kind, you have raised your vibration.

> ✷ *The goal is to feel good, and we do that through changing our thoughts.*

The way that you rise up the scale is by entertaining a new, higher thought. Let's take another example. Let's say that you are feeling depressed about money. You are looking at your stack of bills and thinking "I never have enough money for all of my bills". This is likely to be a thought attached to the emotion of fear, insecurity or worry. All of these are low vibrations. If we consciously know that this is making us feel bad, we can then change our thought to "well, never is a strong word; sometimes I have enough money, but, not this month." That is a truer statement and could raise your feeling up as high as frustration or disappointment. Check to see if that thought gave you any relief. You could then think, "but, if I stop buying soda pop for this month, that will give me a few extra dollars for gas and that will free up some money for the power bill". That could take you up as high as hopefulness and optimism, which is now in the right direction of what you really, really want—peace of mind and prosperity. Always remember the goal is to feel good, and you can do that through changing your thoughts until you feel better and at least feel some relief.

The Law of Attraction—you get what you think about most, not always what you want—is still true, but keeping your mind and thoughts on what you want instead of what you don't want is a challenge. Knowing that your feelings will always tell you what you are thinking is one of the most powerful things I can ever teach you. What people don't understand is that the law of attraction is always working—24/7. It is always bringing you what you are thinking about, and spending 15 minutes a day in mediation thinking about what you want is a good start, but, what about the rest of the hours and minutes in the day? Monitoring your feelings is the key to manifesting your dreams and desires.

We are going to spend an entire section of this course on Spiritual Energy; however, you need to know now that spiritual energy, which is the highest vibration of all, always flows towards joy. That means that if you are experiencing fear, despair, depression or any of the other lower emotions, YOU ARE SWIMMING AGAINST THE TIDE. You are making life harder than it was ever intended to be. Remember, the scriptures say: "Men are that they might have joy". It is not only possible, it is intentional! Just think about this for a moment. If you are feeling "joyful", do you feel loving towards life or hateful? Easy question, huh? So joy should be our goal. Let me tell you about a funny little thing I happened upon while I was contemplating writing this chapter.

As I have aged, I have had difficulty losing or even maintaining my weight. Most of the time I eat really good food and have this year tried many different "diets". I have even tried diets that were pure hell—eating only to the point beyond starvation, and eating "yucky" things that I really disliked. I started thinking about joy and how, while I was on these diets, I felt anything but joy when I was eating—and the pounds didn't come off anyway! Then I was not only disappointed, but depressed over the fact that I couldn't get weight off and feel good at the same time.

Then it hit me—why don't I eat only foods that I truly love. Now, I *like* a lot of different foods, but, I *love* only a few foods. I sat down and made a list of foods that I love, and committed to myself that I was only going to eat food that I love. An amazing thing is happening—not only am I happier eating these wonderful meals, but, I am joyful shopping for them, as well as preparing them. And guess what? I am eating far less food than I would normally eat, because I am satisfied with what I am eating and I feel able to turn down other food easily, since I don't love it. All I am doing is monitoring my feelings about food and choosing those that bring me joy in eating—or I don't eat. I have lost a few pounds doing this, but, that has no longer become my goal—being happy about eating again instead of feeling guilty or hateful about food has become a favorite pastime of mine. What a concept!

There are three basic steps in the manifesting formula:

1. Ask. This is work for you to do.
2. The answer is given—always. This is not your part to do.
3. Receiving the answer that is given. This again, is your part.

Asking isn't hard to do, but, getting specific and staying focused on what we want is, of course, the hard part—that is why we are learning to monitor our emotions. You don't have to worry about "how" the answer is going to come about; in fact, you will usually slow it up if you try to figure out how it is going to happen. Very often when we try to think of the "how", we start putting limits on it and it slows down the "answering" part of the equation. The receiving part, Step 3, is the part we need to understand, and it is more accurately called "allowing", which we will cover in great detail in the Spiritual Equity Section of this Course. But, for now, just know that the Universe is always looking for a perfect match to your desire. Everything—all potential—is already in the Quantum Soup and your vibrational offer goes out to find its mate. If you are not getting what you desire, it is usually due to one of two things. *One,* you are not staying focused on what you want, and going back and forth from "I want to be healthy" to "I don't want to be sick", which is the opposite of what you want. That confuses the Universe and you will either get nothing, or the one that has the most dominant thoughts. Or, *two*, you are not allowing the answer to come in. How do we allow it—by raising our emotions up the scale—because remember, the Universe only acknowledges love and/or joy. Getting to the joy and love point is always the goal. Do whatever it takes to get you there.

From time to time I'll get a client who says they feel "guilty" if they do what makes them happy. They honestly believe that if they are happy that will make someone else unhappy. That's like thinking that there is a limit on the supply of happiness, and if I take too much joy out of the Universe there won't be enough for you. Sounds silly, doesn't it—but, this is how some of us think. Now, summon up all the good sense you can muster and tell me if that is really true. I actually know from experience if I am happy, everyone around me is happier. Where do you think that saying "If Mama ain't happy, ain't nobody happy" came from? Just remember that you can't give something that you don't have. I can't give a nickel if I don't have a nickel. You can't give happiness and joy to your family if you don't have happiness and joy in yourself. You think you are "making" your family happy by sacrificing your own happiness—let me break it to you gently—THAT DOESN'T WORK!

Emotional Equity

When I first married my Husband, Norm, we set about building our new home and furnishing it, as I have already told you about. A few years after we had been living in the new house, we found ourselves in a furniture store where we were looking for some little thing that I don't even remember. We came to a display of a beautiful bedroom set and I made the comment "If we were ever to do our bedroom over, this would be the set I would want." My normally, sweet, positive husband went absolutely crazy, right there in the store, right in front of the sales clerk. He ranted and raved and said, "You are never happy. You always want more, more, more things to make you happy. I am sick and tired of your wanting. You are never satisfied!" Well, after that tirade, I calmly turned to him and said with much conviction, and accentuating words as I went along, "Listen to me and listen very carefully. I AM A HAPPY PERSON. I don't need you to make me happy, I don't need this furniture to make me happy, I don't need anything to make me happy. I just am happy. So don't you ever forget it. I was happy before you came into the picture, and I will be happy if or when you ever go out of the picture, because I AM A HAPPY PERSON—period!"

I apologized to the sales clerk, and calmly walked out of the store. The interesting part of this story is that, not only is it the absolute truth, but, Norm really got the message that day. He knows that I am a happy person and he now treats me that way. The best part of the story is that he went back later and bought me that bedroom set, which I didn't need—but, I surely loved it, and still do!

The principle here is that love and joy are a state of BEING. Love, which is the only emotion that is real, and joy which is the feeling you get, are your authentic self; and when you are feeling joyful you are a perfect match to your desires. The Bible says it is God's "good pleasure" to give you the Kingdom. That's because God (or the Universe, if you prefer) only knows love and joy, because everything else is made up by us and doesn't really exist. I know that's heavy, and we will get into it more in a later chapter; but, I want you to know that you, too, <u>are love</u>; and if you are feeling happy and joyful, you are fulfilling your purpose here in this life. What could be better than that?

One of the fastest ways to get your feelings to rise is through appreciation. Use the Gratitude Generator if you are having trouble raising your emotions up the scale; go to appreciation and you will feel relief, because when you are appreciating yourself or someone else, you are creating a vibrational match to who you really are—love and joy. The converse is true too. When you are finding fault or criticizing another or yourself, you are going away from who you are, and creating a vibrational match to what you don't want. The emotion you are feeling is your indicator as to whether you are getting close to what you want or farther away.

We should mention here that fear is not always bad. Fear is also our best indicator of danger, and we should pay attention to it as part of an alarm system of our physiology to alert us to situations and people that could be harmful. Fear is helpful in dire circumstances, like when you're being chased by a tiger, or being stalked by someone who wants to rob or kill you; but if you feel fear for any other reason, you are feeling it for either the future or the past. So, the trouble is that fear often comes up in non-life threatening situations. What you fear "might happen" rarely does; but, your body goes through the exact same response as if the tiger were really there. Dr. David Hawkins teaches the game of "what if" that is helpful to me when I start worrying about the future and what "could" happen. Here is how it goes:

When you think the thought, "I can't pay my mortgage this month" you then say "then what". Then you think, "then I'll get behind and I'll get all kinds of late penalties". Then what?" "Then I will be further behind and I might lose my house." Then what? "Then I will have no place to live". Then what? "Then I will be on the street and be poor". Then what? "Then I will have nothing to eat and I will get sick". Then what? "Then I'll die". So what!

Emotional Equity

This is how most of the game goes when you start saying "then what" to your silly fears. Most of the time this game leads to laughter, or at least a smile, which instantly raises your vibration. Dr. Hawkins also teaches that if you are worried or fearful, you are not worried or fearful enough—so he has you really get into it, just like I do with the anger. When you focus and concentrate on the fear or worry, you will see how silly it is and instantly it will disappear.

So, in summary, remember that well-being is the natural flow of the Universe and when you "feel bad" you are going against that natural flow. Monitoring your feelings and changing your thoughts to create a better feeling is the goal. Don't be discouraged if you can only go up the scale a bit at a time, but, continually see if you can find relief by experiencing a different emotion, and always look for things that you can be joyful about. Here's your assignment for this chapter. Wherever you are, gather joyful data. Look at certain things, like homes, cars, flowers, etc., that you really love and put it in your emotional bank account. Also, observe other people having experiences or being in situations that you desire and purposely stash that in your "things to want" file. You're not being envious—there's no exclusivity on what you or anyone else can have. Notice how you feel when you see things that you would like to have or experience. If you feel good—you are creating a match—if it makes you feel bad—you're not. Simple? Yes. Take time to observe what people, places and things truly bring you joy—and pursue that.

> ✺ *One of the fastest ways to raise your emotions is through appreciation.*

CHAPTER SIXTEEN

The Art of the Dream

*"Dream as if you'll live forever,
live as if you'll die today."*
~James Dean~

*"I like the dreams of the future
better than the history
of the past."*
~Thomas Jefferson~

We've been talking about ways to "feel better", which raises us up the Emotional Frequency Scale and takes us closer to what we desire. One way that I have discovered which almost always works for me when I am in an emotional "funk" is to look for beauty.

Beauty, especially in nature is a quick fix for balancing your energy. It is an instant neutralizer. If you will just take a moment to find something beautiful to look at, you will immediately become centered. Let's say that something has happened that is making you angry and you can feel the anger rising up your neck. Just stop and look at a flower, a plant, a baby's face a cloud or an animal—anything that is naturally beautiful and your Spirit will take over and you will become calm. The best part is that once you have calmed down, you can respond to the situation in a high-energy way instead of reacting from the same low energy as the person or situation that caused the anger in the first place.

We live in a beautiful country, and most of us can merely look out of our windows to see something lovely. One of my favorites is watching a sunset. No matter what is going on, or what I am feeling at the moment, looking at a sunset will instantly raise my energy to gratitude and I find myself appreciating the beauty all around me that is free for the taking. Flowers work for me—I always feel better instantly just looking at or working with flowers. Getting your hands in the dirt or walking barefoot on the lawn will work, too. Just reach out to nature and you will find yourself rising up the scale fast—towards your desires.

Since love is the only emotion that is actually "real" it would seem logical that love would be the one that we would aspire to at all times. However, we have already discussed that this is sometimes very difficult to do. There are, however, some precursors to love that will help at those times when you just can't muster up authentic love. One of those precursors is kindness—which is a virtue, but, it works to help you feel better.

I loved the movie "Pay it Forward" because it is a perfect example of using kindness to create a positive "state of being". If you have not seen it, I highly recommend that you rent it and show it to your entire family. The theme of the film is that a young boy, as an assignment from school, decided to do a kind deed and ask the recipient of the deed to pay it forward by doing another kind deed for someone else. This, of course, caused a ripple effect, and pretty soon everyone in the town was on board doing kind deeds—and it changed the emotional climate of the town towards love. Kindness definitely pays—for both you and the receiver of the deed.

> ☀ *The serotonin levels go up in both the giver and the receiver of kind words.*

You can become a hero in your family, in your community, in your world, just by consciously looking for ways to be kind. Dr. Wayne Dyer tells us in his book, "The Power of Intention", that the serotonin level (the feel good hormone) goes up not only in the person who received the kind deed, but, also in the giver. However, the most amazing fact of all is that the serotonin level went up in those who merely **observed** the kind deed, as well. That means that, if you allow someone to get into line in front of you in traffic, you will feel better, that driver will feel better and all the drivers that saw you do that will feel better. What a way to advance the world closer to love! You see, you don't have to be a world leader to make huge contributions to world peace—just be kind. If you are ever in doubt of what to say or do—choose kindness and you will always be correct.

Just remember that being kind to yourself counts, too. This is where a lot of us mess up. We are so hard on ourselves. You can desire to be slender and fit, but, what do you say to yourself every time you pass the mirror? Be kind! The cells in your body respond to kind words just the same as the people in your life. If you keep telling your body that you are ugly and fat, the cells which are highly intelligent are dutiful servants, and they will keep you ugly and fat. Treat your body the same way you would treat a member of your family—with great love and care. One way I have found to do that is to just take a moment for an oil rub before I shower. This is how you do it according to Dr. Deepak Chopra, who taught it to me. Use cold-processed sesame oil (this is the only oil that doesn't go rancid) and put it in a small bottle in your bathroom. Just before you jump in the shower, rub the oil all over your body and also in your hair if you are going to shampoo your hair too. This only takes a couple of minutes. Then take a dry body brush and rub vigorously all over your body (I use a long handled brush so I can get my back, too) until you can feel the circulation really rolling. Then shower as usual. Not only is this a fantastic "spa treatment" for your skin, it is also a subtle way of saying to your body "you matter". Some people tell me they don't have time for such a routine—get real—it takes a total of three minutes and will do wonders for your skin and your mood—it sends a great message to your body that you are worth the time. Think how lovingly you run lotion all over

Emotional Equity

your infant's body. Do that for yourself—you will be glad that you did.

Now we get to one of my favorite subjects — passions. Passions are the loves of your life—things that are extremely important to you—things that light up your life. Since we are talking about raising our energy and making our dreams come true, we absolutely need to know about passion.

Dr. Andrew Newberg and Mark Waldman, neuroscientists at the University of Pennsylvania's Center for Spirituality and the Mind, have studied the relationship between what we believe and what we create in our world and have written a book called "Born to Believe". When asked about the idea of whether human beings could bring more feelings of joy and fulfillment into their lives if they aligned themselves with things they love, this is what they had to say:

"The brain is very happy when you're focused on what you love. The more you focus on what you truly love and desire, the volume gets turned down in those parts of the limbic system where the destructive emotions of fear, anger, depression, and anxiety are controlled. This allows you to think more clearly.

"You also turn up the volume in other parts of the limbic system of the brain that generate positive emotions. When this happens, you get a release of dopamine, endorphins, and a variety of stress-reducing hormones and neurotransmitters. The more you focus on what you truly love, the healthier you are likely to be, and the more you will feel the positive effects of those stress-reducing neurochemicals in your body and mind.

"You actually get kind of a double whammy. You can have a decrease in negative emotions and an increase in positive emotions when you align yourself with what you believe is most important to you."

(Excerpt taken from the book "The Passion Test")

The Art of the Dream

Let's get clear on what passions are—they are <u>not</u> your purpose in life which we will talk about more in the Spiritual Equity Section of this book, but are <u>clues</u> to your destiny. Your life's purpose, when you get very clear about it, doesn't change throughout your life and has no bearing on your age, circumstances or experience. Your passions, however, can change and morph as you grow and most people go through their entire life without even daring to explore or understand themselves deeply enough to know what their passions are. You are not going to be one of those unfortunate people because we are going to get acquainted with your passions NOW!

Most people set way too low standards for themselves. I've always liked the saying "aim for the moon, and if you miss, you will at least hit the stars". When I was a little girl, my Mother, who had very low aspirations for herself, tried to keep me what she called "realistic" in my goal setting. She was really trying to help me by trying to get me to understand that I "couldn't do it all". She thought I took on too much, tried to be excellent at everything and never said NO to anything. One day she said in frustration, "For heaven's sake, Connie, when are you going to realize that you are <u>just</u> a girl?" Well, for some girls that might have been a downer—but, luckily for me, I thought "just watch me". My problem was that I had a passion for a lot of things when I was young and she didn't understand that that is actually the way to sort it all out before coming to any conclusion about what my passions were to be in the future.

> *"When you follow your bliss...*
> *doors will open where you would not have thought*
> *there would be doors; and where*
> *there wouldn't be a door for anyone else."*
> *~Joseph Campbell~*

The book "The Passion Test", by Janet and Chris Atwood, tells about a survey of one hundred of the most influential, financially successful individuals in the United States. The survey found that all of these super successful people had one thing in common. The survey found that these people had **totally fulfilled the five things that they felt were most necessary for their ideal life.** That is an amazing finding and can be a great clue to us getting what we want out of our lives. This statistic led to the authors writing their book, which I recommend highly if you want to take the complete test. I am going to give you just the highlights of that test here.

Most people go to jobs that they actually hate, and records show that there are more heart attacks at 9:00 a.m. on Mondays than on any other one single day, or time. That is a travesty since one of the first glaring requisites to success in any area is having a passion for doing it. Enjoying what you are doing arises from both a love of the activity and purposefulness in the doing of that activity. More people stay with a job because they feel appreciated than they do for the money.

However, you can probably think of someone, maybe even you, that always chooses the "safe" route — the job with the security or the insurance or whatever, even though they hate the job, and it pays a low salary. Contrast this with a person who goes for broke, takes on the challenge, willing to do whatever it takes to live their dreams. I am so admiring of people who start a small business because they give up all the security and usually get paid last, if at all and work twice as many hours as they would at a regular job. That doesn't mean that everyone should be an entrepreneur, but, I do believe that everyone has a "song" in them and there is a stage somewhere for that song to be sung.

To make this passion test work for you, it is necessary to think big and to definitely not censor your own personal list. So, to get started, get out a Journal or a notebook of some kind with a pen or a sharp pencil. The first part of the test is to make a list, a long list of your passions. Now remember, passions are not goals. Goals are about outcomes—passions are about the process to get you there. Passions are those great feelings that drive us to reach our goals. Your list should contain all the things you love most, are the most important to you and are absolutely critical to your well-being and happiness. After we name your passions, your goals and your purpose in life will become much clearer. When making your list, begin each passion with a verb that expresses how you are living your life when your life is ideal. For example:

1. Living in a beautiful home and feeling perfectly at peace.
2. Having fun.
3. Working with a supportive team of people.
4. Enjoying perfect health.

You get the idea. Now write your list—have fun and let your imagination run wild. Remember, there is no limit to your passions and there is nothing that is considered impossible. Go for it!

If you are having trouble, here are a few springboards to get you going:

1. What kind of people do you love to be around?
2. What are you good at?
3. What do you do better than someone else?
4. Do you have unique skills or talents?
5. What kinds of situations get you really excited?
6. What are you doing when you feel most fulfilled?
7. How would you like to spend your days?

It is best to do this exercise in one sitting and to not do it with anyone else. Don't take advice, and don't help anyone else either. This is about you, not your Spouse or child—there are no "shoulds", or have-to's on this list. Now, when you have at least ten (I prefer more if you can) you can go on to the second part of the test according to the Passion Test book.

Emotional Equity

You are now going to do the comparison step of this test. What you do is look carefully at the first passion on your list and compare it to the second on the list. Ask yourself "If I had to choose between having the first or the second passion, which one would I choose?" Now, don't panic, just because you choose one or the other doesn't mean you are losing one of your passions, we're just comparing for now. This gets you in touch with what is deeply important to you and makes you think. After choosing one or the other you go to number three and compare it against the one you chose out of one or two.

Let's say for example that when comparing one and two you chose number two, then you would compare number two with number three and you still chose number two. You then go down the line to all of your passions and compare it against the one you choose. You don't go back to the beginning, just go down the line and keep choosing one until you get to the end of your list.

Once you have completed this exercise, go back to the top of your list and start again. Beginning with the first one on the list that you did not choose, repeat the exercise as before. Keep comparing the ones you did not choose, starting the list again until you have your top five passions. While doing this entire exercise keep in mind that you need to be brutally honest in what you choose. We are not talking here about what society expects from you or what would please your parents or spouse. These are your passions and are extremely important to your happiness, regardless of how someone else feels about them. Don't be surprised if your choices change as you go through the test—and you might feel a little frustrated in having to choose. That's O.K. because according to Dr. Newberg this is the first step in changing one of those old "ruts" in your brain into a new pathway towards what you want. It is a very valuable step in the process—creating new neural circuits.

Here's some good advice:

The Art of the Dream

"Whenever you are faced with a choice, a decision, or an opportunity, choose in favor of your passions".
~Janet Atwood~

After you have written your list, the Atwoods suggest that you put them away for at least 24 hours and don't look at them or edit them in any way. The next day, take them out and see how you "feel" about them. If you question your choices in any way, go back and take the comparison test again. It's perfectly all right for you to change your mind. I did when I took the test the first time. I suggest that you take this test three or four times a year because it becomes a good measuring stick to see if you are actually pursuing any of your passions, and gives you a chance to add new ones that come up as you grow personally.

Now the only thing you need to do after you have your five favorite passions is to post them on index cards or small pieces of paper, make multiple copies of them and put them everywhere so you will see them all day long. Post one on your bathroom mirror, in your car, by your bed, on the fridge, etc. This is a critical step in getting to your ideal life, which we will write in a future chapter. But, for now, I want you to see your passion statements many times a day and notice how you "feel" when you read them. When I read mine, my heart races a little faster and I find myself grinning which is a good sign that I really have hit on my true passions. Monitor your feelings and see if you can create the feelings of love and joy—that is the goal; to find your passions in order to create the highest emotion possible so we can manifest our desires.

CHAPTER SEVENTEEN

Language of the Heart

"Beliefs, and the feelings that we have about them, are the language that "speaks" to the quantum stuff that makes our reality."
~Gregg Braden~

Now I want to try to tie together all the parts that we have been learning in both the Mental Equity Section and the Emotional Equity Section. Keep in mind that the goal is to raise our frequency. Why would we even want to raise our frequency? Because, we can both solve problems and create what we desire in our lives with higher vibrational energies, that's why!

We have been discussing emotions and I want to make certain that we all understand this very powerful energy; so I am going to summarize what we already know and give you a few new things to think about.

First of all remember that emotions are powerful turbo-chargers that take you to what you want or don't want fast. The key here is speed. Fortunately, if we attach a positive emotion to a desire we really, really want, it will show up faster. The problem is, as we learned, that there are really only two emotions, love and fear; and fear is usually the strongest emotion and takes us to what we don't want much faster, as well.

Let's discuss the difference between an emotion and a feeling again. We know there are really only two emotions, but, we can have many, many feelings that fall from those emotions. Fear, for example, begets feelings of anger, hate, resentment, guilt, remorse, jealousy, etc. Love begets feelings of compassion, joy, happiness, peace, contentment, etc. Science can now explain how that actually happens in our bodies.

Thoughts, by themselves, have very little power and could be considered to be made of "scalar energy", which is a potential force, and could lead to a possible situation. This is kind of a safety net so that not every one of our passing thoughts becomes reality. However, emotions are an actual force (vector energy) and when combined with a thought becomes directed and very, very powerful. That's why wishes and hopes are weak. But, when we marry a thought with an emotion (either love or fear) we create feelings—and then watch out!

This is where beliefs come in—and we discussed them at great lengths in the Mental Equity Section; however, now you need to know that beliefs are a form of feeling and very often a strong one. If you doubt this statement, just check your beliefs about politics or religion and see how much feeling is attached to your beliefs. That's why when you have a strong belief about something and you hear somebody say or do something that "resonates" with that belief, you believe that it is true. It doesn't have anything to do with whether it is actual fact or not, but, for you at that moment it is true. Some of us even have body signals that tell us when we are hearing truth or not such as goose bumps or a sensation in the chest.

Resonance also works in the reverse. We can get a feeling of "fear" that resonates with a person or experience or situation that warns us of danger or tells us that something is "untrue". We can often immediately feel in our bodies if someone is lying to us—this gut reaction can be a valuable tool to keep us safe. It is well, then, to pay attention to the signals our bodies are giving us.

Because beliefs are so powerful, being attached to such strong emotions, they are also very difficult to change. But, since we know that our beliefs are really running our lives, changing those that are no longer working for us becomes a necessity. A scary fact is that the thoughts and beliefs that we all have as individuals are really just miniature "fractals" of what all human beings are believing. When we look at our world, we can see what the strongest beliefs really are—fear and all the fallouts from fear, like hate and anger.

All of our thoughts are stored in our brain—either in the conscious or the subconscious mind. One is the pilot, the other the autopilot. The subconscious mind is much larger than the conscious mind and has stored every thought, feeling, success, failure and belief that we have ever had. Why should we be concerned with what is in there from the past? Because every new thought that we might have goes through the past "filter" to see if we believe it or not. Take for instance someone who believes that they were born with a weak immune system and, therefore, always gets sick. What happens then, when someone comes to visit them that is coughing and sneezing?" You're right; they get sick—because they "know" that this always happens to them. Your subconscious mind not only records all of your thoughts and beliefs and experiences, but, also how you felt about them. So, if you know that you always get sick, you probably feel like a victim—poor me!

This is really, really important because it has been estimated that about 90% of our daily lives is directed by our subconscious minds. The conscious mind processes huge amounts of information every day, but does it kind of slowly. Bruce Lipton, PhD describes the conscious mind as operating with the computer-processing power at about 40 bits of information per second; while the subconscious processes at **20 million** bits per second. That means that the subconscious mind is 500,000 times faster! That gives us the ability to react instinctively and helps us make quick decisions. If we had to always wait for the slower mind to process everything we would be hit by the truck before we jumped out of the way.

Studies have shown that up to the age of seven, a child's brain is like a sponge which absorbs everything that it hears and sees in its surroundings with no filters to tell him whether it is true or not, safe or not—and those things that he hears over and over again become beliefs—which determine the direction his life will go. William James made a very poignant statement regarding this when he said "Could the young but realize how soon they will become mere walking bundles of habits, they would give more heed to their conduct while in the plastic state." And, we as adults should watch more carefully the words that we say to our children, because we are told that 90% OR MORE OF OUR DAILY ACTIONS ARE RESPONSES THAT COME FROM THE RESERVOIR OF INFORMATION WE ACCUMULATED DURING THE FIRST SEVEN YEARS OF OUR LIVES! Which thoughts and beliefs that were given to you in your formative years are running your life?

> *"Do not believe in anything simply because you have heard it. Do not believe in anything simply because it is spoken and rumored by many, or merely on the authority of your teachers or elders. But, after observation and analysis, when you find that anything agrees with reason, then accept it and live up to it."*
> ~Buddha~

Since our beliefs are so closely connected with our feelings, it is important that we understand what part our heart plays in all of this. Our hearts are the most magnificent organ in our bodies. This miraculous piece of "equipment" has to carry lifeblood to all of our cells, and it turns out to be the most self-healing and longest-lasting part of the human body. Why then do so many of us die of "heart failure". What does failure of the heart really mean? Even though medical science tells us that lifestyle has everything to do with heart problems, leading edge researchers are now showing us that "hurt feelings" and "unresolved negative feelings that underlie that hurt" (or in other words our beliefs about those hurts) have the power to create conditions that we call cardiovascular disease, clogged arteries, high blood pressure, etc. This theory of mind-body relationship was documented recently by a Duke

University Study done by James Blumenthal. He identified that when we have long-term experiences of fear, frustration, anxiety and disappointments, these negative emotions are destructive to the heart and put us at risk.

Other studies done in England show that the failure to heal and forgive old hurts and disappointments "cuts you off from good health" and has proved that perpetual anger and tension can and do lead to high blood pressure, lowered immunity, headaches, stomach problems and heart attacks. Positive emotions rarely cause us problems. Most of us don't complain about having too much joy or peace in our lives. It's the negative emotions of anger, resentment and hate, the perceived hurts that do the damage and are reflected in our body's physiology. We will discuss forgiveness at great length in the Spiritual Equity Section of this book.

> ✸ *The best way to counteract the negative is to put the emphasis on the positive.*

The best way to counteract the negative is to put the emphasis on the positive. Appreciating the people in your life that you love, and spending time doing things that really bring loving and joyful feelings becomes a must and can be our greatest of healing arts. Now would be a good time to bring up how you "feel" about love. Is it hard for you to love yourself? Self-hatred is a killer. Do you feel it unsafe to share your love with others fully? When I was dating my Husband, Norm, it was extremely difficult for him to even mouth the words "I love you", much less say them. We had been going together for over two years, and he still had not said that to me. Finally, I asked him right out about his feelings and he tried to beat around the bush by saying that he had "strong feelings" for me and that he "adored" me and other such lines. I then stated that I didn't think I could continue the relationship with someone who was incapable of truly loving another person and telling them so. He left and went on a trip at that time, and called me from the airport and said, "I don't think I've ever loved anyone more than I do you—so there, I said it!" That was not only a turning point in our relationship, but, it was actually a turning point in Norm's emotional life. He was from a generation that certainly didn't hug and kiss men, and he had never told his only Son that he loved him. After our experience, he began to speak his love to his children, including his Son, his Brothers and Sister, and my children, too. It has been a very powerful and rewarding experience for all of us to see him able to express his love verbally—and I know it has increased his love for himself.

Emotions then, which lead to feelings which lead to the results we are getting, are extremely important and we need to be very aware of them. As a review, always ask "is this coming from love or fear?", and monitor your feelings on the scale of emotional guidance. Try to raise your feelings so that you are coming at life from a higher frequency. Remember, you do that by choosing a different thought that at least brings you relief.

Now that you have your desires written as affirmations, and emotional words attached to these affirmations, and have identified your values and your passions, it is time to put them all together into a "life design". Take out all of your notes that include all the aforementioned information and we'll get started.

First, take out your journal or notebook that you can keep for all of these exercises that we are doing. Looking at all of the information that you have documented, let's title this page MY IDEAL DAY. I want you to start writing what an ideal day would be for you. What are you doing? Who are you with? Describe your surroundings and be sure to write in your feelings about this day. What time do you get up; do you go somewhere or stay home? Do you work or play—or both? What is the weather like? Are you somewhere besides where you live now? Just go through an entire day looking at all the details, writing it all down, and including some of your passions. Write this day as if it had already happened—your ideal day. Have fun with this exercise—let it all out.

When you have finished this part of the exercise you can put your notebook away if you like and do the second part another day; however, if you are on a roll, go right to the next part. Turn to a new page in your notebook and entitle this page MY IDEAL LIFE. Now we are going to broaden our horizons and write down how our life looks as if everything we have ever desired has already come to pass. Describe your house, furnishings, car, and toys, people who live this life with you, your finances, career, your passions, your contributions to society, and most of all your feelings about all of this. Make sure that there are plenty of emotional words scattered about your essay that describe how happy, proud, peaceful, joyful, abundant, independent you are feeling because of all these wonderful things that are going on in your life. Take your time and have a good old time describing your ideal life. When you are finished with everything you can possibly think of, put it away for 24 hours, then come back to it and see if you (a) have thought of something else or (b) you still feel the same way about this delightful imagining. When you just love the look and sound of this treatise, write it or type it in final form and make a couple of copies of it. I suggest you carry one with you at all times and put the other one by your bed. Then read it to yourself when you get a minute, while waiting for an appointment, and definitely read it before you go to bed at night. Read it with lots of feeling and passion. If you got it right, you should feel a tingle somewhere in your body whenever you recite this — it never gets old. Feel the excitement building whenever you think about having all of this deliciousness in your life. Remember the child at Christmastime. Expect nothing less than all of your desires.

If all of the reasons come up as to why you can't have what you want, just remember that it is part of the process—chaos becoming order. Thank your brain for reminding you and state that, THIS IS WHAT I WANT. There are parts of my ideal day that I have memorized, and when I start to feel a negative feeling creeping over me, I recite that part and feel the fun all over again. Some people think this is "Pollyanna thinking"; if you believe that, this won't work for you, but, I highly recommend that you go with the science that now confirms that what you think and what you believe coupled with how you feel is definitely creating your reality. For me, the proof is in the pudding—it certainly can't hurt anything to "feel good" and dream.

I am reminded of a story that Wayne Dyer tells about his Daughter when she was about seven years old. This little girl had a serious skin problem that she called "her bumps". They had taken her to several doctors who had all told her the same thing—that she would have to just grow out of them, probably when she was about twelve. Her Dad then told her about the power of the subconscious mind and how if she refused to believe what the doctors had told her she could create a new belief—that her bumps would go away now and stay away. He sort of forgot that they had had this discussion, and a few days went by and he noticed that she didn't have any bumps on her face. He commented on this and she told him, "Oh, no, I just go into my room each night and talk to the bumps and tell them that I really don't need them anymore and I want them to leave because I know that I have beautiful, smooth skin under the bumps, and I am so much happier without them." Those bumps never came back. So, if you are hesitant to try some of these exercises because your "adult mind" knows better, I suggest you become "as a little child". The Universe is a marvelous place and we are just beginning to understand some of its ways. It's with our thoughts, beliefs and feelings that we become the bridge between reality and all that we could ever imagine.

Mark your days in ways that bring your heart joy! Put your seat belts on because next we move up to the Spiritual Equity —this is where the real power is—if you know how to use it.

Emotional Equity

IMPLEMENTING THE EMOTIONAL EQUITY

1. **Thought→Belief→Attitude→Perspective→Emotion→Behavior→Result**. You always move in the direction of the strongest emotion. There are really only two emotions, love and fear, the others being derivatives of the two. Which is your dominant emotion? The mind and body are one – what you think about is experienced by the body and vice versa. To release negative emotions, follow the exercise instructions on page 174.

2. The body always responds to the dominant emotion. Denying your feelings doesn't work; but you can change your dominant emotion from negative to positive by using the Gratitude Generator in any unpleasant circumstance. Create your own mission statement by following the directions on pages 165 through 167. Focus on what you love.

3. If you feel good, you're going in the direction of your desires. If you're feeling bad, you're going away from your desires. Your feelings always tell you what you are thinking. Remember to always think of what you **do** desire, not of what you don't want. Having what you desire does not deprive anyone else of having their desire – the Universe is unlimited. When you are being critical of yourself or others, you are creating a vibrational match with what you **don't** want.

4. Be kind to yourself. Try Dr. Deepak Chopra's suggestion of massaging sesame oil into your skin and hair before showering. Identify your passions, following instructions on pages 186 through 189.

5. Describe your Ideal Day in detail (pg 195-196). Then describe your Ideal Life (197), again in detail. If negative thoughts and feelings come up during this process, thank your brain, but firmly state, THIS IS WHAT I WANT.

RECOMMENDED READING FOR EMOTIONAL EQUITY

1. *Living the Heartlife*—Steven and Cynthia Wand

2. *Spontaneous Healing of Belief*—Gregg Braden

3. *Strengths Finder*—Tom Rath

4. *Steering by Starlight*—Martha Beck

5. *Fear and Worry*—Dr. Joseph Murphy

6. *Everything You Need to Know To Feel Go(o)d*—Candace Pert, Ph.D

7. *Ask and it is Given*—Esther and Jerry Hicks

8. *The Passion Test*—Janet and Chris Atwood

9. *Heal Your Body*—Louise Hay

10. *The Gift of Love*—Joel Goldsmith

11. *A Return to Love*—Marianne Williamson

12. *Love is Letting Go of Fear*—Jerry Jampolsky

13. *Focusing*—Eugene T. Gendlin

SECTION FOUR

SPIRITUAL EQUITY

CHAPTER EIGHTEEN

The Unseen Power

*"The universe is sacred.
You cannot improve it.
If you try to change it, you will ruin it.
If you try to hold it, you will lose it."*
~Lao-tzu~

Soft as a powder puff and as strong as steel—that's how Dr. David Hawkins describes Spiritual Energy which we are going to discuss, and try to understand, in this Section.

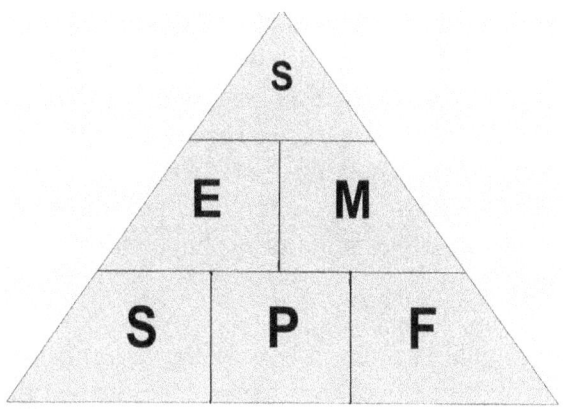

If we take a look at the pyramid, you will see that Spiritual Energy is at the top. This is the highest frequency there is— and like all of the other equities, there are levels of vibration within that level. Our job in this section is to learn how to access this energy and use it in our daily lives. If we are truly able to do that—miracles will happen!

Spiritual Equity

To begin to intelligently discuss this vast subject we must all have three major assumptions, otherwise none of the following will make any sense at all. The three assumptions are:

1. There is a Universal Power—call it God, Creative Intelligence, Supra-Consciousness, etc.
2. In order to release this power called spiritual energy, we must all agree that we already have it within.
3. Everyone has a direct connection to this power—you do not have to be or do something special to be given the right to this power.

We have already learned in previous chapters about what I call The Quantum Soup—which we shall now refer to as Consciousness. This "field" is where all possibilities are located. If that isn't mind-blowing enough, this field is also where every thought, word, and action that has ever been made is also kept. We discussed the ramifications of this when I told you the story about the "blue couch". This consciousness field is very alive and dynamic as well as intelligent and is accessible to all of us whether we use it consciously or unconsciously. We are all creating out of this Quantum Soup all of the time 24/7. Knowing that this "soup" contains all wisdom and is all-knowing, there really is no limit to what you or I can create from it—except, as we have already found out, we have to believe it.

The ultimate goal is to learn how to harness this power and use it for our own personal desires; but, before we do that, I want to use this chapter as a bridge between what we have already learned and what we have ahead of us. So, a discussion of power vs. force seems appropriate.

Power and force are not the same thing at all. There are a lot of forces in this world; in fact science says there are four major forces. We will not concern ourselves with the forces of nature at this time but, I would like you to know the major

The Unseen Power

differences between the two so you can always tell which you are dealing with.

The major difference is that force always moves against something and therefore creates a counterforce. Force causes movement—from here to there. Power is still. Power is whole—force is incomplete and therefore has to be fed energy at all times. A good example of force is war which continues to gobble up energy such as manpower, money, ammunition, etc. Power in contrast, energizes supplies and supports. Force takes away energy—power gives energy and life. Power seeks to unify, force polarizes which implies conflict. Force always produces a win/lose situation where power has no counterforce. Force creates opposition and enemies—power is friend to all equally. Power is associated with meaning and has no needs—force appeals to the lower nature of beings and is constantly in need of something. Force is concrete, literal and arguable—requiring proof—power is self-evident, therefore non-arguable. The only accurate statement that can be made about power is that it just "is". True power comes from consciousness, and what you see in this world is the visible manifestation of this invisible power.

> ✵ *Power and force are not the same thing.*

If this were a scientific treatise, we would go into discussions of M-fields, Chaos Theory, Nonlinear Dynamics and Attractor Fields, all of which are extremely interesting studies that, if you are interested, you could pursue. I will include an extensive bibliography at the end of this Section to assist you in that investigation, if you so desire. However, I will try to explain some of this in simple terms so you can get a hold of this super power. One of those concepts is this: most of us think that the future is being created out of a sequence of experiences from our past. Attractor field science tells us just the opposite—we are being pulled along from our future because of who we are "being". For now, just hold that thought, and I promise we will come back to it in great detail. The important point is that powerful attractor patterns make us strong and weak patterns make us weak. Powerful patterns are associated with health; weak patterns with sickness, disease and maybe death. Those individuals throughout history who have aligned themselves with strong attractor fields have been those with great power, and those truly powerful people all attribute the source of that power to something greater than themselves.

History has shown that there are "imitator patterns" which are really weak patterns trying to appear as strong patterns. Hitler and the Third Reich is a good example of this. This regime disguised its motives as "patriotism" which is a strong attractor, when its' real motive was "force" as a Demagogue. Powerful attractors never create opposites such as enemies. We need to be aware of the difference at all times.

Science has up until now always told us that to solve a problem we need to start with the known and work to the unknown, or A=B=C. That system would be called Linear Dynamics; however, Nonlinear Dynamics is just the opposite, start out with the unknown to find the unknown. That amazing study lead to the discovery of a science called Kinesiology—which means the "study of muscles and their movements, especially as applied to physical conditioning." Dr. George Goodheart was the noted pioneer of the specialty that he called "applied kinesiology" after he found that beneficial nutritional supplements, a benign physical stimulus, would increase the strength of certain indicator muscles where harmful stimuli would cause those same muscles to suddenly go weak. This opened up the possibility that, far below conceptual consciousness, the body "knew" what was good and bad for it.

Later, in the late seventies, Dr. John Diamond refined this new specialty into a discipline he called Behavioral Kinesiology. The amazing finding of Dr. Diamond was that muscles would strengthen or weaken in the presence of positive or negative emotional and intellectual stimuli, as well as physical stimuli—such as a smile strengthening the muscle, and the statement "I hate you" weakening the muscle. Can you imagine how life-changing these discoveries were? The most amazing part of Dr. Diamond's work was how predictable and repeatable his experiments were. There was no rational link between who was being tested, their backgrounds or belief systems or even their ages. Hundreds of thousands of people were tested and the results were universal.

You can all try this out for yourselves and I suggest that you do after reading these instructions taken from Dr. Diamond's outline, in his 1979 book, *Your Body Doesn't Lie*.

It takes two people to perform a kinesiological test. Choose a friend or a family member for testing. We'll call him or her your subject.

1. Have the subject stand erect, right arm relaxed at his side, left arm held out parallel to the floor, elbow straight. (You may use the other arm if you wish).
2. Face your subject and place your left hand on his right shoulder to steady him. Then place your right hand on the subject's extended left arm just above the wrist.
3. Tell the subject you are going to try to push his arm down as he resists with all his strength.
4. Now push down on his arm fairly quickly, firmly and evenly. The idea is to push just hard enough to test the spring and bounce in the arm, not so hard that the muscle becomes fatigued. It is not a question of who is stronger, but, of whether the muscle can "lock" the shoulder joint against the push.

Assuming there is no physical problem with the muscle and the subject is in a normal, relaxed state of mind, receiving no extraneous stimuli (for this reason it is important that the tester not smile or interact with the subject), the muscle will test "strong"—the arm will remain locked. You can then repeat the test in the presence of negative stimuli (such as artificial sweetener) and push again. Although you are using the very same pressure, the arm will fall down easily. Another good way of testing is to have the testee say "my name is____," filling in the blank with his real name and then test to see if it is strong. Follow this statement with "my name is____," giving a false name, and test again—the arm will weaken. For some reason, unknown to me and most of the so-called experts, a few people are unable to do kinesiology testing. We have also found that it is very difficult for some husbands and wives to test each other. The key here is that the one doing the test cannot have a preconceived answer already in mind, and that is probably why it is difficult to do because there is so much emotional "stuff" around marriage partners and parents. If you are invested in the answer—don't do the test. Just try it out with stimuli that don't matter either way. Another good test is to do regular ascorbic acid vs. natural vitamin C. Put each of them in an unmarked envelope and have the testee hold the envelope near his solar plexus and test. Another good test to do is with your teenagers—test their music. Try putting a rap c.d. next to their solar plexus and test—then try classical music or even The Beatles and see the difference. Just remember, strong attractor patterns attract those things that we normally think of as desirable; health, abundance, joy and peace. Weak attractor patterns attract those we know as undesirable—pain, disease, poverty, conflict and death. The object of the game is to surround ourselves with those things that make us strong and eliminate those that make us weak.

Another fascinating thing happened in 1975 during a demonstration by Dr. Diamond. He had subjects listen to tapes of known deceptions, such as Lyndon Johnson perpetrating the Tonkin Gulf hoax and Edward Kennedy stonewalling the Chappaquiddick incident—both recordings caused a weak muscle response. This opened up a whole new research study by Dr. David Hawkins on the kinesiological response to truth and falsehood. He did extensive experiments over many years in double-blind testing and mass demonstrations involving huge audiences and found that the subjects tested universally weak when exposed to falsehoods and strong when in the presence of truth. Dr. Hawkins explains this in his landmark book *Power vs. Force* and refers to the power at work here as the "database of consciousness".

Two of the fascinating discoveries Dr. Hawkins made while doing his research with truth and falsehood testing, was that questions had to be phrased so that the answer would be a clear "yes" or "no". This led to the finding that there really is no such thing as "false" in the universe, just the absence of truth. We liken this to there really being no such thing as "darkness", just the absence of light. After hundreds of thousands of clinical tests both in his huge psychotherapy practice and other venues, Dr. Hawkins asked "Is the human brain, at some primal level, a wondrous computer linked with a universal energy field that knows far more than it knows it knows?"

After 20 years of testing and research, Dr. David Hawkins came up with his Map of Consciousness, which is in essence the geography of man's experience. This map is actually a profile of the entire human condition allowing a comprehensive analysis of the emotional and spiritual development of individuals, societies, and the race in general. This is a guide that can be used to see where we are on the ladder of spiritual enlightenment and gives us, for the first time, an actual scientific way of seeing man's relationship to the universe. The way he came up with this map was by doing thousands of calibrations using kinesiology as his testing methodology. A calibration is done by using the "arm" in a pulsing manner to see the degree of truth that is contained in the person, the book, the music, the movie, etc. This method of calibrating led to such huge numbers, that Dr. Hawkins was forced to go to a logarithmic scale—which means that the numbers used in this guide would be unbelievably large if using regular arithmetic numbers.

Therefore, when perusing this scale, which you can find in any of Hawkins' books, or on the internet at www.VERITASPUB.com, you will see that Dr. Hawkins has quantified human action and emotion by frequencies. On that scale even a difference of five would be a huge difference in reality. This scale is most useful when calibrating the levels of human consciousness, and takes the form of a scale from 1 to 1,000; these numbers indicate the degree of power of all possible levels of human awareness. This stratification of levels shows the remarkable distinction between power and force and their respective qualities. He then correlated the levels with emotional states which we have discussed previously; however, in contrast to the Emotional Guidance Scale that was referred to earlier, the emotions calibrated by Hawkins give you a better idea of the actual "power" in the emotion and the level to which it is attached. This map is another way of helping us to see how we can move from the slower vibrations of shame, guilt and fear into the higher frequencies of willingness, acceptance, reason, love, joy and peace. I know you are going to want to read his book, which I highly recommend. This, along with several of his other books, is listed in the bibliography.

Remember, there is no falsehood, just the degree of truth. There is really only one truth—the Absolute; however, the degree of truth that can be understood by a level of consciousness is what is actually being measured. All the numbers listed in the Map of Consciousness are measured against the totality of truth which is called The Absolute. The only other thing for you to remember at this point about this Map of Consciousness is that one level is not "better" than another. You would not say that your Fifth Grader was "better" than your First Grader, would you? More educated, more mature, wiser, but definitely not better.

This anatomy of consciousness correlates well with the Emotional Guidance Scale insomuch as when you are at the level of grief (which is at 75) you would do well to increase it to at least anger(150) which is still a low level, but, then you can creep up to maybe pride (175) and eventually courage at 200. The Map of Consciousness denotes level 200 as the level of integrity—therefore, anything higher is considered to be as having integrity, and below this line, lacking integrity. Even though a person's consciousness (spirit or soul) might calibrate at 400, we find ourselves going through a myriad of emotions and other levels many times during the day, until we have mastered that level.

Since this lesson is about the difference between power and force, I want to give you an idea of how much power is in your spirit. When you can raise the frequency of your consciousness to the higher levels and master that level, you will see how much of a difference you can make to this world. (Keep in mind that a Jesus or a Buddha would calibrate on this scale at or over 1000 which, according to Hawkins, is as high as you could go and still survive on this planet.) It has been noted that Jesus would only have to enter a village to raise the consciousness of those in that village. As Dr. Hawkins states: "In this interconnected universe, every improvement we make in our private world improves the world at large for everyone". Here are some examples: one person at level 300 counterbalances 90,000 people below 200, one person at level 400 counterbalances 400,000 individuals below 200, and one person at 500 balances 750,000 people below 200. Knowing this, just becoming ALL THAT YOU CAN BE, is enough to save the world. Because of this amazing fact, that was discovered through calibration testing, the United States calibrates at an average of 405—even though 51% of Americans are below 200! Can you see the miraculous in that statement? You are holding up entire towns, just by being your wonderful self who is trying, every day, to become better and better. Give yourself a big old pat on the back! Make a commitment to raise your frequency every chance you get, by being as kind, generous and loving as you can be in every circumstance.

I know this has been fairly heavy, but, I wanted to create a context for you that would take you from the linear to the nonlinear energies. Up to now we have discussed mostly the linear—we are now starting to get really close to the most powerful frequencies of all—stay tuned.

CHAPTER NINETEEN

Divinity is an Inside Job

*"The solution to the problem of the day
is the awakening of the consciousness of
humanity to the divinity within."*
~Hazrat Inayat Khan~

Before we get started on this chapter, I need to explain a few caveats regarding discussing anything to do with "spiritual energy". We are now entering the non-linear energy and yet trying to explain it with linear language. I want to make it quite clear that with the following information I am not trying to convince anyone of anything, nor argue in any way. I am quite well aware that some of the things I am going to say will butt right up against some of your beliefs. That's perfectly O.K. I just have one suggestion about that: When you read something that you are not quite sure of, instead of rejecting it outright, I suggest you do what I do, and just hang it on a hook in your mind to see if at some later time you know how to interpret it, or where to put it within your philosophy of life, or discard it permanently. The information is meant only to inform and inspire and most importantly to broaden your perspective. I have found that this actually enriches and deepens most belief systems and have had many students come to me after taking one of my seminars and sharing with me how this happened. Here is a statement from one student (name withheld):

"After taking your class I wasn't really sure how some of the things you taught us fit in with my religion. However, when I did my daily scripture reading, I found that I understood some of these familiar scriptures at a much deeper level than before. I believe that as we learn and grow that we do understand things that we were not

able to grasp before. I thank you from the bottom of my heart for opening me up to such unbelievable wisdom."

I also believe that what I am about to tell you is so benign that it could not possibly hurt anyone by including it within their beliefs. Remember, we are not talking about religion here—only spirituality, and we are only discussing it for the purpose of learning how to raise our energy to the maximum for greater problem solving and a more balanced and successful life.

The truth is that spiritual energy is the fastest, most powerful energy and it is available to us at all times. Our job is to learn how to access it. The only difference between a Jesus or a Buddha and us is that they were operating from this spiritual energy all of the time and they performed what we call "miracles". Jesus told us that "these things I do, ye shall do greater". All we have to do is believe that!

We have discussed at great length how fear is the strongest emotion (but not the most powerful), and how our beliefs are running our lives. Well, now I am going to drop the bombshell: There is really only one fear, and our belief in that one fear is running our life. Here it is:

Our greatest fear is that of abandonment—and our belief that we are separate is what brings us all of our misery.

We know that fear is not real—that we made it up and it only exists here on this planet with human beings. Love is the only emotion that is real. So, our fear to begin with is an illusion. The reason we really, really fear abandonment, is that we really, really believe that we are separate—and that is a lie.

Imagine with me for a moment that you can see the big, round beautiful sun shining up in a clear, blue sky. Now, imagine that you see thousands, maybe millions of tiny, rays beaming out from this magnificent sun. Imagine that you can see a little, old shack out in the middle of a field that is all boarded up. Windows and doors are all covered with boards and you are inside this hut in the dark. However, there is a mini crack in the ceiling, and through this crack you can see one, lonely sunbeam shining down with all its glory. You are now not totally in the dark; but, just for a moment imagine <u>you are the sunbeam</u>—you think you are alone and separated from the sun just because you can't see it. That sunbeam is us!

If you get the gist of this example, you will see that the ray of light was not really disconnected from the sun at all—we are not separate from our Creator either. Let me share with you a personal story.

When my Son, Todd, was about 18 months old, he was a holy terror—into everything—and had to be watched 24/7. Back then we didn't have conveniences such as clothes dryers, so I had to wash clothes in the basement, climb up 13 stairs with the wash basket and walk clear out to the farthest point in our back yard to hang the clothes on the line. Not only was this a chore, but, it was next to impossible to do it with Todd around. So, since it was such a nice warm day, I decided to put both of the children in the sandbox which was near the basement door. But, since I didn't trust Todd to stay there, I got a rope and tied it around his coveralls and then onto the railing. I carefully measured so that he could have a little freedom, but, that he couldn't go far enough to get into trouble—or so I thought. While I was going up and down the stairs, I heard this big crash—and Todd had fallen right through the basement window! He was still attached to the rope and that rope had saved him from falling clear down to the basement floor. Now he was really hurt, and had to get 24 stitches in his head, but the rope had kept him from killing himself. This is how we are protected by our Creator.

Just imagine, if you will, that at some point in time we told God (or the Universe or any word you feel more comfortable using) that we wanted to experience being an individual sunbeam for a change—so God created this beautiful world and gave us everything to work with to have this glorious adventure. However, the Creator was much smarter than we were and knew that even if we did crazy things, we could hurt the costume we were wearing (our bodies), but, we could never really damage our Selves (our Spirits); because we are always still connected—we just BELIEVE THAT WE ARE SEPARATE AND ALONE. Since we have freedom of choice, we can make some detrimental choices that will definitely slow our progression; but since we are still <u>always</u> connected to THE CREATOR, we cannot be permanently lost.

> *Our greatest fear is fear of abandonment.*

When I was a little girl we sang a song in Sunday School called "Jesus Wants Me For a Sunbeam"—I loved that song, and it was close to being right. We are not trying to be a sunbeam—we already are!

As soon as we became "human", we were given a mind (which is not the same as our brain), and that mind is now split in two—even though it was not meant to be that way. Our belief that we are now "separate" became our mind's Ego—which is nothing more than this erroneous belief that we are not only separate from God, but, that we are separate from everyone else, too. And, we can prove it, just look at us, my skin ends here and yours starts there so we must be separate, don't you think? The most important thing to remember about this is that the Ego's existence depends upon you believing that you are separate so it does everything in its power to keep you in that belief system. And, guess how it keeps us locked into this lie—through blame and judgment! That's right, our Ego knows that if we can constantly judge others as being "wrong" or "evil", that gives us the false sense of security that we are "good" and that makes us better! Blame and judgment intensifies the belief and keeps it alive by making it "real".

Just think how insane this whole thing is—our greatest fear is being abandoned and our strongest belief is that we are! Another word for our ego according to Dr. David Hawkins would be the "Experiencer". The ego's main job is to get—get more of everything; more money, more pleasure, more love, etc. and we spend our entire lives trying to get these things because we believe that if we just get enough, we will be whole again. But, remember, we wanted to be individuals, and we wanted to feel "special". Our whole life becomes a journey of trying this and then that and nothing really works to make us feel whole again—because we are looking in the wrong place!

I told you that we have a split mind—one part is the Ego, the other side is the Holy Spirit which was put there by our Creator to remind us of our heritage. Now, the whole purpose of me explaining all of this is to show you who you really are.

Let's look at an example: If I take a seed—let's say a tomato seed—we know that all the possibility of a full-grown tomato plant is inside that seed. Now I plant the seed and in a short while, if I water it, we will see green sprouts appearing. When you see that little bit of green showing do you scream and yell and rip the plant up, and say "you are not a tomato—so you are no good?" No, you wouldn't do that if you were in your right mind—instead, you would keep nurturing this little plant and pretty soon you would have a seedling. Is that seedling a tomato yet? No, but, we know that under the right circumstances this seedling has all the potential of being a nice ripe, red tomato. Why?—because all the possibility and potential of "tomato-ness" is inside that seed and that seedling. When the tomato finally appears, it is small and green—not red at all. We still understand that it is a tomato and will be mature in time. It was always a tomato—from seed to fruit; it couldn't be or become anything else, could it?

When a baby is conceived involving two human beings, we could not expect any other animal to appear at the time of birth. Humans beget humans. Why?—because within the egg and the sperm of the human is all the potential of creating another human. Are you with me?

If you don't believe in a God, then none of this is going to make any sense, but, I believe that you do, so I will continue. We know that this body that we carry around is not who we truly are—so we'll call it the little self with a small "s". We also know, at some level, that we have a Spirit that we did not create nor did our parents. This Self is the big Self with a capital S. Now muster up all the sense that you have, and tell me, that if God created our Spirit, in His own image, and God is Divine, then our Spirits must also include "God-ness" and contain all the potential and possibilities of Divinity. I know that is a hard one for some of you to take, but, how could it be otherwise?—like begets like. The truth is that we do have this heritage, and our right mind—the Holy Spirit side—is trying to get us to listen. Jesus said "The Kingdom of God is within"—and that is what he meant. But, our Ego loves being an individual, loves being "special" and screams so loud in our ears that we have a hard time listening to our Spirits. Listening to this voice and creating a brand new belief is the secret to solving problems at the highest level of frequency possible. There is nothing for you to become or to get—you are already perfect. You might still be a seedling, but, you are a perfect seedling. We don't call our babies imperfect just because they are infants—they are perfect infants. All we need to do is keep growing.

How do we do this—by simply changing our minds—literally! If you knew for an absolute fact that you and I and God are one—what would happen to all of your fears? To picture this oneness, imagine looking at the inside of a human body. Inside you would see vital organs, hundreds of miles of blood vessels, bones and tissue—but, if you looked closer under a high-powered microscope you would see millions of cells. Each one of these cells operates individually but at the same time as a part of the whole. A heart cell does not think it is more special or "better" than a rectum cell. All cells work in harmony with all the rest of the cells in the body and as long as they do that, the body enjoys health. As soon as one cell thinks it is "different" it starts to act up and becomes part of a diseased state instead of health. This is how it works with us humans, too. We are little fragments of the Whole (God) and we contain all the characteristics of God, even though we are in a seedling form; however, we are only a part of the Whole, and when we work in complete harmony with this notion, life goes well—as soon as we think we are "better" than another, or more "special" than another is when we get into trouble.

Remember, the Ego's very existence depends on us feeling separate, so it nudges us to keep trying harder and harder to get to heaven only knows where. And, to continue the fantasy that we are indeed separate, it teaches us to blame others for our problems, which makes us the innocent victim.

Now for another bombshell: THERE ARE NO VICTIMS! I know, you are now going to start shouting at me and saying "Oh, yeah, what about the innocent child who is raped and murdered? Tell me she wasn't a victim!" I hear you and I am in no way telling you that this is not a terrible tragedy, and I am not in any way shape or form telling you that it was the child's fault. That's precisely the point. Lots of horrendous things happen to us humans down here on planet earth and since we planned this entire journey, we have to know that that child's Spirit existed before and we have no idea of the agreements that were made before we came here. There are no accidents in this life—but, we do have freedom of choice and the choices we make can alter our experience here—but they do not alter our true Self. Just remember that if you think you are a victim, and our culture loves to play the victim (entire careers are made by gathering up so-called "victims" for expensive lawsuits), you have given up your power. However, if you want to play victim, you have then given up your power. If you take responsibility—not blame—for all that you experience in your life, then you have a swat at changing it.

Remember, you just have to change your mind and get a new set of beliefs. Blame is one of the favorite games of the Ego to keep you in the lower frequencies and keep you from listening to the Holy Spirit. Like the Course in Miracles says: "you are not a victim of the world, because you invented it".

Blaming yourself doesn't work either—taking responsibility is just saying, "If I am powerful enough to create this mess, then I am powerful enough to change it". That's how you start raising your frequency and start getting in tune with the high spiritual frequencies. Here's what Valerie Hunt, a scientist, says in her book "Infinite Mind":

> *"In my laboratory, we found that when a person's energy field reaches the highest, most complex vibrations, from imaging or meditation, that person had spiritual experiences, regardless of their beliefs."*

We know by looking at Dr. Hawkins' Map of Consciousness that the lower frequencies include humiliation, blame, despair, hate and scorn. These are the emotions that are the result of blame and/or judgment. When we blame someone else, it is an effort on our part to feel better by making someone else the cause. Judgment is our effort at looking and feeling more "special" and making the other person wrong. The problem is that both of these responses gives us more of what we don't want and intensifies the belief that we are separate, which perpetuates the entire illusion.

> ※ *"If I am powerful enough to create this mess, I am powerful enough to change it."*

I believe that you would not even be reading this book if you didn't have a strong desire to grow, and that is what this entire course is about—how to raise frequency and solve problems. Judgment will keep you in the lower frequencies more than any other single cause. It is not easy to stop judging—but, it is the key. Let me tell you about an experience I had.

A few years ago I was studying the "Course in Miracles"— a course that calibrates at 600 and I highly recommend you read. This Course consists of 365 lessons with the purpose of you taking one lesson per day until you complete all of them. However, you are not to go on to the next one until you feel you have mastered the lesson. I was working on non-judgment and I realized that even when you say something nice to someone such as "you sure look pretty today", that is still making a judgment. The reason it is considered a judgment is that you are comparing it with…what?—How they didn't look pretty yesterday? Or that they are looking prettier than some other person?, etc. This was particularly hard for me to grasp; it was easier to stop the negative judgments than it was the positive. Just at that time we went on a trip to New York City and I was fairly driving myself mentally crazy by focusing on this non-judgment principle. As we were strolling down a NYC street, I had to step over a "wino" to stay on the sidewalk. Just as I passed him, our eyes met and he winked at me. At that very instant I got it! I understood at a very deep level that this life is like a drama on stage and all of us are pretending to be characters in this play—and we are all playing our part perfectly. This Gentleman was playing the part of a "wino" and he was doing a superb job of it. As soon as I realized the perfection in all of this—judgment went away.

In order to understand this "perfection" idea I need to explain it the way it was taught to me by my friend and author, Wally Minto. He calls it the "O.K. Theory" which can be found in his book "*Alpha Awareness Training Manual*" which unfortunately is out of print. If you can find one in a used book store—buy it. You'll love it.

Spiritual Equity

Start seeing everything as perfect or okay. For example, the bouquet of roses I have is an illustration of this very point. In the bouquet is a perfect bud, a perfect, full-grown rose and a perfect dead rose. All are being perfectly WHAT THEY ARE. Take for example if you cut off your finger—it is a perfect, cut-off finger. You see, everything is perfectly expressing what it is at that moment—and so are you and everyone else. If someone is being a "creep"—they are being a perfect "creep" at that moment. However, by observing the "okay-ness" in everything, we are not labeling it. The "creep" who is acting "creepy" is not a creep. That would then be judging. Just observe the perfection in all that is and you will automatically get yourself out of judgment and raise your frequency.

To help with this non-judgment idea, just remember that a 12th Grade Student isn't "better" than a First Grader. All of us are perfect in this moment—expressing who we are; however, you do have freedom of choice and you can choose moment by moment which part of your divine potential you wish to express. In the following chapters we are going to discover ways to make higher frequency choices which will keep us in the powerful vibration of our Creator.

As Wayne Dyer so neatly expresses in his book *"There is a Spiritual Solution to Every Problem"*:

"In essence, when you finally come to know and understand the world of spirit on an intimate basis, you will see clearly that all problems are illusions in that they are concocted by our minds because we have come to believe that we are separate from our source. Your ultimate choice, once you understand these principles, is whether to align yourself with a high energy field or a low energy field."

CHAPTER TWENTY

Human Being— or Being Human

*"Sounds of the wind or sounds of the sea
Make me happy just to be."*
~June Polis~

Chapters 18 and 19 were written for one purpose—to show you who you really are. You are divine—you are a fragment of the Source—The Creator. Some New Age devotees like to say that they are God. That is not true; however, the potential is there. It would be like saying all of us are the President of the United States—which would not be true; but, it is true to say to any child in our country, that it is possible for any one of them to become President if the desire, and all circumstances line up with the possible potential. So you see, we are not God, but, we have God-like potential within our Higher Selves—the real us. Therefore, we have been given all we need to work with to operate from these higher states, that I am calling Spiritual Frequencies. To be able to do so, will turn our lives into what other people would call "magical" states. Obviously, we would not still be here on this planet if we could do it all of the time; but don't you think it fun to start honing our talents? We are now going to discuss some ways to do just that.

One of the fastest ways to align ourselves with spiritual vibrations is to flow <u>with</u> the Universe. Unfortunately, most of us are trying to swim upstream most of the time instead of going with the flow. Here is why this is true. Let's say, for ease of discussion, that one of our desires is to become rich. Most of us think that to be rich we first have to <u>have</u> money, then we would <u>do</u> what rich people do and then we would enjoy <u>being</u> rich. It can work that way; however, it is the slow-boat-to-China way and it never really works out for most of us. If you really wanted to be rich, it would be faster to start out in the being, then the doing and then the having. The Universe answers immediately to what you are BEING. So, let's break this idea down so we can get our minds around it a little better.

Let's make a chart around the desire of being rich:

HAVING   **DOING**   **BEING**

Now, underneath these categories let's start naming what we would have if we were, indeed, rich. We would <u>have</u>:

1. Money
2. Big house
3. Nice, new car
4. Lots of friends
5. Boat
6. Stocks and Bonds
7. Investments

You get the idea. Now, let's name some of the things we would be <u>doing</u> if we were really rich:

1. Travelling
2. Shopping
3. Running our own business
4. Having fun
5. Playing
6. Giving
7. Relaxing

Finally, let's name some things that we would be <u>being</u>, if we were rich:

1. Happy
2. Generous
3. Retired
4. Peaceful
5. Free
6. Relaxed
7. Relieved

Now for the fun part of this exercise. Since flowing against the current (the Universe) is starting with the having and going towards the being, let's do it the other way and start with the being and flow towards the having. Look at our list of what we would BE if we were rich and tell me, do you know anyone who is happy that isn't rich? How about generous, retired peaceful, free, relaxed and relieved? You see, you can name quite a few people, maybe even yourself that is one or more of these values without actually being rich. The good news is that the Universe flows from whatever you are BEING AT THE MOMENT. Think of someone like Mother Theresa—do you think she was happy, peaceful and free? You'd better believe it! And she didn't have any money of her own—but, was she generous? So you see, starting out in the being—just *being* happy, peaceful and generous, will lead you into doing the giving, playing, having fun which will then end up with you having money, cars and houses. I know this is sometimes hard to believe, but, the truth is that you could put down this book right now and start BEING RICH. Isn't the whole idea of being rich so that we can be happy, peaceful and generous? Sure it is—so the trick is to get into those feelings and be it now! The widow's mite, in the Bible, wasn't much to the world's way of thinking, but, it was enough—and she was being more generous than the rich person who gave only a pittance of his wealth. So, being generous doesn't really have anything to do with amounts—just the intention of BEING GENEROUS. I love this saying that I have printed in my office for me to see each day:

"All that I have, all that I am, I give."

Human Being – or Being Human

I have no idea who said that so I can't give them credit, but, I try to live by this creed. You see it doesn't limit me to money or even material possessions, but, to all that I am—which means I give away my cheerfulness, my optimism, my knowledge, etc. Giving is the key (and we will get into this side of BEING when we get to the Financial Equity). I just want you to see right now, how to start living from the being, because that is a very high frequency, one of the highest frequencies possible.

You could start with saying you want to BE PEACEFUL—which calibrates at a very high vibration. So if your goal was to BE PEACEFUL, what things would you have and what things would you be doing if you were actually peaceful? See, you can start from either direction, and when you do, you will find that you can be whatever it is you desire right now. If you can, you will see miracles happen in your life—right in front of your very eyes. I have included a page called States of Being at the end of this chapter so you can look at other states that you wish to be and start there and work backwards towards the having. Find one or two that you are attracted to and go for it.

We already have learned that if we think happy thoughts and couple them with the emotions of joy and hopefulness that we raise our frequency—that is how we get to the BEING. Make it a habit to see the glass half full instead of half empty. Become known for being the cheerful, optimistic one in your family or group. That is a good start. <u>Being</u> hooks you right into your Higher Self and plugs you directly into The Source—God. Since we are a fragment of the Whole, and we have all the potential of The Source within us, it is imperative for us to know which attributes are of God and which ones are of humanity only. Just remember that this world is one of duality—purposely—for us to see and experience what is real and what is made up. We need to see evil to understand good, black to see white, hot to feel cold. Since heaven, or wherever God is, is a world of NON-DUALITY— there can only be good, love, peace, etc. Here's an exercise for you to do to

Spiritual Equity

understand the crux of this principle. Get out a piece of paper and write down all of the traits or attributes that you think God possesses. Some people think God is judgmental, or that he is capable of becoming angry or jealous. Write down whatever character traits you think describes your God. One lady told me in a seminar that she thinks God can be disappointed in us. I know people who think God is a biased God, since the winners of a game often give thanks to God or Jesus for them winning—which means He (or She) says "no" to some and "yes" to others.

It is important while you are doing this exercise that you get down deep to your real beliefs about God and write down what you think and believe—not what someone else has told you to believe.

Once you have your list made, you have my permission to BE any of those attributes that you have given to God, because that's who you are made in the image of, and then those traits are also yours. However, I don't believe it is possible for God to be anything but good, loving, kind, generous and peaceful. So, my list will only have those values on it. I'm not here to change your beliefs, just to point out to you what they are so you can consciously keep or change them. I will show you the main attribute that does belong to God—Love. However, it's not the kind of love that we think of when we say that word such as: romantic love, motherly love, passionate love, love of country, etc. God is not doing love, He (or She) is BEING LOVE—He just is—and you can't really say anything else after that. His kind of love, though, is even above unconditional love—it is called ALLOWING.

This allowing business will take us to an entirely new level. On the Map of Consciousness, Unconditional Love is at 540— which is high, but, not the highest. Dr. Hawkins doesn't even show Allowing—which would be off the charts. Let's discuss this highly volatile subject for a moment.

God doesn't just love—he allows us all to be whatever we are, and to NOT BE whatever we are not. This is really a high frequency and we can try our best to follow the lead. How do we do that? Start by not judging, which we talked about in the last chapter—"live and let live" becomes a nice mantra. But, the truth is that we do judge—others and ourselves—so, when we do, we have to FORGIVE. This is an absolute necessity to clear ourselves from the low frequencies of judgment, criticism and hate that we all get into from time to time.

Forgiveness is essential to our spiritual well-being. True forgiveness is complete erasing from our "minds". Some people say they can forgive, but, not forget. Forgetting is hard to do, but not impossible. One way that I like to really forgive someone, or myself, is to close my eyes (or better yet, do this in meditation) and envision the person and the terrible thing that I think they did. When I can see it all clearly, I encapsulate the entire image in a helium balloon and then see me holding the string and when I am ready, letting it go. When you do this, watch carefully as the balloon starts to ascend into the sky and don't stop watching until it is completely out of sight. Then give thanks and gratitude for this and FEEL THE GRATITUDE in your heart—then it is erased.

> ✸ *Forgiveness is essential to our Spiritual well-being.*

Another really important step to take if you feel you have been hurt, or "the victim" of someone's unkindness or thoughtlessness, is to ask your Higher Self to tell you what the lesson was. Remember, there are no accidents—we attract to us what we really need at the moment in order to keep growing. Once you have learned the lesson, there is no need for the further "hurt" or crisis. Learning to contact your Higher Self and/or the Holy Spirit is essential to really being able to raise your energy. There are several ways to do this that I know.

Spiritual Equity

Prayer, of course, is one way to tune into the Spirit—and can raise your frequency if you pray correctly. Praying is talking; correct prayer renews, relieves stress, restores harmony and produces guidance when driven by deep belief. Gratitude is the most powerful type of prayer and really the only one you ever need. When you are praying always affirm goodness—don't whine or use negatives—remember God (or the Universe) is non-dual so only hears positives. Pray for others—send high energy and protection their way. My Daughter Amy is so convinced that I have a better connection to God than she does (which, of course is not true), that whenever she is about to get on a plane or do anything that she thinks has any risk whatsoever, she calls me first and asks me to send positive and protective energy her way. The way I do that (and yes, I have taught her how) is to see a white beam of energy going out from my forehead straight to hers and then I visualize her being encapsulated in a ball of white light. Anyone can do that—if they believe they can.

One word of caution about praying—please don't beg! You know how you hate it when one of your children begs for something over and over again. And, besides, that kind of plea is full of negatives. God is not Santa Claus. Stop asking for "things". Things belong to this world—values and attributes belong to God. So, if you are going to ask for something, ask for this:

"Please, dear God, help me to see this situation differently"

OR

"Please, dear God, help me to feel peaceful about this problem"

Your Higher Self knows what you need and so does God—we don't always know what we really need—just what we want or what we think we need. In the Bible God says he "knows" before we ask! Ask to see clearly, to have a different perspective or to learn the lesson that is hidden within this so-called "problem".

I was meditating about a situation many years ago and I was given an answer right then—and it was so powerful that I got up and wrote it down immediately. I could never have written anything as beautiful as this and it is from this guidance that this entire energy system was born. Here is what I was told:

> *"Whenever you experience physical, mental, emotional, spiritual, social or financial crisis—your Soul is seeking transformation. As soon as you surrender to the transformational flow, there is no longer a need for the crisis".*

You can imagine how dumb-struck I was after reading this over a few times. Just going with the flow, and understanding what the bigger opportunity is hiding within this situation, is also the relief. I can tell you from personal experience, that when I remember to pray this way, (and I don't always remember) that I am given information that helps me to see the lesson or the opportunity masked as problems. Such was the case with my Son, Brad.

I already told you how devastated I was to learn about Brad's drug addiction, and I shared with you how I had to grasp to gratitude to even be able to get through this awful experience. However, the good and the opportunity that has come out of this situation, was probably worth all the terror that we went through. Brad's life has been spared several times (I wrote about his first one in the Prologue of this book), and I think, until now, he thought, as do a lot of young people, that he was "indestructible". But, this time, he came out of it with an entirely different perspective. First of all, he acknowledged that he would not have made it without all of the support from his family, and he is dearly sorry for those addicts that do not have that kind of support. But, the most important lesson he learned was that since his life has been spared several times, that he really must have an important purpose or some special mission that he needs to perform. That was a huge "Aha" for him—and one that we hope will keep him climbing to higher states that he has never experienced before.

I want you to know that YOU ARE MAGNIFICENT—you are so much more than you think you are. Marianne Williamson tells us that we are more afraid of who we really are and what we could become, than we are of the person we are being now. In order to understand your divinity and your magnificence, it would be very helpful for you to have a relationship with your Higher Self. I have referred to it several times previously, but, I don't know how many of you really know how to get to know, and how to contact this part of you. Being able to relate to this higher me has been a true blessing in my life. I remember the first time I was able to meet my Higher Self, I was taking a seminar from Wally Minto. He had us do a meditation and then walked us through the exercise to get in touch with this REAL SELF. I have put this very exercise on my meditation c.d. that you can order if you like, and I have included a transcript of the exercise with this chapter if you want to walk yourself through it or record it on a tape of your own to play during your meditation. Whichever way you choose, please do it—I am sure it will change your life for the better.

I will describe for you my own experience of this wonderful meditation the first time I did it with Wally. As he asked for us to see our Higher Self, I saw, in my visualization, a person that looked like me but, had her back turned to me. She was sitting at a desk and even though I cleared my throat and said "Ahem", she didn't turn around. However, she finally did say "what do you want". I then told her that I wanted to meet her, and she firmly said she didn't know whether I really was ready or not. I asked her politely what I needed to do to be ready and she laughed and turned around and said "lighten up". I was so grateful for this cheerful approach that I too began laughing. We talked for a while and I can say that I truly liked this person—she looked like me but, was everything I would like to be. She was funny, smart, and optimistic; she had a sparkle in her eyes and a glow to her that reeked of confidence. I truly loved her. We decided I would call her "High C" (after the juice) which I thought it was terribly appropriate, and I call her by that name to this day. Whenever I need her, I close my eyes, get really calm, and ask for her to join me. Most of the time she does—but, like me, she doesn't like to be "summoned"—she prefers to be invited. I have received so much guidance and help from Hi C and I am certain that you too will form a relationship with your very own Higher Self.

Remember, your Higher Self is not the same as the Holy Spirit, but, I know that High C has a direct connection to the Holy Spirit and that is my fast way to get answers. I hope this has been helpful to you and that you enjoy the meditation.

THE HIGHER SELF MEDITATION
By Connie Hayes

As you get ready to meet your Higher Self, you must first be seated in a comfortable chair with your back straight and your feet flat on the floor. Place your hands in your lap with your palms up, and slowly close your eyes. Now take a deep breath through your nose, hold it for the count of three and slowly, slowly release the breath through your mouth like it is coming out of a straw. Be sure to lower your shoulders as you exhale. It is lovely to feel so relaxed.

Again, a nice deep breath through your nose and as you exhale, think the word Relax, Relax, Relax. It is so nice just to take a few moments to completely relax. Another breath, this time as you release the breath think the words I Am, I Am, I Am. Lower your shoulders and feel that beautiful breath swirling down from the top of your head, down through your torso and legs and out of your big toes. Another deep breath, and this time as you exhale think the word Within, Within, Within. Feel the deep relaxation swirling down from your head, into your body, down the legs and out the big toes.

Spiritual Equity

Now, take a check of your body's state of relaxation. Check your scalp, tense and release your face, tighten and let go; your neck and shoulders, raise them slightly and then lower them down. Feel that relaxation flowing down from your head, down your body and legs and out your big toes. Now, check your back and buttocks—tighten, release; your thighs and calves—tense and release, and feel your body starting to let go.

As you take the next breath, go up through the top of your head where you'll find a beam of bright, pure light, and grab some of this light and bring it down through your body and legs and out your big toes. Again, a deep, deep breath; go up through your head, grab some light, swirl it down through your body and out your big toes. If you are feeling nice and relaxed, we are ready to meet our Higher Self. Remember to keep breathing.

Using visualization, I want you to imagine that you are out in nature somewhere; pick a place that you like, maybe a forest, or a beach or a meadow—somewhere beautiful and peaceful. Take a deep breath and enjoy where you are at the moment. Look around and see with your mind what season it is—what do you see? Are there trees, flowers, water, snow, animals—look carefully and take in all the sights. Keep breathing. Now try to hear the sounds of this peaceful spot. Listen carefully. Can you hear the creek or the waves of the ocean?—maybe a bird or the crickets?—try your best to hear something. Just to sharpen our senses a little more, try to smell something at this wonderful, peaceful spot. Can you smell mint by the creek, or the flowers, or the salt of the sea? Just try to smell something, but don't be upset if you can't.

Now, with your imagination visualize a path of some kind that leads from you to way off in the distance. Clearly see this path. Now, if you look closely, you can see a figure far off coming towards you on this path. Keep your mind's eye on this figure. It is coming closer and closer to you—closer and closer. As you look at this figure, can you make out whether it is male or female? Keep breathing. Can you tell how this person is dressed? Bring it closer and closer. Can you see more detail now? How about the hair, the shoes? Look for detail. Bring them closer and closer. Do you recognize this person? Is it someone you know personally or someone from history? This person is now almost close enough for you to touch. Greet this person—either shake hands or give a hug, whatever seems appropriate to you.

Ask this person, "Are you my Higher Self?"—and wait for the answer. If they say that they are your Higher Self, ask for a signal somewhere in your body where you can feel that they are with you any time you need them. Wait now and see if you get a bodily signal, something like a tingle or an electrical twinge somewhere in your body.

Thank the person for coming and tell them how grateful you are to meet them. Now, ask them if they have a message for you? Wait for the answer.

Now ask them if they have a gift for you, if they do, take it from them thanking them graciously. If you know what the gift is and understand its meaning, thank them for coming and tell them goodbye. If you don't understand the gift, ask for more information, and accept whatever they say. If you have brought a gift for them, give it to them now.

Again, thank them for coming and say goodbye in any way that seems appropriate. Take your time and keep breathing. Now, watch the figure turn away and start walking slowly back on the path from which they came. Keep watching until you can't see them any more. Keep breathing. When you can no longer see this person, take your visualization back into your own home or somewhere that you feel safe, and see yourself taking your special gift and putting it in some wonderful place to take out any time you choose. When you feel satisfied that the gift is safe, you are ready to come out of your meditation.

Spiritual Equity

Take a few normal breaths, open your eyes, look around the room, and stretch your arms and legs. You can return to this meditation anytime you wish, but, best of all you can call on your Higher Self anytime you feel you need extra help; and if you feel your body signal, you know they are with you. Don't forget your gift. Look at it often so you will eventually understand the full meaning of it and how to use it in your life.

STATES OF BEING

Accepting	Exuberant	Musical
Adaptable	Fanciful	Neutral
Adventurous	Fearless	Now
Affectionate	Feeling	Open
Amazing	Flexible	Optimistic
Assertive	Focused	Original
Athletic	Free	Outgoing
Authentic	Fresh	Peaceful
Balanced	Friendly	Perceptive
Believing	Frolicsome	Persistent
Blissful	Funny	Physical
Bouncy	Giggly	Playful
Bright	Graceful	Positive
Capable	Gregarious	Powerful
Carefree	Happy	Present
Cheerful	Harmonious	Resilient
Clever	Healthy	Responsible
Colorful	Helpful	Sensitive
Compassionate	Imaginative	Sharing
Confident	Ingenious	Silly
Connected	Innocent	Spiritual
Consistent	Inquisitive	Spontaneous
Creative	Intelligent	Strong
Disciplined	Joyful	Trusting
Eager	Kind	Warm
Empathetic	Limber	Wise
Enthusiastic	Loving	Zany

CHAPTER TWENTY ONE

The Sum and Substance of Spirit

*"Within everyone there is light and shadow,
good and evil, love and hate. In order to be truthful,
you must embrace your total being. A person who exhibits
both positive and negative qualities, strengths and
weaknesses is not flawed, but complete."*
~Deepak Chopra~

    What you are BEING in this moment is drawing to you things and experiences that match that frequency. Like I stated before, you are being pulled into the future from what and who you are at this moment—not from your past. I am repeating this thought because of its great importance. What you see in your life today is solely because of WHO YOU ARE. Being is the highest energy vibration of all! The Law of Attraction will not be fooled by your affirmations and thoughts if your BEING is not a match. The whole purpose of this Section of the book is to show you some ways to strengthen your "beingness".

    We know that the fast-track to "being" is non-judgment. We cannot even attempt to not judge if we don't notice when we are judging—so bringing it up to the conscious mind is a must. When you notice that you've made a judgment about yourself or another, don't slide into blame and guilt—just notice and immediately go to forgiveness. Socrates told us that "the only sin is ignorance" and I believe that is true. So, as we are learning and trying to give up judgment, we are going to make mistakes. What is the correction to judgment? Forgiveness! I always say when I catch myself, "forgive me

Father, I'm so sorry—next time I'll _____." The reason I say "next time I'll_____" is that it gives me a positive idea with which to replace the judgment. Louis Tice teaches that method because that gives us a "visual" as part of the correction.

It is true that we all have a dark side—and even though we like to keep those parts of us hidden, it is useful, albeit terrifying, to take a look at our shadow. Knowing that the capability for murder, theft, lying and cheating is within all of us certainly is humbling. Owning this notion is also freeing, because it is much easier to forgive someone else for acting out those possibilities when we admit that we could also make those choices. Sometimes as we hear the news of the day which includes horrendous acts of brutality by human against human—it is difficult for us to forgive, much less understand. It is at these times that I say "forgive them Father for they know not what they do". During the September 11th tragedy, I was having difficultly dealing with acts of terror and how to forgive the perpetrators for such violence. I printed up cards to put at each place setting at our Thanksgiving dinner that said: "God, please forgive them FOR me THROUGH me". This was my way of expressing that I wanted to be able to forgive, but, I needed help.

So, how do we manage our darkness? First, by identifying what is in our shadow, and then by TRANSCENDING those traits. Ignoring them, or stuffing them down farther into the recesses of our mind and pretending they are not there do not work. Transcending is like the caterpillar turning into a butterfly. The caterpillar has to be willing to give up all his "caterpillarness" in order to be "born again" as a butterfly. We too, need to transcend and acknowledge our shadow by choosing another form of BEING. You see, if you are BEING an honest person, it would be impossible for you to lie or cheat. Being is the key, which reminds me of a story.

When my first Husband left me and the children, I was in the deepest, darkest despair I had ever known. The electricity was being turned off, and I had no idea how I was going to support my family. I had been educated in business and had experience as a legal secretary, but, I knew that wouldn't pay me enough if I was to be the main provider in my home. So, one night as I was meditating about this issue, I was perusing the idea of what I could BE. Out of the blue came the idea that I could be a Trouble Shooter. Now, I had never been such a person and I didn't know anyone else who had either. So, I then thought to myself, what does a Trouble Shooter do? Solve problems—I guess. How would I go about telling the world that I was now BEING a Trouble Shooter? My first thought was to go to an executive that I knew who was Vice President of a big department store. At our appointment, I asked him to name his biggest problem that he was dealing with at that time. He didn't hesitate a moment to answer that his most serious problem was some of his employees. These "problem" employees were ones who had been there for 25 years or more, and most of them were not only old, but, cranky and irritable—and customers were complaining. He didn't know what to do with this situation since he couldn't fire them, and they had not responded to his reprimands or suggestions.

I then asked him some very pertinent questions. First I asked him how much it would be worth to him to solve this problem. He said "a lot". I then asked him to put a number to the meaning of "a lot"—to which he said "around $10,000". Now remember, this was 1973 and that was a lot of money. I could make around $750 a month as a secretary, so if I could solve this problem in six months or less, that would be a small fortune for me. So I asked the next question, How will we know when I have solved this problem? He told me that he would consider it solved if he started to get complimentary letters from customers instead of complaints. I then told him he was on—and he didn't have to pay me a dime if I didn't solve the problem. He said "great"; and I then started BEING a Trouble Shooter.

To make a long story short, I devised a contest and made up

a slogan that said, "Courtesy is Contagioius—Come Catch the Bug at Auerbachs". I put ads in the paper, ballot boxes on each counter and had a meeting with all employees announcing the grand prize for the most courteous clerk—a Caribbean Cruise! The best part of the story is that the oldest, most cantankerous clerk won the contest—and I solved it in two months, which gave me enough money to get out of my hole and my funk! I then went on BEING a Trouble Shooter for many more companies. And my one claim to fame was that every company I represented ended up offering me a permanent job—apparently trouble shooters are in high demand! That's actually how I eventually BECAME an Interior Designer. I had never had any formal training as a designer, I just had to become one out of necessity, and then I started doing those things that designers do and having all of the things that designers have—including my own design studio called Interiors by Connie Lynn. So, get started BEING who and what you really want and get on the fast track to the higher spiritual frequencies.

Now I'm going to explain one of the best kept secrets to getting what you want. We have spent a lot of ink and paper talking about controlling your thoughts, checking your beliefs and adding powerful emotions to your desires. All of that works, but, there is a faster way—through ESSENCE. Essence is another word for being, and it means CORE. So, getting to the core or essence of what you desire is the key. How do we do that?—glad you asked. Go back to one of your listed desires or affirmations and look at what you are asking for. I'm going to use "money" just because it is something tangible that we can all understand. It's not because I think that money is the most desirable goal—but, there's nothing wrong with it either. If money had anything to do with one of your desires—let's dig a little deeper into that desire and find out what the essence of that "want" is all about. For example, wanting money for what? You might name more things, like houses, cars, etc. but, I want you to dig deeper than that. What would having more money represent to you? When I think of having a lot of money, the essence of that desire would be "safety—security—freedom". You see, those are the essence of the desire. If I had to choose just one—it would be safety. Once I've identified the core of my desire, knowing that the fast way to get it is to start out in the being, it would be important for me to get the FEELING OF SAFETY first—wouldn't it? How can I feel safe without actually having enough money, you ask? By going back to what I know is true, I am always connected to my Source, I am not really alone or separate, and I have faith and trust that I always will be safe—and when I don't feel that way, I am giving into my fears. My own personal trick is to go directly to gratitude and start thanking for what I have and asking forgiveness for even entertaining the thought that I could not be "safe".

One of my favorite ways of giving gratitude is with my THANK BANK. I've alluded to it before in this book, but, here's how I do it: Each night when everything is quiet and I am about to go to bed, I go over my day and pick out one thing that I am particularly thankful for. Sometimes it is something big—like a new Great Granddaughter who was born that day—but, most of the time it is something relatively little—like having my favorite ice cream with two of my Grandchildren. By taking just a minute to actually put a name to what I am grateful for, rather than lumping it all into a big category of being thankful for my family, gives it a personal touch and immediately puts me into the FEELING of gratitude. I also have a Gratitude Angel on my nightstand to remind me to make a deposit into my THANK BANK, just in case I had forgotten to do it.

Here's another way to transcend some of the negative attributes of our characters. I call it the Law of the Boomerang—a form of blessing. It's actually a little game that you play with yourself each day and it goes like this: Every morning you bless the first five people that you see that day. Throw out a blessing to your Spouse, children or milkman or whomever you meet at the beginning of the day. Maybe it will be a pedestrian crossing the street or another driver who cut you off. Try to personalize the blessing to something that you think would be helpful for them that day. We are in no way convincing ourselves that we know what another person needs, but, if a driver was discourteous, or passed you exceeding the speed limit, you could bless him with patience for the day, or good decision making, or safety. If you see a person having difficulty crossing the street because of a physical problem, you could bless them with a pain-free day or lots of loving assistance. It doesn't really matter—just bless them with something that you would want for yourself, because remember this is a boomerang—what you throw out comes right back to you! Of course you can bless lots more people than five a day—but, at least consciously bless five a day—that will bring you back a good day's worth of blessings for yourself.

However, don't play this game for the sole purpose of "getting" something for yourself—have the intention that you are giving something to someone else that is valuable. We know that energy is tangible and we can hoard it or give it away. This is one way for you to give something you have to someone else without them even knowing it—but, they will feel it and it really will affect their day. Just remember that it works in the reverse, too. If you send out hate thoughts and less-than-complimentary epithets—they come back to you, too. The boomerang always works, but, to get into the higher spiritual vibrations we have to do it on purpose. Always affirm goodness—no negatives.

> ✺ *Meditation is a bridge to the higher states of being.*

We have talked a great deal about meditation, which is a great way to get you into a higher frequency. Remember that praying is talking, and meditating is listening. Getting into the silence, what the Buddha called "the gap", is where all of the real power is located. I am a big fan of meditating mostly because it is a form of discipline—a way to start quieting the "monkey mind" which chatters incessantly. It is also what I consider a bridge to the higher states of being. Having said that, the draw-back to meditating is that it is something that you DO and sometimes you don't DO IT. We all live very busy lives and may regularly meditate for weeks; then Aunt Martha comes to visit and we don't do it for a week. It is very difficult to get started and back into the habit again. That's why I am fonder of contemplation—which is something that you can do all of the time.

Contemplation is another way of BEING as you go about your day. To begin to incorporate contemplation into your life it is best to do it consciously at first which means that you can pick a value or a subject to contemplate all day. Let's say that you choose "peace" for the day. If that were the case, you would constantly apply that value all day to whatever you are doing, whomever you are around, and wherever you find yourself. Just looking at a field of sunflowers or a mountain would instill peace into your heart. Attending a business meeting would take on a completely different flavor if peace were on your mind, wouldn't it? Listening to the children argue in the backseat of the car would affect you differently if peace were the goal. You see, this is a way of being the value, not just thinking about it or doing it for 15 minutes a day and then going back to your usual life.

When you first start a habit of contemplation, you will find yourself going in and out of it all day long—that is quite normal. Even when you have been attempting a contemplative life for a long time you will still go in and out of it—that's the nature of the beast. But, you will, with practice, get better and better at pulling yourself back into the value and you will get good at identifying the times when you were completely out of it. I personally think it is easier if you have a topic picked out at the beginning of the day—but, there are days when I change from one value to another just because of an experience. There are days when I am so struck with the sheer beauty of this earth, that I am overcome with that observation, and continue to contemplate beauty for the rest of the day. In fact, you could choose beauty every day and be way ahead of the game because it is an instant neutralizer.

When your life is hectic and far from acceptable, you can immediately get centered if you will just take a moment to find something beautiful to look at. Let's take an example: Some one is yelling or criticizing you and you feel your anger start to rise. Just stop and look at a flower, a plant, a baby's face a cloud or an animal—anything that is naturally beautiful and your Spirit will take over and you will be calm. Then you will be able to respond in a high-energy fashion instead of reacting from the same energy the other person was coming from.

I am fortunate to live on a lovely mountain and just looking out of my window gives my Soul a lift—but, there is beauty everywhere. Please take time to see the magnificent world you live in and thank God for the blue sky, the many variations of green of the grass and trees, the sound of the birds and the crackling of leaves under your feet. This earth truly is a masterpiece of art when you start to look around and appreciate the Artist. Always remember that peace, beauty, contentment and harmony are all ours for the taking. We just have to open our hearts, our minds and our souls as well as our eyes to be able to see, and feel balanced. Beauty is a great value to begin with, as you practice contemplation.

Probably one of the most important principles to remember about spiritual energy is that you can't get there if you are uptight. This is another reason why mediation works—you have to relax to meditate. However, you can learn to relax regardless of what you are doing, if you know how.

Proper breathing is critical for you to align yourself with higher frequencies—you can't contemplate or meditate with little, shallow breathing. If you find yourself tensing up or starting to exhibit one of the emotions in the lower frequencies, changing your breathing pattern will start you going back up in vibration instead of spiraling down. When this happens to me, I like to employ what I call Velvet Breathing. This is how you do it: Take in a nice big breath, and count to four, one—two—three—four—; and immediately exhale to the same count, one—two—three—four; and again inhale without creating a space to the same count, and exhale again to the same count. Keep these smooth rhythms going until you feel calm and relaxed and then go back to your regular breathing. It is a good idea when using this method to look at something beautiful while regulating your breathing. It is almost impossible to look at a magnificent waterfall, do velvet breathing and be tense and nervous all at the same time. I can't always look at a real waterfall, but, I have a beautiful painting of a waterfall hung directly over my computer, so that when I feel tense or have "writer's block", I can check my breathing and look at my wonderful painting to bring me back to center. It is a bonus that this painting was painted and given to me by one of my very best friends.

Essence is a huge topic and I have barely scratched the surface of it in this chapter; but, my hope for you is that you will take time to contemplate on what essence means to you. Getting to the core of your beliefs and your desires will take you higher and higher in frequency, and will change who and what you are being. Never forget that your future is a direct response to who you are being at this moment. One of the deterrents to spiritual energy is the constant noise that is going on in our homes, and in our environment. It is impossible for most of us to maintain a high vibration when the TV or stereo is blaring, and incessant chatter is dominating our own minds and our space.

> ✸ *Your future is a direct response to who you are being today.*

Spiritual Equity

Silence is absolutely necessary if you are serious about getting to and actually making use of spiritual energy. I know it is difficult for young people to find a moment of silence; but, unless you make it a priority, you won't do it. Some days I have to get in the car and drive to a peaceful place just to have a few moments to myself. I suggest you pick out a spot in your home that you can call your own—even just a special chair and let everyone in the family know that when you are in that room, in that chair, that you are not to be disturbed. Teaching your spouse and children to do the same would be a huge step forward and would also bring a higher vibration into your home.

I know I am suggesting a lot of new actions for you to take; but, my intention is for you to pick out the ones that resonate with you and implement them daily.

CHAPTER TWENTY TWO

What is the Purpose of All This?

*"I long to accomplish a great and noble task,
but, it is my chief duty to accomplish small tasks
as if they were great and noble."*
~Helen Keller~

I get a real kick out of all the arguments over evolution vs. creation theories. When you stop to think about it, it is really both. Evolution is continuous creation—the unfolding of potentiality depending upon favorable conditions. Life is constantly creating and we are all evolving moment by moment—the Divine is continually expressing itself through us. The important part of knowing this is understanding that we are part of the creation process and we have choice—but, only if we are aware of those choices—otherwise choices are being made for us by society. We are learning in this Course how to become "conscious creators", and we now know that the most powerful way is to avail ourselves of the high spiritual frequencies.

We also have learned that manifestation takes place depending upon the "essence" of the desire and that love is the organizing power. I have tried to explain that truth is relative to the foundation of the understanding of the individual, which is masterfully described by The Map of Consciousness created by Dr. David Hawkins. What a person can understand as "truth" at consciousness level 300 would be considered "incomplete" to a person at level 550. It wouldn't be "not true", just not complete. Thus, explaining non-linear truths becomes most difficult using linear language. It is important that you go to your spirit within to help you define and use some of these more difficult principles.

One of the best ways to "choose" to align yourself with higher vibrations is to always be present in the NOW. Now means this very moment. If and when you start becoming totally aware of your thoughts, you will notice that most of them are either in the past or the future. We constantly rehash what has already happened and incessantly plan our next move. Very little time is actually spent in this minute called NOW. The irony of this is that the only place from which we can create is the NOW. We can not change the past and we can't actually create anything from the future—our power lies in this very instant and only in this instant. Knowing this, it is imperative that we learn to place our attention, and our intention, on the present. No matter how many problems you are facing, it is usually truthful to say that in this moment you are O.K. If every person and every thing is perfectly expressing who it is being at this time—then this moment is also perfect. Women are particularly guilty of doing many things at one time and planning, planning, and more planning.

> ✸ *Our power lies in this very instant, and only in this instant.*

Sometimes I can even be fortunate enough to be having a massage, but find myself planning and figuring out the rest of my day instead of totally enjoying the massage—how wasteful is that?

Training ourselves to "be here now" is a very worthwhile exercise—and it needs to be done constantly. Can we do it constantly—probably not, but, we can learn to keep bringing ourselves back to the present when we notice that we have slipped into the past or the future again. Does that mean that we never plan? No—it means that when we do plan, we do it on purpose in the now. We sit down and plan our day and then

What is the Purpose of This?

we are done with that instead of letting our awareness drift to the future constantly. Dwelling on the past is probably the most insidious—because it almost always brings up negative emotions such as regret, anger or guilt. Future thinking can bring up fear and apprehension. Remember, the Ego loves you to be in those lower emotions as much as possible, and its' tools are blame and judgment—even, and especially, if you are blaming yourself.

If you find your mind drifting to the past, just tell yourself "that was then, this is NOW". One of my favorite little tricks that I do when I find myself projecting myself into the past or the future is to picture myself as a little girl in school when the attendance roll was called. When the teacher called my name I had to raise my hand and say "I am here"—which is the image I use to remind me that I am here now. This is not an easy skill to refine, but, I promise you that it is worth all of the effort you can muster because you cannot create with this marvelous "quantum soup" anywhere but NOW. We know that we can create consciously or unconsciously, but, it is still being done in the present moment. I highly recommend a marvelous book by Eckhart Tolle called *The Power of Now,* if you want more information about this important topic. For the time being, let us continue to diligently practice becoming conscious and aware of our thoughts and making proper choices for creating in this moment.

When you really are in the present moment with all of your awareness, you will find beauty wherever you are and it is easy to be grateful for what you are experiencing. When I am present while writing this chapter, I find myself being totally overwhelmed by the magnificence of language, thoughts and the process of communication—not to mention the marvelous electronic wonders that I have at my command. I am overwhelmed by the perfection of this moment. And, as you learn to accept this moment—just as it is—you will find yourself experiencing true peace. Peace is my main goal and I can find it when I am totally present in the NOW.

Stillness is where creativity and problem-solving can be found. That is why we do meditation and contemplation—to find that stillness and to silence the monkey mind chatter in our heads. When we concentrate on the present and go to the stillness, we are aligning with our natural state of consciousness, which is love, peace and joy. "Man is that he might have joy" was not an idle statement—you and I are meant to have joy, but, the problem is that we always think that our "joy" is off in the future and is connected to an "only-if" experience. For example: we think we will be happy when we get married and some people think they will be happier when they get divorced. Or, we will be happy when we have children, and then happier when they finally leave. We are sure that we will find joy when we get a better job, or when we have more money or if we could get a better education. You see, we put off our joy to the future when it can't ever actually happen. We can only experience joy in the now and if we are not happy now, we won't be happy in the future. " Only-if's" are a neat little tool of the Ego to keep us trying to "get more", because that keeps us from our big Selves and stops us from listening to the Spirit.

Being happy, joyful, peaceful, loving, etc. has to be who you are—right now. It doesn't matter what the circumstance; if you are being peace—you will bring peace to the situation. Anything less is an invention of the Ego.

Since our natural state is love, then in truth we don't have to "become" anything, we just have to remove the obstacles that are in the way of our true selves. Think of a sculptor like Leonardo deVinci who said "I don't really create anything when I want to sculpt David; I just remove all the stone that is not David". That is the key to creating consciously—to come from our Higher Self which is who we really are. We know that the way we do this is by "being" all the attributes of God every day and in every way to the best of our abilities. That's how we raise our vibration—knowing that joy is always available to us if we just remove the parts of us that don't

What is the Purpose of This?

represent joy—say "yes" to this moment and feel the joy that is the essence of who you really are. By staying in the now and feeling your true core you are aligning yourself with the most powerful energies available to us humans.

Remember, situations don't make you unhappy—only your perception of the experience can knock you out of your true essence. When you find yourself exhibiting lower frequencies, it is helpful to borrow a line from The Course in Miracles that says: "I could choose peace instead of this." That statement brings you back to the now and changes the vibration immediately.

One of the most powerful principles I ever learned and that I hope to now teach you, is knowing your PURPOSE. Americans are very goal-oriented, but, to completely understand purpose, you have to know that your purpose is not a goal. A goal is something that is possible to reach—such as getting a particular job that you desire—then a new goal takes its place. If what you desire has a deadline or can be reached or finished—it is a goal, not a purpose.

Purpose is much broader than a goal—it is something that you can do every day, every moment of your life and you never finish it. Your purpose does not require anything that you don't already have—no skill or talent, no money or particular place—no special people or particular education. You have all that you need right now to be on purpose. When you are expressing your true purpose, it is a function of BEING—it is being who you are. When we discuss purpose, most people are looking for some really big event—like saving the children in Africa. That is a great goal and can be part of your purpose, but, if you are waiting for the money to travel to Africa, or waiting until you have time to devote to such an undertaking,

> ❋ *Your purpose does not require anything that you don't already have.*

it would be considered a great goal—not a purpose. If it really is your purpose, you can do it right now, right here—always.

For example: I have a client who really has had a difficult life—she seems to be surrounded by people who are very low energy, and do not show love or appreciation for anything that she does. She has been physically and verbally abused and even her grown children seem incapable of any of the higher emotions, including love. She, on the other hand, is one of the most beautiful, kind and loving people that I know. She is constantly doing lovely things for her family, friends and neighbors and is trying diligently to come from unconditional love even though she gets very little, if any, in return. She wonders, as would we all, what on earth could her purpose be in this. I invited her to come over for an "exploration session" to see if we could get to the bottom of her purpose. Now remember, when you find your true purpose in life, it will be simple—and you will probably laugh and say, "I can do that". Of course you can, you are already doing it; we just want to bring it up to the conscious mind so that you are doing it all the time—on purpose (pun intended). So when she came over, I put her through the same exercises I am going to describe in a minute, and she came up with this: MY PURPOSE IS TO TEACH LOVE. Well, now take a look at her life a little closer. If you were going to teach golf, would you seek out really good golfers or ones that don't already know how to play? If you are smart, you'll find the ones that don't know how to play golf but want to learn. Since she is here to teach love, who would she find in her classroom—experts on love or beginners? You see, her life became instantly understandable because she is teaching love, and has all along—she just gets frustrated because all of her "students" are beginners and aren't very good at it yet. Once she stopped expecting everyone to love like she does, her suffering went away. Now she looks to see where there is improvement, and takes pride in her work when she sees someone in her life that is starting to "get it". Purpose always brings joy—both to the giver and the receiver.

What is the Purpose of This?

When I was first introduced to finding my purpose, I was in a retreat seminar setting and we were given an entire day to work on it. I suggest that when you do the exercises below that you go somewhere where you can be alone and where you won't be disturbed for a while. This is important business and it is life-changing. At this seminar we would do an exercise, then go off to work on it by ourselves. At the end of the day, I had about four pages of writing, trying to describe what I thought my purpose was. Our Teacher instructed us to take our writings home and work on them each night until we had our purpose down to one or two, very succinct sentences that said it all.

I will share My Purpose with you, knowing that it took me weeks to get it down to this statement:

"My purpose is to raise energy wherever I go and teach others to do the same."

Those of you who know me can decide if you think I am doing that most of the time or not. I have learned to assess energy wherever I go, such as a store; and when I notice energy that is extremely low, I purposely try to raise it—that is my purpose. I don't mind telling you that my only goal, when someone comes to see me for nutritional counseling or life coaching, is for them to feel better when they leave than they did when they came in. Keeping that in mind, whatever else I might do is just a bonus.

I cannot stress enough that when you do these exercises, you go deep within and feel the answer instead of just thinking it—so here we go with the first one.

Take out a clean piece of paper or your journal and write at the top

I AM THE COLOR _____!

Spiritual Equity

Now, finish that sentence with the first color that comes to you. After you have found the color, then go on to the next question that says: WHY? List all the reasons why you are that color.

For example: when I first did this exercise I chose the color purple—which is not my favorite color, and my list as to reasons why went something like this:

1. because I am unusual
2. because I am regal
3. because I am bright
4. because I am not liked by everyone
5. because I am spiritual
6. because I am dramatic
7. because I am confident
8. because I am intense
9. because I can dominate my surroundings
10. because I am tricky to be compatible with
11. because I am powerful
12. because I am unforgettable
13. because I am strong
14. because I can be cool

Now, don't worry about whether it sounds like bragging or not, nor if it sounds uncomplimentary to you—just write down the reasons as fast as you can. This was very eye-opening to me and even though I did this many years ago, I still agree with these reasons because they truly are a part of who I am.

Please notice that when you choose a certain color, your answers will be totally different than another person's reasons even though you're talking about the same color. For instance, when I did this in a seminar, a lot of people chose the color red; however, the reasons for doing so were all over the map. For example: one person saw the color as hot and fiery, and another saw it as cool and intense. Another person saw it as powerful and proud, and another as basic and ordinary. You

What is the Purpose of This?

see, your reasons are your reasons. Now go—do the exercise for yourself.

The next exercise is a lot of fun. I want you to pretend that you are a detective, and you are sneaking into your house (but, you are the detective, not the you who lives there). Start at the front door and notice everything you see and then describe the person who lives there. What would this detective know about you just by going through your home? Here are my answers to this game. The person who lives in this house:

1. likes pretty things
2. has a classic taste
3. is a prolific reader
4. has localized disorder—not general disorder
5. likes drama
6. is sensual
7. is clean
8. likes comfort
9. loves nature
10. is intellectual
11. is a collector of sorts
12. is self-confident
13. is busy
14. is feminine
15. spends money
16. loves words

Now it's your turn—write your answers in a special notebook or journal so you can keep them. I have kept mine for over 20 years—the page they are written on is yellowing. Go!

The next exercise is easy—just name two or three of your best talents—and yes, you do have talents. My Mother used to say she was born with no talents—which was not true. Mother had a great talent for getting other people to do things for her—which shows great leadership. She thought that she had to be musical or artistic to have a talent—not so. Maybe you have a talent for story-telling or arranging flowers or playing with children. You can discover your talents by stopping to think about what other people say you are so good at. When people say you are so good at wrapping gifts—that's a talent. Now get busy and write down all your talents—more is better but at least two or three.

When I really got into this particular exercise I found and verbalized a talent that I had not thought about before. I realized that I have the ability to read and take in large amounts of difficult-to-understand material, spin it in my head and spit it out in a relatively easy-to-understand way. Wow! That was really neat and it fit right into my purpose—teaching others to do the same. I was really happy to discover this talent and I am trying to use it in writing this book. How am I doing?

Take all of this information from these various exercises where we were getting to know you better and start writing your purpose. Keep these facts in mind as you write—and remember my first go at this was four pages—so write all you want at first. To be a true purpose it must:

1. have a feeling of destiny
2. be bigger than self
3. be a compulsion—you just have to do it
4. can never be finished

I sincerely hope that you take the time to do this properly—you don't have to do it all today or any one day. This is something that you continue to work on until you have it down to one or two sentences that really speak to you. You should feel a rush of feeling as you recognize that, "YES", that is what I am here for—and I love it.

Check out your "Ideal Day" exercise and your "Passion" exercise answers to help give you some more clues. Finding your purpose is one of the most freeing things I can ever guide

What is the Purpose of This?

you to do. When you find yours, if you feel like sharing it, email it to me at connie@connielynnhayes.com—I'd love to know your purpose and I will do all I can to help you stay with it.

One other thing—organizations have purposes too. If you are a member of a club or a business, it is wise to either discover their purpose, or come up with one and see if it is truly compatible with your purpose. I like to use my purpose as my measuring stick, or ruler if you please, to measure everything that I do against. If it is not compatible with my purpose—I don't do it. If a group's purpose is diametrically opposed to my purpose—I get the heck out of there. You will also find it useful to know your purpose when choosing lifetime companions or even business partners. Knowing and living your purpose is probably the one, most powerful thing you can do in this life to stay in the high vibrations. Being on purpose is the driving force of high-energy people.

Before we leave the Spiritual Section of this book I want to give you one more thing to do. I have been criticized for giving you far too many exercises and things to do in this book, but you can come back to this book over and over again for multiple readings. I promise you that each time you read it you will find something that you didn't remember before. So, having said that, here is one more thing that I recommend you do if your intention is to raise your frequency. I use these little gimmicks to keep my mind focused, and most of the ones I have suggested take only a few moments to complete—it's just a matter of getting into better habits.

Our life experience is based on what we focus upon—as we know. The following questions are designed to cause you to experience more happiness, excitement, pride, gratitude, joy, commitment and love every day of your life. Remember, quality questions create a quality life. The following page has two categories: The Morning Power Questions and the Evening Power Questions. I suggest you put them either on your bathroom mirror or near your bathroom mirror where you will see it first thing in the morning and last thing at night. Come up with two or three answers to all of these questions. If you have difficulty discovering an answer, simply add the word "could" to the question. For example: What <u>could</u> I be most happy about in my life right now instead of what <u>am</u> I happy about.

I would love to give credit to the person whom I got these questions from; but, it was at a seminar over twenty years ago, given by a man named Mac—I don't remember his last name. I am grateful to him, however, because I have used them personally since then and taught them to hundreds of students. I suggest you make copies of them and put them in an appropriate place for you to see twice a day.

I sincerely hope that this Section of the book has been inspiring to you, as we are going to use these powerful vibrations as we go into the next two sections—Financial equity and Social equity. I purposely kept those two sections for the last so that we can use our new-found abilities to solve problems from the highest frequencies possible. Check out the Bibliography for wonderful books that will help you broaden your knowledge about spiritual energy.

What is the Purpose of This?

The Morning Power Questions

1. What am I happy about in my life now?
   What about that makes me happy? How does that make me feel?

2. What am I excited about in my life now?
   What about that makes me excited? How does that make me feel?

3. What am I proud about in my life now?
   What about that makes me proud? How does it make me feel?

4. What am I grateful about in my life now?

5. What am I enjoying most in my life right now?

6. What am I committed to in my life right now?

7. What and who do I love? Who loves me?

Evening Power Questions

1. What have I given today?

2. What did I learn today?

3. How has today added to the quality of my life or how can I use today as an investment in my future.

Spiritual Equity

IMPLEMENTING THE SPIRITUAL EQUITY

1. Spiritual energy is the fastest and most powerful energy available to us. We can connect to Spirit by seeing the beauty in everything and eliminating blame and judgment. We also connect to Spirit by taking responsibility for our lives—remember, "If I am powerful enough to make this mess, I am powerful enough to change it."

2. All things can be calibrated through kinesiology to determine their level of weakness or strength. I suggest you read Dr. Diamond's book *"Your Body Doesn't Lie"*, and Dr. Hawkins's book *"Power vs. Force"*. Try doing the kinesiology test with a partner.

3. The Universe responds to what we are BEING. Try the exercise on pages 225-226; identify the attributes of God, then BE those attributes. This will take you to a higher level of consciousness. Be grateful and feel the gratitude deep within your Soul with daily contemplation.

4. Meet your Higher Self through the meditation exercise on pages 231-233. And remember, YOU ARE MAGNIFICENT!

5. In order to HAVE what you want, figure out what the true ESSENCE of it is, what it really represents to you. For example: why do you want more money? The true essence might before security or safety. Then ask yourself if you could feel safe without having more money. Chances are you can.

6. You can choose to align yourself with higher vibrations by being present in the NOW. This also raises your level of joy. There is no power in thinking of the past or future.

7. Identify your purpose in life—to help you along, re-read the story on page 250; then do the exercise that follows.

8. Consider putting the Morning and Evening Power Questions where you will see them easily and answering them each day. This will start and end your day knowing if you are going forward or backward.

9. Learn to allow—which is the highest form of love—Godlike love. Remember, the only sin is ignorance. Allowing people, including yourself, to be who they are, and who they are not, will lead you into non-judgment; which is necessary to partake of the highest Spiritual Energies.

10. Know that we are all one—the sunbeams of the Sun—there is no "other". Practice acknowledging the divine in yourself and others. Namaste.

RECOMMENDED READING FOR SPIRITUAL EQUITY

1. *Power vs. Force*—David R. Hawkins

2. *The Contemplative Life*—Joel S. Goldsmith

3. *Seven Spiritual Laws for Success*—Deepak Chopra

4. *Essays of Emerson*—Ralph Waldo Emerson

5. *Your Sacred Self*—Wayne W. Dyer

6. *The Power of Now*—Eckhart Tolle

7. *The Isaiah Effect*—Gregg Braden

8. *The Four Agreements*—Don Miguel Ruiz

9. *Steering by Starlight*—Martha Beck

10. *There's a Spiritual Solution to Every Problem*—Wayne W. Dyer

11. *The Four Insights*—Alberto Villoldo

12. *The Greatest Secret of All*—Marc Allen

13. *The Eye of the I*—David R. Hawkins

14. *Peace is the Way*—Deepak Chopra

15. *The Power of Infinite Love and Gratitude*—Darren R. Weissman

SECTION FIVE

FINANCIAL EQUITY

CHAPTER TWENTY THREE

The Abundant Life

*"You are already rich,
you were born that way."*
~Peggy McColl~

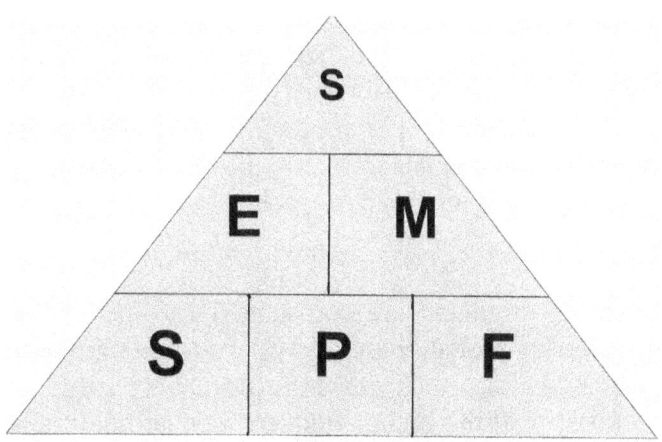

We've traveled up the Pyramid Frequency Scale right up to the top—which was the Spiritual Equity, and now we're going to go back down to the bottom row where you will find Physical, Financial and Social Energy Equities. Here's the reason I started with the Physical Equity and have devoted seven chapters to it: I figure that if you don't feel good, you are not going to be able to focus your attention on any of the other equities—and most people really don't feel all that well. So, if you are tired, in pain, or dealing with health problems, you really should go back to the first seven chapters of this book and see where you might not be giving yourself all the help that is available to you in a safe and natural way.

Financial Equity

Then we went up the scale and visited the Mental, Emotional and Spiritual Equities to learn how to raise our energy as high as possible so that we can solve problems and live our lives at the highest level that we are able to at this time, understanding that it is our goal to constantly work on incorporating the powerful spiritual frequencies whenever possible. Now, when we go back down to two of the lowest energy equities—financial and social—we should have a terrific toolbox full of ways to deal with our money issues and our relationships. So, let's tackle the world of finances.

How would you feel if I told you that wealth is your birthright? That doesn't mean that you are entitled to a stack of greenbacks just by the fact that you were born, but it means that wealth is an energy force and you have all rights to this source of abundance. The problem is that most people don't know of this force and don't know how to access it—but, you do now, and I am just going to point it out to you in case you have forgotten.

Financial problems are surrounded by one of the lowest energy fields—probably the lowest rung on the ladder—and many of us get so stuck at this level that we really never get beyond it to find the higher frequencies that hold the answers. The main reason I think we get stopped by financial issues is because of what I call THE BIG LIE. If there were a devil and he really wanted us all to fail at our adventure here on earth, he would just have to whisper to one person this lie: "There is not enough to go around", and fear would take care of the rest! That lie has spread so viscously throughout time that it has kept the majority of the world in poverty and has made crime our continual world nightmare. Crime and wars are all built around someone trying to take something from someone. If we all believed that there is more than enough to go around, there would no longer be a need for theft, embezzlement and the likes. Abundance, however, includes much, much more than just money. You see, abundance and true prosperity has to include all good things, such as enough love, peace, freedom and joy. Money and all those "things" that we associate with abundance, are merely symbols of prosperity—if you have lots of these symbols you have been manifesting them into your life using the laws of energy whether you knew you were doing it or not. Our job is to do it on purpose, and at will; and to do that we have to become "conscious" of what we are doing and why.

A lot of these last chapters are dedicated to the purpose of learning how to use some of the principles and concepts of the past 13 chapters, and applying them to our daily problems. We already know that there is only one Source, call it God, or the Universe or Consciousness, or whatever appeals to you. We are not that source, but, we all have access to it. We also know that we live in a world of duality—good/evil, black/white, etc.—and that The Source doesn't recognize opposites. So, in order to tap into the higher frequencies to solve problems, we need to "talk" the language of The Creator. One thing that we learned was to find the "essence" of our desires. That is one of the greatest principles you can have to solve so-called money problems. Get to the bottom of what you want money for—usually it is something like freedom, safety, peace, joy, etc. We learned in the Mental, Emotional and Spiritual Equity Chapters that we need to feel the *feeling* that we desire first—by BEING joyful, peaceful and free—by *feeling* rich! Jesus gave us the perfect example of how to do this—he taught us to start with what we already have—give gratitude and appreciation for it and "feel the joy of already having what we are asking for." Remember the parable about the loaves and fishes? Jesus asked for the crowd to gather up what they had in the way of food, and it came to just a few loaves of bread and some fish. He then blessed it, gave thanks for it, and PUT OUT THE INTENTION OF FEEDING THE MULTITUDE—and then proceeded to feed five-thousand people and never ran out of food. Now, that's what I call masterful manifesting! We probably aren't quite ready to do that on that level—but, we could—if we truly believed it; however, the principle is sound and we must emulate the "essence" of the teaching.

Financial Equity

We've talked a lot about the process of manifesting, by first knowing exactly what you want—this is usually where we mess up. It is not enough to say "I want to have money", or "I want to be rich". I could ask every one of you what it means to you to be rich and I would get a myriad of answers. You have to be explicit and exact in what you really want. I have always been much better at manifesting what I want the money for, than I am at actually manifesting money—unless it is an exact figure—then it seems to appear like magic. I can't tell you how many times I have faced an approaching due date for a particular bill, having that amount in my mind, firmly stating that that amount of money come to me in perfect time—and having it show up almost to the penny when adding up the cash intake from my business. It used to surprise me, but, now I expect it to happen. I understand the basic concept that the world is abundant, and that my Creator wants me to be happy and peaceful, so I just surrender to the knowingness that it will come. Here is one of my favorite affirmations that I have printed up in my office so that I see it many times during the day:

> *"What I desire is on its way. It will arrive precisely on God's timetable, not mine. Everything that I'm experiencing now is disguised as a problem, but, I know that it is a blessing. What I desire is on its way, and it's coming to me in amounts even greater than I can imagine. This is my vision and I'll hold on to it in a state of gratitude, no matter what!"*

When I was doing personal counseling and a client would not show up, years ago I would be upset—but, I learned a better way of looking at it. I started seeing that I was not ever losing anything—I just exchanged more money for more time which is also an asset. When this happened I would say, "thank goodness this person is not my source—my good comes to me in ways I cannot even imagine—but, I know it will come." I'm not bragging to you about this, I am just trying to explain to you that I have come a long way from my days of

The Abundant Life

poverty thinking. That doesn't mean that I always have loads of money—it just means that I always have enough which brings me to my own description of what I think it means to be prosperous:

"Prosperity means having enough money to do what I want, when I want, and not having to do anything that I don't want to do, to get it".

Sometimes students ask me why I don't manifest millions of dollars if I really know how to do it—and believe me I have seen many people do just that and I know it is possible; it's just that prosperity has many meanings to many people and having enough to do what I want when I want pretty much covers it for me. You have to do the thinking and get very clear about what you need in order to be, and feel, abundant.

Some people, like me, have a need to be surrounded by beautiful things like furniture, paintings, sculptures, plants, etc., so those are part of my prosperity thinking and I am pretty good about conjuring "things" up when I feel very passionate about them. I already told you how I got my grand piano and beautiful bedroom set and cars; but, the key, I believe, was my feeling about those things. I not only wanted them, but, I could feel the joy of possessing them before I actually could see them in reality. However, the magic happens after you have become clear about what you want, felt

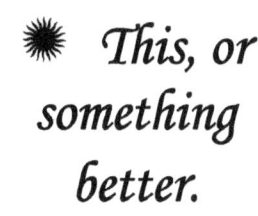

This, or something better.

the "essence" of the desire and then detached from the outcome —that's when I let it all go and say "this or something better". I have found in my old age that I am quite limited in my imaginings and The Creator has a bigger and better imagination than me—so, I think of the best I am capable of and then surrender the outcome to the Universe. Do I always get what I want? No—but, as I have told you, I always get what I think about most. So, if I am obsessing on what I don't have—you know the drill—I always get more of what I don't have. However, when I do what I have taught you here in these lessons, yes, I do always get what I want—if it's what I have been thinking about.

As a review, remember that everything that you can see in this material world has been manifested out of the unmanifested (Quantum Soup), and this "soup" is composed of all potentiality—so whatever you can desire has already been created as an energy pattern, you just have to match up to it and it will show up in your world. The Creator doesn't think about cars and dollar bills, He (or She if you prefer) just "is" and that "isness" includes everything—or the whole. We are mini-creators, so to be a conscious co-creator we need to emulate the characteristics of The Creator—which would be unconditional love, peace, joy, etc. Do you believe that The Creator knows that He is capable of creating anything at any time? Of course, that is where we need to get to—complete and total belief in our ability to create—that is our birthright. I get perturbed at people or groups of people who believe that poverty, or going without, is somehow "spiritual". That is bunk! God made us "so that we might have joy"—and I don't know anyone who is very joyful while in a state of poverty—pious perhaps, but, not joyful. If you knew without a doubt that you could create anything you truly wanted or needed, would you be jealous of someone else? Some people I know seem to think that frugality means denying yourself of goods and services to show your obedience to God. I don't believe in waste, and I certainly don't believe that all of us require the same things in the same amounts in order to be joyful; but, to purposely go without because of some notion that it makes you more "spiritual" or "holy", in my opinion, is a huge misinterpretation of God's will for us.

Knowing that we are creators-in-process, also carries with it the obligation to be good stewards of what we have already created. For example, I have created things that I no longer need or want, so giving them to someone else who needs or wants them is a form of creation for them. You see, giving away a suit that no longer fits me, to someone a size smaller, fits into the scheme of creation perfectly—giving and receiving which brings me to my next point—receiving.

Kaballah, which is an interesting spiritual philosophy, teaches that when we were all together in the spirit world everything was always provided for us and we were in a constant state of receiving. All of our needs and wants were constantly provided for us without us having to do anything in order to get it. It would be sort of like getting a hole-in-one every time you played golf—you probably wouldn't get much of a kick out of playing golf any more, and would go on to something more challenging. Or, if I gave you a million dollars every day without you having to do anything to get it, the money would eventually lose its glitter. The story goes that we all became bored with this and noticed that The Creator was able to always be the "Giver" and we were always the "Receiver"; and we desired the experience of giving. So, as the philosophy continues, the world was created and we now have an opportunity to give and receive. This is a very important principle to remember because it takes both giving and receiving to complete the manifestation loop.

The other important part of this principle is to know that the whole point of receiving is to share. So, in a nutshell, The Creator gives—we receive for the purpose of sharing. Now listen up: if the purpose of your desire to have something is for the purpose of sharing, you are using the highest spiritual frequency there is. So, check your desires—if just having stuff (or money) is for the sake of having it, you have created a stopping point and the energy will be blocked. Keeping energy moving is critically important. Some of us are better givers than receivers. For example: how do you receive a compliment? Do you shrug it off and act as if the compliment doesn't belong to you—or do you graciously receive it and thank the giver. Other people are continual receivers and never think about giving anything away. I often see people "hoarding" things in their garages and basements thinking that they might someday need it. I think that's why some welfare programs work better than others. When we keep giving people money without them doing anything for it, we are creating a culture of "takers" and it is no wonder that they never get out of the state of poverty. The Church of Jesus Christ of Latter Day Saints, I believe, has the best welfare system in the world. They do give to the needy—but, they require recipients to come and work at their supply warehouses or factories so that they are giving of their time in return for the food or clothes that they are in need of. They rarely give money; and if they do, it is for a very limited time—that gets people out of the "crisis" mode and into the "production" mode which actually turns lives around. Our government could take a lesson from this model.

With this business of giving—it needs to become a mindset for you at all times. Start giving every day in every way. Does that mean it has to be something big? No, size isn't the critical part of giving, but, the thought in the giving is! Start by doing this: never go to someone's home without taking a small gift—a rose, a poem, a thought, and wrap the gift if possible—this really makes it a gift. When you start doing this, you must also be ready to receive. For example, I have taught this principle to hundreds of my students, and most of them remember it and bring me gifts all the time. At first, it was not easy for me to receive all these nice remembrances, but, now I realize that it is the other side of the coin and it is a requirement to complete the flow. I love to give—most people do—but you must also learn to love receiving. Just remember: whenever you receive, you have given someone the opportunity to give—and both are absolutely essential to the process of manifesting.

We already learned that going with the flow of the universe is much easier than going against it—and hoarding is definitely going against it. That brings us to another energy principle—THE LAW OF THE VACUUM.

Basically, what this law refers to is that nature abhors a vacuum—so it usually rushes in to fill up the empty space. Think about this now, if you have filled all spaces with something (junk or useless stuff) there is actually no room for what you say you desire. Let's take an example—most of our closets. A lot of women are famous for saying "I don't have a thing to wear"—and when you inspect their closets you will find they are stuffed full of clothing. Sound familiar? We all justify it by saying that we are saving clothes that we don't fit into because we plan to go on a diet—or if we hold the style long enough it will come back in fashion. Well, if one of your desires is a new wardrobe—you won't get it until and unless you are willing to let go of all the old wardrobe. This is a terrific exercise to get you into the flow of financial energy — clean out your closet and dare to give it all away! Most of the clothes we actually wear fall into a group of seven or eight outfits—and the rest just takes up space—valuable space that the universe can use for creation. This same principle applies to other closets and drawers as well as entire rooms of "junk" that you neither like nor need. Get busy cleaning and clearing out space and you will be amazed to see your financial needs and wants improve almost immediately. I highly recommend that you give those unwanted things away and then claim your ten-fold return.

> ✸ *Start giving every day, in every way.*

There is a principle that is just fabulous for raising your financial energy quotient—THE LAW OF THE HARVEST. This law says that you reap what you sow; so, if you want corn, you must seed corn — if you'd rather have wheat, you'd better plant wheat. But, what if you want money? Like begets like, and giving away fruit cakes is a nice thing to do, but then don't expect money in return — food maybe, not money. Most people believe they have to have money first, but,

Financial Equity

remember starting out in the BEING is going with the flow. So you can be generous and seed money, no matter the amount. If you want money—give away money, and remember to claim your ten-fold return. When you plant corn, do you get just one cob of corn per seed? No, you plant a seed and get an entire corn stalk with many cobs of corn on it. That's the same way with money—you give away a small amount and claim a ten-fold return. Remember, we aren't giving just to get—but, we are investing to get a reasonable return which is your right. If you give a 10% tip, that's expected as part of the waitress's salary, but, if you give more than that, you can claim you've given a gift.

When you first plant a seed, do you check it every day and pull it up and ask "are you growing"? That would be futile—but, we tend to do the same thing with seeding money. You are planting a seed and in its own time it will return to you a nice little money plant—just be patient. And, as we've already discussed, sometimes that return comes in the form of a savings or a refund on something that you didn't expect, so keep your eyes open. The universe always gives a nice return on your generosity.

Now, I don't want you to get in the habit of giving just for the sake of getting; but, you are entitled to a return on your money when you invest it, and you are also entitled to a reasonable return on your items that you give away. Don't expect it from the person who receives it—it's not your job to know where it is going to come from. You are, however, obligated to claim the return—that's the receiving part. When I leave a tip or take clothes to the Good Will, I mentally claim my ten-fold return. Why ten-fold? No particular reason other than that seems reasonable—however, I have at times, when I really, really needed it claimed one-hundred-fold return. Let me demonstrate this with a story.

When I was a struggling single mother, I was in dire need of cash to pay my rent and my utilities which were due. I had no

The Abundant Life

money and I wouldn't be paid for another two weeks. I was thinking of how Jesus turned the loaves and fishes into dinner for the multitude, and reasoned that if I needed money I had to start with what I already had—but, remember, I had no money—or so I thought. So, I started to search through my belongings and came across 16 real silver dollars that my Father (who had passed away when I was 17) had given me on my 16th birthday. Now, as you know, real silver dollars are worth much more than the face value of a dollar since they are real silver. At that time, each one was worth about $15.00 which would mean that my 16 dollars had a value of around $240.00, if I could find someone who would give me that for them. Besides that, they had great sentimental value to me which actually meant more than the money. However, I realized that I had to give something to prime the pump, and the better my giving, the better my receiving. So I did something really brave. I boxed up all the silver dollars and shipped them off to a charity that I loved. I kissed them goodbye with love AND CLAIMED MY one-hundred-fold return—so I was looking for around $2,000 to come from somewhere. Does that take guts, or faith? Both!

Days went by and I was late on all of my payments, but, I kept saying my affirmation that I gave you at the beginning of this chapter. About a week after I sent off my precious package I got a call from a former employer who wondered why I hadn't come and picked up my final commission check? Obviously, I didn't know that I had one coming or I sure would have gone to get it; but, he said that their accountant had located an error in his computations and found that they still owed me $2400! I know, I know—that is kind of spooky—but, it was exactly my one-hundred-fold return on my silver dollars. Would I have received the check anyway? I don't know, but, I do know that I got into the flow and started the whole process by giving what I had—even giving the best of what I had—and remembering to claim my just return.

Get busy looking around your house, garage and basement,

Financial Equity

to see what you are storing or hoarding that you definitely do not need. Clear out and clean up and give it all away. You will be doing two things that will instantly help your prosperity situation—you'll create a vacuum so the universe can fill it with new desires, and you will start the giving/receiving loop that gets the energy moving; and, you will be employing one of the most amazing principles we know about, the LAW OF THE HARVEST. Don't forget to give thanks and appreciation for what you have, bless it and give it away in love—then watch for the magic.

CHAPTER TWENTY FOUR

Wealth Consciousness

*"Expect your every need to be met.
Expect the answer to every problem.
Expect abundance on every level."*
~-Eileen Caddy~

The world we live in is very, very abundant. The dictionary defines abundance as: plentiful supply, ample, copious, affluent, flowing freely, generous, wealthy, bounteous and rich. That's a pretty good description of nature. I can just look out of my window in the winter and see copious amounts of snow, or in autumn I see a bounteous supply of leaves. Even when I walk through an orchard I can often see an overflow of apricots rotting on the ground. The principle here is that there is more than enough of everything—for everyone—it's just when people get involved that we start to see lack and scarcity. The reason for this poverty mentality is beliefs. We spent a lot of time discussing how our beliefs are running our lives, and there is no better illustration of this than with money or wealth.

I was brought up with sayings like this:

1. Money doesn't grow on trees.
2. You have to work hard for a living.
3. If you don't save your money you'll go to the poor farm.
4. Money is the root of all evil.

How about you? Did your parents or teachers "lovingly" teach you any of these concepts? Knowing what you now know, do you believe these statements? I certainly do not, but, they were buried so deep in my consciousness that they definitely did some damage and I have had to purposely with discipline replace these false concepts with positive, more accurate beliefs. I was saved to some extent by my dear Grandma who thought that I was "born with a silver spoon in my mouth" which was her way of saying that I had a lot of opportunities that went well for me and talents that I used to bring me some abundance even at an early age. I did, however, believe that I had to work hard to get ahead—which I have done for most of my life. Let's take some of these erroneous beliefs one by one and see what they really mean.

<u>Money doesn't grow on trees</u> — what Mother really meant was that money was hard to come by and you couldn't just go pick it up whenever you wanted or needed it. I thought it was a rather stupid statement—and quite obvious—but, since then I have taken a different point of view. Actually, money is made out of paper and paper comes from trees. (Ha, ha). Seriously though, I have learned that money is only another example of what can be manifested out of the Quantum Soup—and the universe has a plentiful supply of this unmanifested energy. Listen to what Deepak Chopra has to say about this in his book: Creating Affluence:

> *"Behind the visible garment of the universe, beyond the mirage of molecules, lies an inherently invisible, seamless matrix made up of a nothingness. This invisible nothingness silently orchestrates, instructs, guides, governs, and compels nature to express itself with infinite creativity, infinite abundance, and unfaltering exactitude into a myriad of designs and patterns and forms.*
> *"Life experiences are the continuum in this seamless matrix of nothingness, in this continuum of both body and environment. They are our experiences of joy and sorrow, of success and failure, of wealth and poverty."*

<u>You have to work hard for a living</u> — my dear Father believed that you did have to give something to get something—and he saw that as being in the form of "work". My Mother added the hard part—which conjures up images of

sweating and fatigue. So, I started working at age 14 teaching dance. But I thought it was fun; and in 1953 for a youngster to make over a hundred dollars for six hours of work on a Saturday was phenomenal—and I didn't think it was hard—I just thought it was fun. That started to change my belief because I reasoned that if "hard" was what it took, wouldn't ditch diggers be the wealthiest people in the world? Hmmm! However, I have heard myself saying from time to time that I was born a "worker bee" instead of the "queen bee" which indicates I still believe that I have to work, work, and work. Actually, I'm working on that one (pun intended).

<u>If you don't save your money you'll go to the poor farm</u> — now, I didn't actually buy this one, but, my Brother certainly did, because I heard his kids tell me over and over again that they were afraid they were going to have to go to the poor farm if they kept wanting and needing so much. Obviously, my Brother kept that lie alive or they would never have heard it. I'm certainly all for saving and being smart with your money, but, I watched my own Mother, as late as in her nineties, squirrel away money—a few bills at a time—in her purse for her "old age". I gave her a beautiful robe on her 85th birthday and found it years later still in the gift box and was told that she was saving it for her "old age". Saving money is great—hoarding or denying yourself a little pleasure is over the top. We've all heard the story of the old hermit living in a log cabin in the woods of West Virginia who died all alone with over a million dollars under his mattress—just think of all the joy and happiness that man could have had by using and giving away his money while he was still alive. Remember: desiring money for the purpose of sharing is using the highest energy frequency possible.

<u>Money is the root of all evil</u> — this is something we have been fed for a long time by well-meaning religious leaders. Actually, this is a misinterpretation of scripture—what it actually says is "For the *love* of money is the root of all evil" (NT, 1 Timothy 6:10). I have amended this saying to my own

preference by saying that the *lack* of money is the root of all evil. Who does most of the stealing?—those who need money and take it from those that have it. Same with embezzling. Loving money leads to hoarding and this stops the natural flow of abundance. I have learned that money doesn't solve money problems—if it did, welfare would work. I personally believe in the old adage "give a man a fish and he eats for a day; teach him to fish and he eats for a lifetime". I think education is the answer to solving poverty—not money. This misleading statement of money being evil is akin to another one found in scripture that is misunderstood. It says "it is easier for a camel to go through the eye of the needle than it is for a rich man to reach the kingdom of heaven." We now know through scriptural research that the "eye of the needle" was an actual place, a gate so to speak, where camels had to get down on their knees in order to pass through it. It also was more difficult to accomplish this task if the camel was laden down with a heavy load of material possessions.

Having things, even lots of things, is not bad—having a lot of money is not bad—in fact, in most cases it is very good. Who is it that creates the symphonies, the ballets and the operas as well as the cancer research centers and libraries? It certainly isn't the poor people. Your purpose for wanting and having the money or the possessions is the key to getting it and keeping it coming. I was touched lately by Bill Gates, who recently retired from his position at Microsoft to spend more of his time on his charities. We have learned, I hope, that our intention sets the tone for the level of energy that we are choosing to come from. Always remember: YOU CANNOT SOLVE A PROBLEM FROM THE SAME FREQUENCY AS THE PROBLEM!

That's why money doesn't always solve a money problem —but, having a money- or wealth-consciousness does. That's what we are learning here. It is impossible to talk about developing an abundant way of thinking without revisiting some of the principles that we have already discussed in this book. We will be reviewing some of these laws of the universe and directly applying them to our financial problems.

Prosperity thinking is actually a math game—we are constantly either adding to our good or subtracting from it. How do we do that?—with our thoughts. What are we thinking about most in regards to money?—what we have or what we don't have? Most of the time, if we are honest with ourselves, we are thinking about what we don't have and that just creates more of what we don't have. Lack is a disease of the mind—always talking about what we can't afford or how we were born to be peons instead of princes. Those are pretty powerful beliefs. Is that what you really want? If not, then you must change your thoughts and your beliefs about money and wealth, and you can't do that if you don't first examine your own beliefs. I've shared mine with you, and at the end of this Section I will give you a few affirmations that I have replaced those insidious notions of my childhood with, which is what you must also do if you want things to change and get better in the pocketbook.

Since we brought up working, let me share with you my new understanding about work. I believe that we all have a song to sing and we all have a stage somewhere on which to perform. What that means is that I believe that we all have the right to do something that we love—and get paid for it. That's why we did the Passion Test, to find out what you truly love to do. If you are not already performing a job that you just love, take out your list of passions, also the list of talents that you wrote, and check in with the exercise we did about your ideal day. What did you come up with that you are truly passionate about? And how could you earn money doing it? A fun way to do this exercise is to make a list of all the ways you can think of that would incorporate your passion. For example, when I did this assignment, I found that my main passion was teaching, and my main love was personal growth, with an emphasis on energy. I made a list of ways that I could accomplish this:

1. teaching seminars
2. doing personal counseling sessions
3. writing a book, or books
4. making audio seminars
5. teaching other teachers

When I look back on this list, I am happy to say that I have been doing most of these methods of teaching for over 40 years—even when I had to do them on the side or as a hobby. This book is a first-time attempt at being an author on such a large scale, but I have done, or am doing, all of the other things on my list. I would love for you to be able to do the same thing. I truly am convinced that you can and should be doing what you love to do, and I know that the world will pay you well for doing it. We can all tell when someone loves their job or not. I am reminded of a young man down at the local Taco Bell Restaurant. He has a disability called Downs Syndrome; but, I have never seen anyone perform a job with any more precision and love than he does. When I asked him about this he told me, "I just love my job and look forward every day to meeting such nice people, and helping to keep my restaurant clean and tidy." This wonderful person is gifting us all with his presence and his love, and I am grateful for people like him. Norm and I went to China a few years ago and noticed a street sweeper who was just beautifully cleaning every last speck of dirt off of "his street". He didn't understand what we were saying nor did we understand his words, but, we understood that he loved his job and was very appreciative of it. That's what I'm talking about—it isn't what you are doing, but, if what you are doing is what you love, what you are good at, and what makes your heart sing.

> ✹ *We all have the right to do something we love, and get paid for it.*

Wealth Consciousness

Most people think it is a pipe dream to do what you love—but, can you imagine a world where all of us are doing just that? If you truly want peace and love in the world—which I believe we all do—start with what you are doing for a living. I know a boy whose father insisted that he go to medical school and become a doctor, which he did. He tried really hard to be a good doctor for a few years, but, finally he left his practice to do what he loved—painting—much to his parents' chagrin. However, he is such a wonderful artist and is bringing not only joy to his own soul, but, to everyone who is fortunate enough to see or own one of his paintings.

Another way to bring more energy to what you are doing is to give more value than what is expected. Find little ways to do just a "tad" more than what someone is actually paying for—it doesn't really have to be much. When I sell nutritional products, I found that putting them in cute sacks, or sending the item free to them if I had been out of it temporarily, or delivering it to them if I had to order it, were ways that I could add value and make sure that they felt like they were getting just a little extra on my part. How do you feel when the baker puts an extra cookie in your sack or you get a shipment from a catalog company that sends you a small "gift" with your order? The gifts seldom have a lot of value, but, they are still a gift. I am often taken aback when I hear someone say that they didn't like a gift that they were given—for heaven's sake, IT WAS A GIFT—it was free to you and it should be received with grace and appreciation. Always remember that receiving is the other side of giving—start priming the pump with your giving, and then be ready to receive. I used to not stoop to pick up pennies off the ground—I had the haughty attitude that I was too good to stoop for pennies—but, I changed my mind about that and realized that even a penny is a gift—and if you are not gracious about receiving small gifts, who says you will be for large ones?

Give more value than what is expected.

One night, when I was in particular need of solving a financial problem, I went into a meditative state and was immediately aware that someone else was in the room—I asked who was there and he answered "Sir Rubin". I then asked why he was here, and he told me that he was "the Keeper of the Spring of Abundance", and he had come to give me a message. I had to jump up and write down what he told me next because it was so awesome that I was afraid I wouldn't remember it. Sir Rubin was an interesting fellow with an English accent, and dressed up like a sophisticated banker, complete with a watch hanging from his striped vest. He then proceeded to give me his rules:

SIR RUBIN'S LAWS OF ABUNDANCE

1. There is an endless Spring of Abundance.
2. Everyone has equal access to this limitless spring.
3. You cannot divert it for your own use.
4. You can come back to the spring as often as you desire.

Then, as if he could read my mind as I was thinking "what if it isn't enough?" he added:

5. Then bring a bigger bucket!

Wow! This experience changed my life—and I am hoping that it will open up your perspective about money, too. Let's look at each of these laws.

There is an endless spring — that pretty much gets rid of the belief of scarcity or lack doesn't it? We have a lovely natural spring near our cabin at Fish Lake, and no matter how much everyone takes out of it, it still just gushes forth beautiful, clear, clean water. That's the vision I want you to get when you see in your mind this Spring of Abundance—it is always there, and it flows freely to you.

Everyone has equal access — I love this part, because it means EVERYONE; but, you do have to know it's there to be able to use it. This is why knowledge is so important. You have now been told that the Quantum Soup is endless and you can create anything you really, really desire out of it, just by first knowing of its existence, and placing both your intention and attention on it. Sounds easy—are you doing it yet?

You cannot divert it for your own use — this part of the law is a terrific protection so that no one can hoard it and take it all for themselves. I can just imagine if someone tried to do that with the Fish Lake Spring. I know that some uncouth people have tried to divert irrigation water only to their own property instead of letting it run freely to all who happen to be in its path. That's not possible with the Spring of Abundance—Sir Rubin is warning you not to even try. Just let it flow and let everyone have their share of it.

You can come back to the spring as often as you desire — this rule takes all of the fear out of the subject. If you need more—come more often. This is the same as if you and I are in the same room breathing the same air—if I breathe a little harder, I am not stealing oxygen from you—there is plenty for both of us. Also, if I have air here in my office, I cannot hoard it and prevent it from going into the hall and the living room—I don't even know where this air starts and the other room's air begins. Same with the abundance spring—there is plenty for everyone and if you come back more often than your neighbor, you are not depriving him of anything. Endless supply means just that—endless.

Then bring a bigger bucket — this one just cracks me up! How did he know I was worried about my little thimble-sized bucket not holding enough? Now, I know that not only can I go back as often as I want to, but, I can take a huge bucket with me if I need to—the universe doesn't care how much you take! Get over thinking that if you have a lot someone else doesn't—you are not taking it from someone else. I always laugh at the quotation by Maharajah who, when asked "where does all the money come from", quipped, "from wherever it was before." You can have all you want or need as long as you play by the rules—give value, get in order to share, and receive graciously.

Pay attention, and try to notice all the opportunities that you might have to seed money. It's just like the Law of the Boomerang—you don't have to know what they are going to do with the money. Many times when I give money to a vagrant, I find myself thinking that he is probably going to buy drugs with the money. But, THAT'S NOT MY PROBLEM. My only part of the deal is to give—without being attached to the outcome—and claiming my ten-fold return. Try it—it really works.

CHAPTER TWENTY FIVE

Claiming Prosperity

*"I always have enough for all of my needs,
most of my wants,
and still have plenty to share."*
~Connie Hayes~

In this final chapter of this Financial Equity Section, I want to bring out all the principles we have learned thus far and apply them directly to our finances, our careers and our prosperity. Let's begin with our thoughts.

We know that we have thousands of thoughts each day and most of them are the same ones we had yesterday, and the day before that. Our job is to take conscious control of our thoughts and not let our minds wander because when we are thinking "unconsciously" we are usually going in the direction of the cultural mind—and 85% of the time it is going to be negative. Watching our thoughts is critically important because that is the beginning of the manifestation loop. Remember, you are always adding to or subtracting from your growth, and it's no wonder that we don't make any headway, as we're going back and forth all day. The best way I have found to control our thinking is to first notice when we are being dragged back into the past or when we're worrying about the future, and to insert an affirmation or a sentence that we love into our mind to stop the freefall. To do this, you need to have one or two sentences ready—such as my favorite: "my cup runneth over". Especially when I am thinking "lack" or "scarcity" thoughts, I love that one because it conjures up an image of a glass of water with the water running over the top. I also like "God is good" or "My Father and I are one".

Financial Equity

Choose sayings or scriptures that you like that are short that you can have ready to use whenever you notice you are going in the opposite direction of your desires.

But, to make this work, of course, you have to have desires. We were created to desire—and when we fulfill one there is always another one to take its place. I personally think that this is healthy and it does usually keep us going in the direction of growth—so don't be disturbed that you have so many wants. I am more concerned about the people who don't know what they want. The biggest step in the manifestation process is knowing what you want. Go back to the list that you made, where you wrote down fifty or so things that you would like to have, do or be. Check this list and make sure that you have also asked for the money with which to purchase these things or take care of them. I made that big mistake one time. I had my eye on a particular house that I really, really wanted, and I pictured it, saw how I would decorate it and saw the Owner giving me the keys to it. All that happened just as I visualized it—except after just a few months, I could not keep up the payments on that gorgeous home and I lost it. So make sure you have written your desires in detail. And since we are addressing our finances, make sure you have included all the money you will need to keep your desire and maintain it.

Affirmations are a slick way of keeping your mind focused on what you want instead of what you don't want. I write mine down on several different cards and put them in many places where they can be seen. I even, on occasion, record my affirmations into a tape and listen to it while I am vacuuming, exercising or going to sleep. This does take effort! Are you just interested in this idea, OR ARE YOU COMMITTED TO APPLYING IT?

The next step is to check your beliefs. As you know, I am a great proponent of the philosophy that our beliefs are running our lives, and if you don't check them out, your life really isn't your own. Most of our beliefs were handed to us by someone else, and we let them sink into our subconscious mind as "true", and have not questioned them ever since. This can be lethal—especially to your finances. Remember that a belief is just a repetitious thought—one that we have heard over and over again—and most of them seem ridiculous to you now if you take a long hard look at them. So become a watch-dog on your beliefs—question them, and if you can't agree with them wholeheartedly replace them with a new one. I often hear people refer to money as "filthy lucre"—which doesn't leave a very nice impression in one's mind of cash, does it? If you find yourself or anyone around you saying these kinds of things, immediately cancel them out and say something positive like "I like money and money likes me". Tight little clichés are some of the most insidious thoughts that we have in our culture, and lead to repetitious language. Don't for a minute think that these little sayings are harmless—they are not!

One little trick that I use to keep my beliefs straight about money is to put a $100 bill (or $1,000 bill) in your wallet and not spend it. Then, you won't usually be able to say that you "can't afford something"—you just choose not to purchase it at that time. That's a better way of looking at it, don't you think? I always "have" the money; I just may or may not choose to buy.

What's your attitude about money and prosperity in general? Do you think that having money makes you less spiritual or that if you have lots of money you wouldn't be as good a person as you are now? The best way I know of to change your attitude about this is to know what you want the money or abundance for—how are you planning to use the increase—are you going to share it in some way? Knowing in advance that you plan to use it wisely for the good of all concerned is a terrific way to put your attitude on the right track—for remember attitude is usually benevolent or malevolent—and you want to be on the benevolent side for sure.

Changing your perspective just means standing back and looking at your situation from the big picture instead of focusing on just your little view of things from where you are standing. You limit yourself in a big way if you get tunnel vision—especially with money. You may only know of one way that you can bring in more cash—but, the Universe is not limited in any way; so let go of your attachments to "how you think it must look" and open yourself up to many possibilities and unlimited potential. If you think that you know everything (and we all know people who think they do) you are deluding yourself. Smart people know that the more they learn, the more they know they don't know. So be wide open to new ideas and creative ways of thinking. Let me give you another example with a story.

> ✹ *Affirmations keep your mind focused on what you do want, instead of what you don't want.*

I already told you in another part of this book about my just BEING a Trouble Shooter. Well, after my first stint with the department store, I had an opportunity to apply to a Private Men's Club for a similar position. I went through the application and pre-qualifying steps with the Manager of the Club only to find out that there were ten finalists for the job. And, the worst part was that it now went to committee, which meant that no one person was going to make the decision—an entire group of people had to vote on it. Well, we all know that not much gets done in committees, and they certainly don't do anything with any amount of speed. So after around six more sessions with committee members it came down to just two of us. After about a week more of waiting I got a call from the Manager who said that the committee had chosen the other woman—not me.

Claiming Prosperity

I was really bummed out about this as I had invested about six weeks on this process and I had never, up to this point, interviewed for a job that I did not get—so I was angry and upset. But, after calming myself down and meditating on what I should do next, I got up and wrote the Manager a letter. I thanked him sincerely for his help in this matter and told him that this was the first time ever that I had not been offered a job that I had applied for. I told him I would appreciate it very much if he would explain to me why I had not been chosen. Two days after I sent that letter, the manager called me and told me that after just one day on the job for the other woman, they all knew that they had chosen the wrong person; and did I still want the position? Well, I certainly did want it and I went on to perform such a great service for them that that lead to my next position as an interior designer. The point is that after not getting what I wanted, I stood back and looked at the situation and asked how I could learn from this so it never happened again—I took a different perspective on the situation and looked at it from a much wider viewpoint, and it worked. Check out your perspective on your current finances and see if you are limiting yourself to only what you know, or could there possibly be another way of viewing it?

Now comes the big one—emotion. How are you "feeling" about your financial situation? Do you tend to get depressed when you see the bills coming in; are you angry about how much was taken out of your check for taxes? Do you have more month than money? I love what Jim Rohn has to say about this—he said that when he looked at his miserable bank balance he got disgusted—totally disgusted—and that was the day his life turned around. So, you see that a negative emotion can lead you to something good if you use it as a springboard to get where you want to be. I can't help thinking of Scarlett O'Hara in Gone with the Wind, when she said "I promise I will never be hungry again"—and she wasn't. She used that negative situation and the anger and disgust that she felt for it to catapult her to success—it became the driving force for her hard work. Think about Dr. Hawkins' Scale of Emotions and see how you can take the emotion that you have about your money, or lack of it, and find a way to push yourself up the scale; even if it is a little at a time, until you get up to the positive ones like optimism and trust. Remember, every time you jump up even one emotion, you are raising your energy frequency. The goal to using emotions successfully is to notice whether you feel good or not—the object of the game is to feel good—and sometimes disgust just plain feels good, at least better than despair. Getting to a positive emotion and connecting it with your desire or affirmation is a sure way for you to see it show up in your reality faster! Emotions are a huge key to getting what you really, really want.

Take a moment to think about what things make you "feel" prosperous. When I was struggling with finances and didn't even have a winter coat to wear, it was sometimes hard to keep my mind on what I wanted instead of what I didn't want. One little game I played was thinking of things that made me feel rich. I came up with a couple of things: one was wearing a clean nightgown every night, and having crisp, clean sheets every other night just like they do in the nicest of hotels. I also put a mint on my pillow and one flower in a vase by my bed. That was my way of re-creating some of the grandest experiences I had had in my life, when I was fortunate enough to stay at a fancy resort or hotel. It worked for me.

We talked a lot about finding the essence or core of your desire—and when you can do that with your prosperity desires you are introducing the highest spiritual frequencies into your manifesting. Essence leads you into BEING—which as we know is flowing with the universe. We already worked our way through the HAVING/DOING/BEING exercise with being rich. Were you surprised to find that the essences of being rich were things that really have little or nothing to do with having money? We can all be generous, free, happy and peaceful if we choose to be even with very little money. But, I can tell you that when you start being all of those virtues, the money will come—unless your thoughts drive it away.

However, if you were truly BEING free, happy and generous, you couldn't have scarcity thoughts at all—you would look at this beautiful, abundant world and give thanks every day for your part in it.

Which leads us into a really big one—gratitude. This is probably the easiest way to start the ball rolling towards your desires—giving thanks for what you already have. Let's face it, anyone who is reading this book has a lot to be thankful for—and we need to notice what we have and "feel the feeling" of appreciation daily. That's why we feed our Thank Bank each night, it's why we go on the Appreciation Rampage and I have another little game for you to play to get you thinking about what you have instead of what you don't have. If you have lots of dreams that have not yet come true, you probably have a lot of dreams that already have come true for you. Take out a piece of paper or your journal and start looking around and thinking about dreams and desires that you have had that have shown up in your life. For example I always wanted to have four children—and I do. I wanted to meet a Prince Charming who would love me as much as I love him—and I did. I have always dreamed of writing a book—and I am. Now it's your turn. When we start thinking of all the things and people and situations and experiences we have had, we find we have a lot to be thankful for and it primes the pump. This is a great way to get someone to do something nice for you, too—by thanking them first for always doing such nice things for you—they won't be able to resist your request. We always feel better about doing something for someone who appreciates us—well, the universe does, too. When things aren't going so well, start appreciating and showing gratitude—this is truly a magic tool.

While I was writing this section of the book, I thought about ways that I could show more appreciation for what I have. I sat down and wrote letters to my husband and children and dearest friends and told them how much they mean to me. I tell them all of the time, but, I thought it would be something special to see it in writing. It certainly put a smile on Norm's face—

which was worth all of the effort. Have you ever thanked your parents for your education or for the good upbringing that they gave to you? I admit that there were lots of times when my kids and I didn't know where our next meal was coming from, but, they never had to go to bed once wondering if their Mother loved them. I know my Mother loved me, too, and I find myself thanking her every night even though she is no longer with us—she did a good job and I appreciate it.

Giving is another terrific way of getting into the "generous mindset". Of course, it matters what your mindset is while you are giving the gift. If you're thinking that you really couldn't afford the gift, or you don't think the person is going to like it or appreciate it, or if you are looking for something in return— you are sabotaging your efforts. Give with no thought of getting back, and enjoy the awesome rush that comes with truly giving something away. When my children were small, we decided to do a Sub for Santa as a family. I found a woman with two children whose husband was in jail and she had no money for Christmas. So, we all went out and bought toys, a tree and all the fixings' for a Christmas dinner; and just as we were all going to deliver it to the family, I asked each of my two kids (I only had two at the time) to go to their rooms and bring me out their favorite toy. Heidi brought out her newest Madame Alexander doll and Todd brought out his newest Tonka fire engine. I then explained that I wanted them to give these toys to the children we were going to visit. Well, you can imagine the tears and the complaints that I got from my children then! I waited for them to calm down and then explained that if we were going to truly give in the spirit of Christmas, we had to give something away that meant a lot to us—otherwise we were just giving off the top. To really give—like seeding—you must give your best seed corn. I told them then that farmers save their very best potatoes and corn to use as seed and if they sold off all their best, they would not have a great crop next year. So, I said, they needed to give their very best, with love and see what happens. To make a long story short, you should have seen the look on my children's faces when they presented these "special" gifts.

Claiming Prosperity

They were the ones with the look of joy—and to this day, Heidi and Todd will still remember that Christmas as one of their favorites, not for what they got—they probably can't remember a thing they received that year—but, for what they gave. Give from the heart—give your very best—with love, and watch what happens. That's coming from a very high frequency and it is amazingly powerful.

You probably think I do nothing but exercises and play silly games; well I do play a lot of games and I have made habits out of most of the exercises I have given you to do; but, this one is my favorite and I still do it—especially if I sense that the money seems to be in short supply around our house. I take out a new checkbook register, and pencil in a $100,000 deposit. Some people play this game with millions, but, I find it works great for me with $100,000 at a time. The object of the game is to spend ALL OF THE MONEY every day—knowing full-well that there will be more there tomorrow. After making the deposit, then decide what you are going to spend it on today and proceed to write the checks out to whomever in whatever amounts necessary. At first, you will pay bills, get caught up on credit card accounts, but, you can't save any of it—and you must spend it all. Then, the next day another $100,000 is deposited in your checking account and you can then again spend the money. After a few days you have exhausted all of your real needs so you move to some of your wants and dreams. If you do this faithfully for at least three weeks your attitude about money will definitely change—you become really generous, and you have to think really, really hard about how you are going to spend that much money. I was taught this exercise by a multi-millionaire who used million dollar deposits in the game and doubled it each day—do what seems right to you. It works just great for me with the lower amount and I actually find myself looking forward to the next day so I can spend some more money. I start putting a lot of thinking time into what I would spend it on. After a while, I find that I really don't need that much money every day and it becomes quite an effort to spend it all. Try it—silly or not, it worked for a millionaire and it works for me.

When it comes to behavior, you really are going to have to do something. You must take action. I worry that many of you are going to read this book and skim past the exercises. I can't stress enough that you really do have to change your behavior if you want to change your results. I certainly don't expect you to do all of the exercises every day, but, I do expect you to do something. If I could only choose one thing for you to do right away it would be to decide what you want—the rest of this is useless if you don't know your own desires—and most people don't. It would be a travesty, in my opinion, if you purchased this book, took time to read it and then did nothing different.

> ✸ *You have to change your behavior if you want to change your results!*

That's the main reason I have started doing Life Coaching—because people need to be walked through the exercises and to be made to do the work. You might have good intentions, and "someday" you will take time to do it, but, not today—you are too busy. We're all busy; you don't have a monopoly on busyness. However, if your life is just fine and you don't need or want it to change—keep doing what you are doing. But, if there are areas in your life that are not all that they could be, you can't keep doing the same thing and expect different results. Change your behavior—change your results! They tell me that it takes three weeks of doing something to change a habit, so commit yourself to at least three weeks of faithfully saying your affirmations; or of seeding each day; or making a deposit in your Thank Bank; or sending out blessings with the Law of the Boomerang; reading a positive book; or listening to some uplifting music—just do something to raise your frequency. The universe will be thrilled and will reciprocate in kind!

Give more value—at your job, at your club, at your church, in your home—than people expect. Constantly be on the lookout for little ways to add value. Wealth belongs to the world—and we are just leasing it for the time we are here, so the best way to be able to keep wealth is to be able to give it all up. What? Are you saying, Connie, that if I do all this work and attract all this goodness into my life I have to be able to give it all away? Yes, that's what I am saying. You must be detached from the wealth, the things, the stuff and the money. When you surrender what you have to the universe, knowing full well with confidence that you could lose it and re-create it again out of the Quantum Soup, you have truly arrived. You are then among the wealthiest of humans. Some of our billionaires in this world tell us that they have made millions, lost millions, and made millions again. Once they learned how to do it, all the fear went away with regards to keeping it, and yours will, too. Once you know that you are a Co-Creator with God, that you have been given all you need to work with to create the world you desire, you can do it over and over again—and it becomes fun. What can you dream up today? True wealth means to be carefree, happy and joyful and to be in a position to help someone else with their dreams—now that's a worthwhile desire.

Look at the list of affirmations I have listed at the end of this section, and the bibliography, to get you started on some more fine reading. Remember, the word "heaven" comes from a Greek word that means "expansion or growth". Your only job is to keep growing. You don't have to be perfect; you are just expected to be better today than you were yesterday. Cheers!

AFFIRMATIONS FOR FINANCIAL EQUITY

1. I have enough time, energy, wisdom and money to accomplish all my desires.

2. I always have enough for all of my needs, most of my wants and plenty to share.

3. I deserve to be healthy, wealthy and prosperous. All my good comes to me now.

4. I acknowledge the everyday miracles that always happen around me, and I am grateful for all miracles that are yet to come.

5. For all that I am, and all that I have, I give thanks.

6. There is a rhythm and flow to life, and I am part of it. Life supports me and brings to me only good and positive experiences. I trust the process of life to bring me my highest good.

7. I love life. It is my birthright to live fully and freely. I give to life exactly what I want life to give to me. I am glad to be alive.

8. I am very grateful that my life is now full of joy, fulfillment, prosperity and freedom.

9. I am a powerful, dynamic, and intelligent person, and I am manifesting my abundance NOW.

10. What I desire, or something better, is now manifesting in totally satisfying and harmonious ways for the highest good of all.

11. I am really good with money, so financial abundance comes to me in an easy and relaxed manner, and in a healthy and positive way.

12. The genius in me is being released, and I am now fulfilling my destiny.

IMPLEMENTING THE FINANCIAL EQUITY

1. The Universe is Abundant, and there is more than enough for everyone. But abundance and prosperity mean different things to different people. If it's money you want, know what you want it for. Be willing to receive, saying "this or something better". Create a vacuum for what you desire, through giving. In order to keep abundance flowing to you, you need to share; and do it without any strings attached. "Seed" what you want for yourself. Think of something everyday that you can give (it doesn't have to be material), and claim your ten-fold return, without being attached to the outcome. This is the Law of the Harvest.

2. Challenge your negative, false and limiting beliefs about money, examining what you learned from your family and others who had influence in your life. What are your dominant thoughts about money? How are they working for you? Always cheerfully give more than what is expected of you – there is plenty more where that came from. Examine Sir Rubin's Laws of Abundance, and contemplate how you can apply them to your life.

3. Now examine your "feelings" about money. Remember, it's your feelings and emotions that ultimately create your end-result. Now consider what makes you "feel" prosperous (again, that will be different for different people), and see just how many of those things you can give yourself on a regular basis. Now go take action – nothing will change until you do!

Financial Equity

RECOMMENDED READING FOR FINANCIAL EQUITY

1. *The Intention Experiment*—Lynne McTaggart

2. *Changing Your Course*—Bob and Melinda Blanchard

3. *Invisible Supply*—Joel Goldsmith

4. *Spiritual Economics*—Eric Butterworth

5. *Key to Living the Law of Attraction*—Jack Canfield

6. *Creating Affluence*—Deepak Chopra

7. *The Master Key System*—Charles Haanel

8. *Harmonic Wealth*—James Ray

9. *21 Distinctions of Wealth*—Peggy McColl

10. *Spontaneous Fulfillment of Desire*—Wayne Dyer

11. *Feng Shui for Prosperity*—Terah Kathryn Collins

12. *The Science of Success*—James Ray

SECTION SIX

SOCIAL EQUITY

CHAPTER TWENTY SIX

Looking in the Wrong Place

> *"If your compassion does
> not include yourself,
> it is incomplete."*
> ~The Buddha~

It's time now for us to examine the last equity in the Energy Fix System—Social Energy. This frequency refers to all of our relationships—with ourselves and others. If you notice on the Pyramid Frequency Scale, this equity is also on the lowest level along with physical and financial. I call all three of these equities stumbling blocks because we all get stuck from time-to-time in health issues, financial problems or troublesome relationships. The problem is, if we do get stuck on this level, it's pretty difficult to raise our vibratory level. We must first understand the one principle that I have repeated many times throughout this book: YOU CAN'T SOLVE A PROBLEM FROM THE SAME LEVEL AS THE PROBLEM—you at least have to raise the vibration, even if you try to do it on the material level. We know that we can solve these problems much faster and with much longer-lasting results if we go up to the higher frequencies—and that is what we are going to discuss now—how to solve our relationships with some of the more powerful energy levels.

The ancient Chinese identified the basic energy centers of the body over 5,000 years ago and called them "Chakras", which mean "wheels", because they spin. These centers represent a physical part of the body as having an emotional connection with us—thus the mind-body connection. Very often when we find physical problems in these areas, we will find emotional "triggers" that contributed to the problem. For example: The first Chakra at the base of the spine refers to "tribe" or the fundamental groups that we belong to such as our race or ethnicity, or religion or our country—even our gender. When we have problems in that part of the body we often find troubling situations that this individual might be having regarding their "group affiliation". For example when a person tries to leave their religion that their entire family belongs to, there are often separation issues and relationships often suffer. This also happens when an individual is asked to leave the "tribe" because of differing lifestyles. I know of one young boy who finally told his family that he was gay and his father kicked him out of the house at age 16 and they had not seen him again until this past year when he dared to come back because he was dying of Aids and needed help at age 47! These are very difficult experiences and can cause huge emotional as well as physical and mental damage.

Moving up the body to the 2nd charka, just above the navel, we find this center usually means more one-on-one relationships. These usually involve intimacy and/or they can represent parents with their children. Siblings can fall into this group if there is a personal relationship not just a familial one—like twins or those siblings who are also good friends. This area is where we usually find most of what we would consider our "relationship issues." Divorce is running rampant in the U.S.A. and we even are seeing what seems to be more domestic violence that stems from these types of social setups.

If you take a look at the third charka, in the area of your solar plexus, you will see that it has to do with "self", individual self esteem—your relationship with you. This is actually where most of our work needs to be done; in fact it is really the only place that you can solve relationship problems. Here comes another really, really important principle that I don't want you to ever forget: ALL RELATIONSHIP

PROBLEMS ARE PROBLEMS WITH THE SELF! Whew! That one hurts, doesn't it? We are going to dissect that statement right now.

If the main purpose of our human existence is to grow, and I believe it is, what better way than to surround ourselves with "others" so that we "see" on a daily basis those things that we need to develop within ourselves. The problem is that we don't see it correctly because we are looking in the wrong place. We believe that the problem BELONGS to that other person, when in fact, it belongs to us. Let me explain. Every person that you come into contact with is a "mirror" reflecting back to you the places that need transforming <u>in you.</u> That's right, even that most irritating person in your life that bugs you incessantly—especially that person!

How brilliant of The Creator to bring us into families—people that under normal circumstances we are with for the rest of our lives—and those that we find it most difficult to separate from. Wow—how convenient to have parents that we can blame our circumstances on and siblings that we can envy—and what about our own children—now there's a test! We actually have a constant classroom going on right in our own homes and most of us never "get" that the lesson is for US. Now would be a good time to look at all of your close relationships and isolate those so-called "problem people", especially the ones that cause you the most concern. Let's consider this example.

I was once married to a man that did very little around the house to help me. I would gather up the garbage and put it right by the door and ask him to please take it outside on his way out the door. He would always say he would—as he stepped past the garbage and left the house. This would also happen when I asked him if he was going to cut the grass. He always answered "yes, I will" and by Saturday night, the grass still wasn't cut—so I cut it every Monday morning. This relationship was a long time ago and I wasn't clued into this "energy stuff", so obviously I would get angry, and spew out my frustration verbally. Did it help? No—it happened over and over again and of course, the marriage didn't work either. However, using this mirroring concept, if I was faced with the same situation today I would ask myself, where in me am I saying "yes" and meaning "no"? Now that would be a great revelation to me, and probably is to a lot of us. You see, if it irritates you, or keeps happening over and over again in your relationships, you need to look within. Now this doesn't excuse other people from bad behavior; but, it does take your irritation out of the equation.

> ✺ *How brilliant of The Creator to bring us into families – a constant classroom.*

One word of caution when you use this technique—it is not about blame—blaming yourself isn't any more effective than blaming someone else. Also, when you go looking for the part in you that this situation is mirroring, it is rarely the exact same thing that you are seeing. You see, I wouldn't actually tell someone "yes" and then not follow through—that's not my style. However, I often tell someone "yes" when I really would have rather declined. What you are looking for within you is something similar—and it is usually a part of you warring with another part of you. Here's another example:

There was a time when I noticed that a lot of people were showing up late in my life—clients late for appointments—friends late for a luncheon date—my own children late for Sunday dinner. This really started to frustrate me, because one of my virtues is punctuality. I regard time as a valuable asset both for you and for me. In fact, one of my friends calls me a "time freak". That doesn't mean I am never late—but, it does mean that I am very conscious of time and if I can't make an appointment at the proper time, I will at least call and renegotiate if necessary. Any way, I realized that somewhere inside me I was creating this "lateness" in my outer world. Now, as I have just said, I couldn't take it literally and wonder where I was being late for appointments, so I had to dig a little deeper. I asked myself what an appointment represented—and I came up with "an agreement". So then I asked myself where in me am I not keeping agreements. Well, this really upset me because I am really a freak about keeping my word—and to prove it my Grandchildren often say "if Grandma says it you can take it to the bank". That's something I have always been proud of—keeping my word. So where in the world could this problem be coming from? With just a little introspection I finally got it—I was not keeping agreements with myself. When I promised that I would exercise or get a massage or do something for myself and someone else needed something—I always deferred to the other person's need; I figured I could be put on hold. But, what was my Higher Self telling me? That to be impeccable on keeping agreements, it had to include keeping those to myself also! What a find—and it worked. As soon as I got it and started keeping promises to myself, the lateness stopped. Funny thing about that—it always works.

    I can't stress the importance enough about this mirroring method. If you use it, you will solve most of your relationship problems. Remember that we can't change the behavior of another person, but, we can change the effect it has on us, and many times that will change the other person, or another phenomenon happens—they leave. Don't panic—that doesn't necessarily mean that your spouse is going to leave you when you start checking into the mirror. But, it could! What I have experienced is that people that have irked me in the past, after discovering where I was irking within, have sometimes just faded out of my life. There is no fight—no argument—you just don't have anything in common with them any more—AND THE REASON FOR THEM BEING IN YOUR EXPERIENCE WAS NO LONGER NEEDED! You see, once you clear up and transform the flaw in you, their behavior either has to change or they won't be in your experience any more—or at least to the extent that they were. The reason for this is that it actually causes a gestalt—a friction of sorts where your energy no longer matches theirs and you're not as compatible with them as you once were.

I love using the mirror method in families, because you are usually bound to stay within that structure more than you are with your hairdresser—and families are where we find the most irritations. But, this technique works just as well with mere acquaintances. In fact, you will find that certain people move into your life just for the purpose of your learning something—about yourself.

Another principle to remember with your social interactions is to recognize that all of us are teachers and students. We are all either teaching someone something or being taught by someone. Because we play both rolls, it is much easier to listen to what someone has to say for the purpose of trying to learn something new. Being a "know-it-all" is terribly confining and usually makes for uncomfortable relationships. The neat part about this law is that age is not a factor in who the teacher is or who the student is. You might think that you are always your children's teacher—but, more often than not, they are yours. You can raise your frequency fast and furiously if you choose to learn from a child. Take a hard look at the child who always throws a tantrum with you, but doesn't with his Father. If that is the case, the lesson is for you. Also, look at how you react when he acts this way—if you overreact—which most of us mothers do—the lesson is for you.

It's also fun to see how people—maybe members of your family—react to certain news bulletins or people in the news. If you notice an uncharacteristic amount of anger or anxiety, you can be sure they have something that needs attention within. Interestingly enough, children take to this kind of inner work. Calmly addressing where inside them they might be feeling anger is a healthy discussion for you to have with them—and that's when you are being the teacher. When they give you their answer—they are being the teacher! Kids are great—I often say they were born with an extra "chip" in their heads that I didn't get—and they take to this kind of teaching like a duck to water. Try them out—read this to your family and see what they think. Just remember—this is not about blaming anyone—especially not yourself.

Most relationship problems, in my opinion, are basically caused by a person's poor self-concept—more often called "self-esteem". Many years ago I was privileged to know and work with a lovely lady named Susie Wyllie. She developed a company called Success Perceptions which was based around three major points that I think all of us should remember:

1. You are beautiful!
2. You are an unique, limited-edition of one
3. You are the authority on yourself

I was asked to speak to a group of Junior High girls one evening and I started out by asking them this question: "If you knew without a doubt that you were beautiful, is there anything that you would do differently than you are doing now?" and every hand went up. It was a consensus that girls would indeed act differently if they knew they were beautiful. The startling part of this story is that even those girls that the group believed were beautiful—didn't think so. This is how Susie describes what she thinks happens to us.

Let's say that there is a little, three-year-old girl, dancing and twirling around in a dirty and tattered dress. Her hair is a little messed up and she has a smudge on her face. You might say to her, "gee, you're a pretty little girl". She nods and says "I know". You see, the dress, the hair or the dirt had nothing to do with her self concept of beauty. Now try saying that to a 9-year old and she will bow her head and say "I've got this dress on that's too small for me; or, I hate these braces, they make me look ugly." A twelve or thirteen year old is even worse in most cases. They will give you a litany of reasons as to why they are NOT beautiful and not be able to accept the compliment. What happened between 3 and 12 years old? The basic problem here is COMPARISON. Have you ever looked at a painting that you thought was down-right ugly and somebody paid thousands of dollars for it? I know I have. You see, art cannot really be compared because every original piece is unique in some way and defies comparison. Oh, people do compare, just as they compare people; but, if you get the concept, it's impossible to compare one piece of art against another, just as it is impossible to compare one individual against another when it comes to appearance. What I choose to adorn my walls with might be the opposite of what you think is nice—why? Because all are beautiful to someone—so it is speaking truth when you say all are beautiful.

I am reminded of a time when a very high-frequency senior class of a high school, voted for a mentally challenged girl to be the Queen of the Prom. She was dressed in a lovely dress and she wore that crown proudly—and everyone agreed she was indeed beautiful. Another instance I can remember is of one of my teachers at church who was in her late thirties and had never married. She was a very large girl, both tall and big-boned and she towered over most of the men in the area. One night, she glowingly showed us her engagement ring and invited all of us to her wedding. I'll never forget seeing her in that beautiful wedding gown, standing next to her groom who was a good 10 inches shorter than she, and saying to her "you are absolutely beautiful". She responded, "I know—I feel beautiful". I was so pleased that she had the experience of feeling beautiful and I sincerely hope that feeling went with her throughout her life. If we could get that concept over to our young people, things

> ✸ *You are a unique limited-edition of one.*

would change. There would not be bullies in our schools if all our children could adopt the belief that they are all beautiful and they are unique.

Being a limited edition of one means there is no other one like you—so how can you compare? Beauty is everywhere. When we go to pick out a Christmas tree I am often drawn to the asymmetrical ones—the ones that look different—ones that others might think less than perfect. I certainly don't feel sorry for them; I truly love the ones that have odd branches sticking out in weird places. To me, they are the most beautiful. All people are beautiful. I remember Mother telling me that when I was a really tiny girl, that I oohed and ahhed over people with old, wrinkly hands. I have always thought wrinkled hands were a sign of great beauty—and wisdom—(it's a good thing, since mine are getting that way fast). Some people, especially women, try to hide their old-looking hands and I think them beautiful—go figure.

The last principle of being the authority on yourself is a terrific rule. We really get exposed to this with the way our teen-ager's dress, don't we? The trouble is that most young people think they are the authority on themselves, when they are really just following the pack. I am all for them dressing in a unique style—the style that matches their personalities, as long as it is appropriate for the occasion. However, when I see all the boys in the school wearing their pants down so low that you can see the crack in their behinds—I know that is not being the authority on THEMSELVES—it is following a fad. Fads come and go and we would be well to try to teach our young people to dress to bring out their own style—in colors that they actually love—and judge their wardrobes against only their own likes and dislikes. Why? Because this builds self-esteem, and we know that behavior is attached to what we think about ourselves.

What does all of this have to do with relationships—plenty, if we look at ourselves? Where are we thinking less of our self because we compared our looks, our success or our wallets against someone else? If you don't remember anything else that I have taught you in this book, please take the following to heart:

YOU ARE MAGNIFICENT—YOU ARE A BEAUTIFUL, PERFECT CREATION OF THE CREATOR

The truth of that statement lies in the fact that you are already perfect, as we've already discussed—<u>you just don't believe that</u>—and the process of personal growth is not for you to become something or someone else. All that is needed is for you to remove the false concepts that you have built up around yourself to REVEAL your perfect self—that is already there. Like the sculptor, just pick away at the stone that isn't really YOU—and voila—there you are.

Now go to work on looking within to see what your "mirror" is reflecting back to you—especially with your most difficult relationships. And, the best way to make any of these new principles yours is to teach them to someone else within 24 hours—so go!

NAMASTE

(The Divine in me salutes the Divine in You)

CHAPTER TWENTY SEVEN

Love Is All There Is

*"The best place to find a helping hand
is at the end of your own arm."
~Swedish Proverb~*

We have just learned that all of our relationship problems really originate from our very own self. Now, remember that is "self" with a small "s". What we believe and think about ourselves shows up in a relationship so that we can see what it is we need to work on, to grow. I know how difficult this is to accept—since we all have people in our lives that, we think, are truly messed up. The most important thing to remember about this principle is that we are all messed up, and we are all mirroring to others what they need to work on, too. You are surely aware that you don't come across the same way to all of your friends, family and acquaintances—some people resonate with you and others don't. Why do you think that is? It's because not everyone has to work on the same issues.

If you have more than one child in your family you can see this concept immediately. Why is it that each child reacts differently to you when you "think" that you are treating them all the same? It's all in their perception that we are not treating them all the same. We are mirrors, too. The best way to handle all of this is to look at all of your relationships and see how they affect how you feel. The ones that cause strong feelings—good or bad—are the ones that are trying to teach you something. Now remember, they are mirroring fabulous traits back to you also. We're not all bad—so if a person makes you feel terrific when you are around them that is a trait coming from you as well. The most irritating people in your life are your greatest teachers—and, as soon as you learn the lesson you need from them, they will no longer bug you. What a concept!

What you think about yourself is going to be reflected back to you all the time. We discussed self-esteem in Chapter Twenty Six, but, I know that it is hard for a lot of people to think that they are beautiful and O.K. at all times. We are not talking about arrogance here. Actually, arrogance is a mask for low self-esteem. What we want instead is a general understanding that EVERYONE IS O.K. and we need not judge them, or that becomes our problem. Here's one way that I learned to look at everyone as "beautiful".

One of the most difficult situations my children and I had to live through was moving—we actually moved 17 times in 17 years. That was hardest on the children. But, the upside was that we got pretty good at moving—especially my son Todd, and I. I had received several nice pieces of sterling silver as a wedding gift, and since I was so busy and we moved so often, I had wrapped them in plastic bags and just kept them that way for many years.

One day when we were again packing up to leave, I came across the bags of silver, and I was so tired of moving them, and hadn't used them for a long time, THAT I ALMOST THREW THEM AWAY! Then my better sense took over, and I thought "Gee, these are sterling silver—but, they look so ugly. They're black and green and I don't have time to clean them". But, I moved them anyway. When we got to the new house, I purposely set the bags in my car as I intended to find out what they were worth. So I took them to a pawn shop and the owner told me something very interesting. He said that even though they were tarnished and dirty, that the SILVER CONTENT WAS THE SAME, and that he would give me market value for the pieces. I thanked him and took all the silver home, and put all of them back into the garage, except one small bowl. I took that bowl up to my kitchen and set it out where I would see it every day. I got out the silver cleaner and took time just to clean a little corner of the tarnish away. "OOH" I exclaimed, "that is pretty". Every day, I cleaned away just a little bit of it, until, one day it was beautiful and shiny. I filled the bowl with fruit and put it on my dining room table. Everyone who came into my home remarked on the "beautiful, new bowl." Here's a question for you—where was the beauty before? I didn't add anything to the bowl; I just subtracted something from it so we could SEE THE BEAUTY UNDERNEATH. The beauty was really there all the time.

That is the principle behind the EVERYONE IS BEAUTIFUL concept. The beauty is there—however; sometimes it is hidden behind a false belief of who we are. The job here is to polish up ourselves and remove the tarnish. That's what our relationships help us do—except that we have traits, characteristics and behaviors that are hiding our true beauty. But, if we are not brave enough to look at them, and we have the distorted belief that we don't need polishing, we can't reveal our true Self (with a large "S"). Cherish all of the people who come into your life, for they are coming as teachers; and remember, you are reflecting back their "tarnish" as well.

> *"I wish I could show you, when you are lonely or in darkness, the Astonishing light of your own Being."*

Relationships need nurturing to keep them healthy. When you are having trouble with others in your life, try to go to the higher frequencies to solve the problem. Since your social interactions are found on the material vibration level, that means we need to go up to at least mental or emotional to find the solution. First, check your thoughts about this person or problem and see if the way you are thinking about it is actually perpetuating the situation. If you have already fed yourself a false belief such as "He never listens to me"—you will have a hard time getting him to listen. Check your beliefs and change it to something positive like "I know he listens to some people, so I must find a way for him to hear me." If "hearing you" was the problem as you perceived it to be, I would suggest you look at yourself then and see where in your world are you not listening. Maybe you are not listening to someone (a real person) or maybe one part of you is not listening to another part of you. I firmly believe that a lot of actual hearing problems are nothing more than graphic illustrations of our need to listen more carefully.

Next you will want to go to the Emotional vibration and see which emotion is the one that this problem brings up in you. Look at the Emotional Scale to see how you can raise it higher. For example: if you easily get angry when a certain person confronts you, look to see if you could lift your emotion at least up to disappointment or frustration. Now, you don't want to stay at those frequencies either, but, sometimes it is hard to go right from anger to positive expectation—but, you could—and you will solve problems faster if you can. The object of all social issues is to get to love, joy and appreciation as fast as you can. Love, of course, is the goal.

If you find that you really can't get to love, try kindness. I believe that kindness always pays; and before you say or do anything when you are in the midst of the negative situation, check to see if you can say or do something that would be considered by the other person as "kind". This pays huge dividends if you want to save the relationship. Sometimes the kindest thing you can say is "I can't deal with this now—I need to calm down." The key here is that you can't give something you haven't got, and what comes out of you is what is inside of you. Just like an orange, orange juice comes out when it is squeezed, because that's what is inside. And anger can't come out of you unless it is inside. The person who "makes you angry" is trying to show you what is within that needs work.

All arguments and wars are merely coming from fear—the fear of losing something. When in the midst of a negative situation remember to ask if this is coming from love or fear. If you detect a low emotion—you know it is fear-based and fear is an illusion—and it is a call for love. Can you answer the call?

Since love and peace are most of our goals—another good question to ask yourself is, "what do I want—peace or conflict"? Most of the time, when you ask this question of yourself sincerely, the wind will go out of your sails, the adrenaline will drop and you will breathe a big sigh of relief as you admit to yourself that you, indeed do want peace. Sometimes the only thing to do is say that out loud. Since we want peace, not conflict, how do we go about bringing peace?

The best sentence I ever learned was, "you could be right about that." When someone is baiting you and trying to convince you that he is right and you are wrong, try that magic sentence. It immediately eliminates any argument. My Ex-Mother-in-law used to say it was better to be loved than be right—and in most cases I think that is true—at least give them the benefit of them "maybe being right."

Another great trick I learned to help solve relationship problems is to use the Pygmalion Effect—or treating people "as if". What this means is that if you want someone to treat you kindly, you start treating them as if they were the nicest, kindest person in the world. Here's an example:

When Norm and I were first married, I noticed after a few months that we never really had a deep discussion of any merit. Our conversations mostly contained very shallow and "surfacey" kind of stuff—nothing of any consequence; and that is not what I had in mind for a partnership. I knew it wouldn't do any good to bring it up, because he would only say that he would be more than happy to have a deeper conversation if that is what I wanted. That would solve the problem only for that

Social Equity

moment—I didn't believe it would change the relationship. So, I decided to use the Pygmalion technique. You might remember that Pygmalion was a statue that was loved so greatly that it turned into a real person. A more recent illustration of this method was in My Fair Lady. Professor Higgins decided that Audrey Hepburn was to be a princess and he started treating her that way. Well, the way I used this technique with Norm was like this: whenever anyone would ask me how the new marriage was going, I would answer "Oh, it is so wonderful, Norm and I have such wonderful conversations, we can just talk about anything and we do—I always wanted a relationship where we could discuss and share our thoughts and beliefs and dreams." After a few instances like this, I overheard Norm saying to someone on the phone "Oh, we have such a great marriage, Connie and I can talk about anything and we are able to share all of our thoughts without worrying about being judged". Imagine that! The truth is that this works—you are not trying to manipulate anyone—you can't make them do what you want; but, if you start treating people the way you wish to be treated, Voila! Isn't that the Golden Rule?

Another way of clearing up disturbances with people is to watch your own self talk. What you say to and about yourself is going to be reflected back to you, as we have already discussed. So here's a trick when you hear yourself saying something in your own head like "that was a stupid thing to do". Just say (also to yourself) "that was not like me—next time I will _____", and fill in the blank with whatever you think would have been a more appropriate action. Paint the picture with your words so that your mind has a really good template of what to do next time. This is a great way to change your beliefs and your words. It also works with other people when you hear them say something derogatory about themselves. Just offer the same remark: that was not like you –next time I expect you will do it differently.

St. Francis said "Lord, make me an instrument of thy

peace." To bring peace to a situation it is useful to use what I call "emotional hearing". Listen for the emotion that the other person is trying to communicate. If you listen with your heart you are able to tune into theirs. If you sense it is frustration—say "I can feel the frustration in what you are saying—I really get that you are frustrated." This gives the other person a chance to either agree or to correct you and say "I'm not only frustrated, I am disappointed." If you stay with the feeling and not the words you can get to a solution much faster.

I believe that one thing that causes more relationship problems is people not keeping their agreements. We discussed this in an earlier chapter, and it leads to trust issues. Remember, you are constantly either depositing in credits or taking out debits from your Emotional Bank Account with your agreements. Just like with your money account, every time you show up on time, keep your word, do something special for someone, you deposit a credit. Then, if and when you make a mistake, say something unkind, show up 1/2 hour late for an appointment, you have some credit with that person so you are not bankrupt. The thing to remember is that you have a different account with each relationship that you have. Obviously, long-range associations give you a longer span of time in which to accumulate credits and new people in your life don't have such an established Trust Account with you. That's why first impressions mean so much. Let's say, for example, that you are interviewing for a new position. The only possible credits you might have would be on your resume. So, how important is it that your resume looks great and tells your credentials in a nice, easy-to-read manner? Very important! How about how you are dressed? See, you can make credits and debits to any relationship account before you even say a word. However, keeping your word holds the most weight—and will give you a hefty deposit with any person. If you don't remember anything else I say in this chapter, please take this to heart:

KEEP AGREEMENTS WITH EVERYONE!

That includes being on time. Watch what you promise your children—if you promise a punishment—do it. If you promise an ice cream cone—do it. I heard one mother promise her children that they would go swimming on the weekend. When the weekend came, they didn't go swimming, but, they did go to the movie. Problem was, the mother did not re-negotiate with the children so that they would know that the movie took the place of swimming. The children told me that their mother did not keep her promise—in fact; they added that she never does! I'm sure that that last statement wasn't entirely true, but, that was their perception of it. How do you think they are going to react in the future to promises made and not kept? And worse yet, what do you think they are learning about keeping your word. Please keep your word to children—they are keeping track and you might need a great big emotional bank account balance some day to draw upon—like not being able to produce the Hawaiian vacation that was given as a Christmas gift.

This actually happened to my Daughter Amy. She and her Husband, in good faith, gave their four children a trip to Hawaii as their Christmas gift one year. Trouble was, they had a huge financial downturn that no one could have foretold and they had to cancel the trip. I was proud of the way she handled it with her children, by sitting down and explaining the situation and asking them what they would do in the same circumstance. They then decided, as a family, what they could do that would be fun together that wouldn't cost so much money. They decided that once a month they would do something "special" as a family—and as far as I know, they have kept their word. You see, it doesn't mean that you won't sometimes have to change plans—but, it is how you handle it that counts. Most people are extremely reasonable, and more flexible than you would think, especially children. Let them in on the situation and negotiate the solution together—your trust level will go way up and your relationship with that person will grow leaps and bounds.

Love Is All There Is

One of the main purposes of any relationships, especially close ones, is to join energy with that person which makes a stronger, more powerful force. This forms a type of "synergy" if the energies are compatible; and if they are not, it causes friction. Usually, the person with the lower frequency cannot tolerate the energy of the higher one, so he either leaves or tries to start an argument. If you notice this happening, don't lower your own energy to match theirs, add energy to the situation by coming from love (if you can) or kindness or enthusiasm or laughter. Kindness, enthusiasm and laughter are all pre-cursors to love and can be accessed upon demand. It is good to keep in mind that the major purpose for having relationships at all IS TO SERVE. <u>How can I help</u> should become your, and my, mantra.

We have spent a lot of this book discussing The Law of Attraction and how to get more of what you desire out of life. However, the last secret that must be applied I saved for last.. Using this powerful and magnetic law will work for bringing you new homes, cars, and money—it will. But, as we learned in the Spiritual Equity Section, essence is what is important.

> *"Happiness is a perfume you cannot pour on others without getting a few drops on yourself."*
> *~Anonymous~*

What do you hope to BE by having all of these "things"? We decided that the object of the whole game was to be happy, joyous, peaceful, etc. Right? Well, here's the real purpose of the Law of Attraction—to create a happy, joyous, peaceful life for everyone whose life you touch, <u>and for you</u>, IN THAT ORDER! This is the key that The Secret never got around to explaining to you. Your job (and mine) is to help, serve and assist everyone we meet. Is that a huge task? You might look at it that way or you might

Social Equity

look at it with a little different perception—like the Law of the Boomerang that I taught you a few chapters back. What if you looked at serving others as serving God?—because that is what it really is. There is no other way for you to serve The Creator except by helping your Brother—because the truth is THERE IS NO OTHER—we really are all one. Remember the sun and the sunbeams? We are all part of the "Sonship" and when you serve another you serve us all. When we really, really learn that, their will be no need for war. Here's the bottom line:

1. Communicate only love
2. Be first to forgive
3. Do I want peace or conflict?
4. Keep agreements
5. Ask "how can I serve?"

"When you dig another out of their troubles, you find a place to bury your own." ~Anonymous

IMPLEMENTING THE SOCIAL EQUITY

1. Every person you have contact with is a mirror, reflecting back to you the places in you that need transformation. The hardest relationships are the ones that will teach you the most, if you're willing to look and learn the lessons. Blaming yourself or the other person will not help the situation, but do take responsibility for yourself and your lesson. Be willing to be the student; and remember, you can't change anyone else, only yourself.

2. What you think about yourself will be reflected back to you through others, both the good and the ugly. So when a relationship is consistently unpleasant, examine your own thoughts and feelings about it to find what it is you need to change about yourself. Also, consider what you can do to raise the vibrational frequency of a situation or relationship. Saying or doing something kind is an almost sure-fire way to raise the vibration, as most people will respond positively to kindness. Be willing to serve; and keep your agreements with everyone, including yourself.

Social Equity

RECOMMENDED READING FOR SOCIAL EQUITY

1. *Living the Heartlife*—Jeffrey Wands

2. *Love is Letting Go of Fear*—Gerald G. Jampolsky

3. *The Gift of Love*—Joel S. Goldsmith

4. *What Do You Really Want For Your Children*—Wayne W. Dyer

5. *The Path of Heart Resistance*—Fritz

6. *What You Think of Me is None of my Business*—Terry Cole-Whitaker

7. *Love as a Way of Life*—Gary Chapman

8. *Living in the Heart*—Paul Ferrini

9. *Big Mind Big Heart: Finding Your Way*—Dennis Gempo Merzel

10. *Vision of Love*—Cookson

11. *Feel it Real*—Coates

12. *A Course of Love*—Mari Perron

The Final Word

> *"The voyage of discovery*
> *is not in seeking new landscapes*
> *but, in having new eyes."*
> ~Marcel Proust~

    We have come full circle—learning about energy and the Six Energy Equities. We started with the Physical Equity and worked our way through the Mental, Emotional, Spiritual, Financial and Social divisions of the Life Force. Please remember that there is only one Life Force—we just broke it down into sections so that we could learn how to actually use this energy to enrich our lives. I certainly hope that the information has been useful in helping you to do just that.

    As I stated before, I started with the physical energy because it is my firm belief that if you feel physically well and energized, you will have a much better chance of attending to the other equities on the wheel. However, when we discussed physical energy, we had not yet acquired some of the tools from the higher frequencies—so we were only able to talk about raising physical energy within the physical vibration. We learned many ways to lift our physical energy, and since there are levels within levels, I taught you the highest frequencies we know of such as drinking only spring water—and lots of it—eating high frequency fresh vegetables (organic if possible) and taking only natural, whole-food supplements. Since we live in a physical world, we do need to pay attention to the physical; but, since all material things, including our bodies, are vibrating at a slow rate—it takes a lot of energy to keep them going. Think back to the Wally Minto quote that said it takes "three hours in the physical to equal thirty minutes in the mental and three minutes in the spiritual".

The Final Word

Most of us do spend a lot of time in the physical—sleeping, eating, dressing, bathing, driving, working, etc. The key is to balance out your time spent so that you are also spending some time reading, studying a new subject, or creating something new, as well as meditating and praying. Finding time to do all of these things every day is the challenge. Everyone's life balance will be a little different depending upon how much time you spend in the physical. People who work at a very physical job all day and then run right to the gym to work out for an hour or two are going to find it more difficult to find the time in the mental, emotional and spiritual to balance out all of that time. Conversely, those who spend most of their day in a very mental world are going to have the same problem reversed. The object of the game is to find balance—and to go to the highest frequency possible to solve problems which we are going to talk about now.

When I refer to the Physical Equity, I am including health and appearance under that heading. So now we are going to look at our health issues and so-called appearance problems from a different perspective. Knowing what you now know, this next statement shouldn't surprise you: YOUR HEALTH AND YOUR APPEARANCE ARE A DIRECT REFLECTION OF YOUR BELIEFS!

Before you start yelling at me that you certainly don't believe in cancer or heart disease—let me caution you to remember our lengthy discussion about "cultural beliefs". Do you not think that our society has a very strong belief in disease? Cancer is a 49 billion dollar business—and heart disease is our number one killer. How can one not believe in disease? We are bombarded day and night with advertisements for drugs and new diseases that we didn't even know existed. Our hospitals and mortuaries are filled with our friends and loved ones who have succumbed to these dreaded diseases—so when I say that you believe in them—all of us do! We have been totally hypnotized into a stupor over disease as well as obesity. Our lives are cluttered with examples of this "dangerous" world—and we even say to our most cherished loved ones as they go out the door "be careful—drive safely".

The Final Word

We have a huge belief in danger and disease, and our world reflects that belief. We really do live in a dangerous, germ-filled world—and we have created it that way, all of us! Why do we have terrorists? The same reason that we have virus and bacteria that can kill us—we believe whole-heartedly in these things.

Rising above these powerful thought forms is not easy—but, it can be done. The way out of this mess is the same as any other problem—start with your thoughts. We really have to become aware of what we are thinking and saying. Watching your words is a real eye-opener, especially when you hear yourself say "my back is killing me". Once you become totally aware of your words, then you can watch your thoughts. We learned in the Mental Equity Section of this book that you can't change anything until you first become aware—by bringing it up to the conscious mind. Then we need to change the thought. One way is by saying "cancel/cancel" and replacing it with a powerful new thought. One of my favorite ways of negating an unacceptable thought is for me to think or say out loud "not in my world". That little saying sends a very powerful new thought to your subconscious mind that tells it that you are not going to accept the negative way of thinking about that subject. You can use that statement when someone else brings up a new fear or worry, or says "you're going to catch your death of pneumonia"—just look at them kindly and say "not in my world."

Now, please don't misconstrue anything that I am saying here so that you think you don't have to take care of yourself—you do. Because of the power of the cultural belief system—it can take quite a while of constant work to change your belief—but, you will see it working right away. People who are coming from the higher spiritual frequencies get sick less often and less seriously, in most cases. However, those who radiate energy in the high 500's or higher, can often be taking on the burden of society's beliefs and not necessarily their own. The energy becomes so powerful at those levels that many people's nerves and bones have a hard time containing it and they will suffer great pain. But, that is not the problem of the majority

The Final Word

of humanity since 85% of humans are under 200! Most of us just need to pay attention to our own problems, and the thoughts and beliefs that they reflect in our lives. Being overweight is a perfect example. I always weighed around 100-105 until I owned and ran a figure salon. I worked 60-hour weeks with people with a weight problem and talked about it incessantly. I discussed eating problems, hormone problems, exercise problems, digestion problems ad nauseum! And, guess what? I gained 20 pounds which I have never been able to completely get rid of. I really, really believed in fat—my business depended on it—and I didn't have to look far to find it! I took a little different tact to obesity—as a health problem instead of an appearance issue—but, I found all kinds of reasons why people put on weight. All of them are true—but, the bottom-line is that WE BELIEVE IN THE PROBLEM. I'm not telling you that you don't need to eat right and exercise and all of the other things I have taught you about health—keep doing those things, WHILE YOU ARE CHANGING YOUR MIND ABOUT THE PROBLEM.

One of the easiest and best ways to change your thoughts and beliefs about health and fitness is to use affirmations. You know how to write an affirmation and I want to make sure that you have one about your health—even if you are in A-1 condition right now. One of my very favorites is:

My body has the ability to repair itself, and it is doing so NOW!

Writing affirmations for your perfect weight and or shape also works if you say them regularly. I suggest getting a picture of you when you were in top condition and your perfect size and putting your affirmation below it—something like this:

My body is the perfect size and shape for me. I look and feel terrific.

Emotions regarding health and appearance can be double-trouble. For instance, how do you feel about your weight when

The Final Word

you go past a mirror? Does it make you mad or sad or frustrated to look at yourself? Remember, emotions are like turbo-chargers and you get what you think about most—faster! You can be saying the affirmations, playing cancel/cancel and dieting like crazy; but, if you feel some of these negative emotions in connection to how you look NOW, you will be going backwards from your goal. Most of us go one step forward and two steps backward in this regard. That's why a picture can be very helpful—just looking at what you want, instead of what you don't want, will train your mind to stay focused. Try to muster up excitement if you can, when working with a health problem. "Every day in every way I am getting better and better" is a famous saying that still works. Being optimistic and having hope are extremely powerful emotions to employ for your own good. I don't mean "Pollyanna" thinking when you are dealing with a "terminal disease"—but, research shows that those who look at their health problem with hope and optimism live longer. I am reminded of when Norman Cousins was told he had a terminal auto-immune disease and he decided to not accept that diagnosis. He rented dozens of movies, all comedies, checked into a hotel and watched funny films day after day for several weeks until he felt like he had turned the corner—and changed his emotional thermostat. He did just that and lived about twenty years longer than the original death sentence!

We know that laughter and excitement are pre-cursors to love—and that is what you are showing to yourself, or your loved one, when you lighten up the scene. Even when someone is in the hospital with a very real, serious disease—you can bring sunshine into the room. Gloom and doom are detrimental to any condition—and you are going to have to watch who you associate with and who you listen to when you are dealing with health issues. I'm not telling you to refuse traditional medicine or surgery for a health issue—not at all, but, I am telling you that you can certainly augment what the doctors are doing by watching your thought, beliefs and emotions about the matter.

Of course, prevention is the best and that is what we are

talking about here—raising your energy to balance your life, solve problems and experience more peace and joy. Raising your energy up to the higher spiritual frequencies is how to do just that! Try to remember that there are no victims—all experiences are for our growth. There is a lesson in every situation and experience, and if we will dare to go within and look a little deeper we will usually find it. Just as relationships in our lives reflect back issues that we need to work on, physical conditions do, too. Now remember that we are not blaming anyone—especially not ourselves for the condition, just taking responsibility for it. IF I AM POWERFUL ENOUGH TO CREATE THIS CONDITION, I AM POWERFUL ENOUGH TO CHANGE IT, should become your mantra. There are always times when we can't prevent or change a serious health problem—we all have to die of something, I suppose. I really believe that we came into this life to do certain things, and when we have accomplished that, regardless of our age, we are out of here. However, most of our issues are little, nagging problems that we certainly do have control over if we pay attention. Those are the ones we are addressing here.

Meditation and prayer are the best ways I know of to get to the bottom of a health or appearance problem. Finding the basic "cause" of the situation is a very freeing experience. When I was doing weight consulting I found that most weight issues are some form of protection, metaphysically. I am saying this with a "broad stroke", because each instance is very personal; but, my experience found this to be true in a majority of cases. Protection from "what" became the issue. In consulting with hundreds of clients, the "whats" varied greatly. It makes sense that when we put an inch or two between ourselves and others, it is a form of protection or it can be seen as "insulation". Most of us are very sensitive and have been hurt many times in our lives. For example: my first husband told me on our wedding night that he would divorce me if I ever got fat. Now, that became not only a fear, but a new belief. After having four children, I am happy to say that I did not get fat; but, don't you find it curious that when I married my sweet Norm that I did! I have meditated on that one for a long time and come to the conclusion that it was my subconscious's way of challenging Norm's love—was it great enough to withstand "fatness"—since it obviously wasn't with my first companion. So by sharing my personal experience I want you to see that there are many facets to a situation. First, I had a deep belief that fat was connected to love in some way—and then I reinforced that belief with all my clients with weight problems, that told me that obesity was a real, difficult problem that most of us have to deal with. Couple that with society that shows us over and over daily that you are not attractive unless you are stick thin—and you have a very complex problem. Then, just for good measure, add in the protection factor and you can see why obesity is running rampant in this country. The fact that it is affecting our children is a real concern. That is where we need to implant new beliefs. I hear mothers all the time telling their kids that they are going to get fat if they eat a certain thing. Don't you think it interesting that so many thin people can eat and eat and eat—and never put on a single pound?

The highest frequencies you can use for health problems are peace and love—and remember this kind of love is not only unconditional—but, allowing love. Allowing you or someone to be perfect, just the way you are, is God-type love. Most of us are lacking in this kind of love for ourselves. We beat ourselves up daily and wonder why we get negative results. This next statement is one of the most powerful ones that I have given you in this course:

YOU CAN'T LEAVE SOMETHING UNTIL YOU LOVE IT!

If you can internalize that statement and make it yours, you are on your way to a powerful life. That means quite frankly that you can't leave your weight problem behind until you love it—you can't give up the arthritis until you love it. I know, I know, that is a hard one, but, it is true. The reason this is actual fact is because, if you don't love the situation, you have resistance to it. And, we already know that what we resist

The Final Word

persists. If you are "against" fat, or cancer or war or anything else, you will get more of it. That's why our world is filled with war, crime, drugs, disease and unhappy people, because we are "warring" against these problems. A "war on drugs" isn't any more effective than a "war against obesity". We simply can't have a warring mind set if we want something called "peace". So, the most difficult assignment I am going to give you is to bring love, peace and joy into the situation that you are calling "a problem". If you can raise your frequency up to those powerful energies, you can create miracles. This world really could use a few miracles—and who better than you or I to do it?

To change the world, change yourself. Meditate on peace, and pray—not for peace in the world—but, peace within yourself! Take responsibility for all the problems you see in the world, and do something about them. You can't help the world when you feel anger, hate and disgust. You can be a beacon of light, a ray of sunshine who knows that you are always connected to The One. And it is your job to remember who you are, and to remember who every other human being is and say NAMASTE—the divinity within me acknowledges the divinity within you.

"The lesson that life reappears and constantly enforces is 'Look under foot.' You are always nearer to the divine and the true sources of your power than you think."
~John Burroughs~

Following this chapter I have included what I call The Ten Habits of High Energy People for you as a guide as to what to do on a day-to-day basis. Keep in mind that some of the big exercises like Finding Your Purpose, or Your Passion or writing affirmation are drills that you should do regularly so that your daily practice will be effective. Describing your Ideal Day and finding out your Prime Values are worth doing and will enhance your daily plan. You need to know what you want in order to write affirmations, so you can see that everything depends on something else. So, pick out an exercise and do it—that's the part I can't do for you. Just

The Final Word

reading this book helps you "know about" something, but, I want you to experience it for yourself. Just having the information in your head won't help much—you need to do the work to get results.

Everything boils down to habit, making a daily ritual that you do every single day, so that when you don't do it one day you feel strange. You know something is missing when you have made it a habit. I offer this plan as suggestions only; please feel free to add to or subtract from it in any way that makes sense to you. It's only meant to be a guide—you need to personalize it.

If you have come this far in this course, I commend you for your dedication to becoming better—for that is our goal, all of us. This Course was meant to be studied—one reading is not going to be enough. Please come back again and again to the sections that you feel called to. I love the saying that says,

"You don't have to be the best today—just better than you were yesterday."

I know who you are—maybe not in the flesh, but,—I know that you are a perfect, divine soul who has come here to learn how to create and to experience all that this beautiful world has to experience, and to learn from those experiences. I also know that you are loved, that you are safe, and that you can be a light unto the world—a world that can really use a light from you and me.

"Serenity is the final word of all teachings."
~Hung Chih~

The Final Word

TEN HABITS OF HIGH ENERGY PEOPLE

1. The habit of SILENCE — 15 to 30 minutes a day—nourishment for the Soul
   a. meditation
   b. walk in nature
   c. contemplation

2. The habit of EXERCISE — 15 minutes per day minimum
   a. walking
   b. chi machine
   c. yoga
   d. aerobics
   e. stretching

3. The habit of NOURISHMENT — take in only high-energy foods
   a. clean spring water
   b. lots of fresh vegetables
   c. fresh fruit
   d. non-bread whole-grains
   e. fish
   f. olive oil
   g. high-quality, whole-food supplements
   h. eat slowly and chew completely.
   i. blessed food calibrates higher than non-blessed food

4. The habit of SEEKING KNOWLEDGE — ongoing
   a. read only enlightening books
   b. listen to uplifting audio recordings
   c. teach what you have learned within 24 hours

5. The habit of WAKING EARLY
   a. get up one hour earlier than usual
   b. enjoy the silence
   c. meditate

d. journal
   e. plan your day
   f. exercise
   g. eat healthy
   h. say your morning Power Questions

6. The habit of REFLECTION
   a. at bedtime—reflect on your day—good and bad
   b. how could you fix those things that went wrong
   c. listen to good music, have a cup of tea, read good poetry
   d. contemplate on one thought or value—notice your feelings
   e. pray with gratitude
   f. say your evening Power Questions
   g. journal

7. The habit of ASSOCIATIONS
   a. choose your friends and associates carefully
   b. bring light and peace to your relationships
   c. learn from what your relationships mirror to you
   d. use the Pygmalion effect
   e. say "you could be right about that"
   f. use The Law of the Boomerang to bless people

8. The habit of THE SPOKEN WORD
   a. say your affirmations morning and evening
   b. say them while showering
   c. say them while driving or waiting for someone
   d. say them at a stop light
   e. remember: all conversation is a form of affirmation or declaration—watch what you say
   f. play cancel/cancel

9. The habit of LIVING BY YOUR VALUES
   a. be kind
   b. be love
   c. be peace

    d. be joy
    e. be abundance
    f. seed—use the Law of the Harvest

10. The habit of SIMPLICATION
    a. prioritize your wants and needs
    b. do most important things first
    c. successful people don't spend major time on minor things
    d. de-clutter your life—physically and mentally
    e. give things away
    f. keep what you love, enjoy, or can use now

POWERFUL THOUGHTS TO REMEMBER

1. You are magnificent—a limited edition of ONE.
2. You are a powerful creator.
3. You have an unlimited field of all possibilities (Quantum Soup) to work with.
4. We are all one—we are made from the same substance created by the same Creator and have the same common purpose—to wake up to the magnificence of our inherited divinity, and to teach others to do the same.

www.ingramcontent.com/pod-product-compliance
Lightning Source LLC
Chambersburg PA
CBHW022102150426
43195CB00008B/237